*Representative Men of Japan*

写真提供 ● 上杉神社稽照殿
● 報徳博物館
● 講談社資料センター

本書は講談社バイリンガル・ブックス『代表的日本人』(1999年刊)の増補改訂版である。

本書の英文は、現代の表記法とかなり異なるところもあるが、著者・内村鑑三の原文を、原則としてそのまま収録した。ただし、誤りと思われるスペルや名称などは訂正した。

日本人の姓名の英文は、明治時代以降の人物は「名－姓」、江戸時代までの人物は「姓－名」の順に表記してある。

NOTE: The names of modern and contemporary Japanese appear in the Western order, while those of historical figures (pre-1868) are written in the traditional order, surname preceding given name.

English text first published in 1894 by Min'yusha, Tokyo, under the title *Japan and the Japanese*. A revised edition published in 1908 by Keiseisha as *Representative Men of Japan*.

# 対訳 代表的日本人
## *Representative Men of Japan*

内村鑑三 ［著］
Kanzō Uchimura

稲盛和夫 ［監訳］
Kazuo Inamori

KODANSHA INTERNATIONAL
Tokyo · New York · London

著者・内村鑑三（1918年6月、札幌にて。58歳）
The author, Kanzō Uchimura, aged 58, at Sapporo in June 1918.

本書『代表的日本人』刊行の2年後の1910年。著者50歳

In 1910, two years after publishing *Representative Men of Japan*, at the age of 50.

# 序 文

**戦**後50余年が過ぎ、日本は物質的にはきわめて豊かな国になった。しかし、その豊かさの中でさえ、多くの人は満足することができず、不安を感じながら、「どのような生き方が正しいか」「どのような人生を目指すべきなのか」と迷っている。

　学校では多くの知識は与えられるが、人間として最も基本的な「何が正しくて、何が悪いのか」「人間はいかに生きるべきなのか」等については教えられていない。実社会に出れば、お金もうけをすることが一番大切なことであるような風潮がある。

　このような環境の中で、真剣に生きる意味を問い、人間のあるべき姿を追求するような人は少なくなり、ただ楽で安易な道を選んでしまうような人が増えているのではないだろうか。このままでは日本社会はますます荒廃してしまう。日本を健全な社会にしていくために必要なことは、一人ひとりの人間が、明確な生きる指針をもち、それに従い、一日一日を一生懸命生きていくことではないだろうか。

　『代表的日本人』は、内村鑑三が19世紀末、海外との交流が盛んになってきた時、欧米諸国に対し「日本人の中にも、これほどの素晴らしい人物がいる」ということを伝えようとして英語で出版された『日本及び日本人』の改訂版である。

# FOREWORD

More than fifty years after defeat at the end of World War II, Japan has emerged as a materially rich economic power. Rich as it is, however, there are many Japanese who lack spiritual fulfillment and are insecure about their future. They search for answers to eternal questions such as "What is the morally correct way to live?" or "What kind of life should one lead?"

Although schools may provide instruction in knowledge, there is a fundamental absence of even the most elementary moral guidance as to what is right and wrong and how to lead an honest life. In society at large, too, there is a tendency to value money-making most.

Under such circumstances, it is hardly surprising that many fail to seriously question the meaning of life and abandon the pursuit of an ideal, humane existence, choosing instead an easier and more comfortable way. If this trend prevails, Japan will certainly become a spiritual desert. What then is necessary to make Japan a more positive and sound society? The answer is, I believe, for everyone to have a clear set of principles and to live according to those principles.

*Representative Men of Japan* is the revised edition of *Japan and the Japanese*, and was originally written and published in English at the end of the nineteenth century, when Japan's relations with other countries was growing. The author, Kanzō Uchimura, wanted

その中では、西郷隆盛、上杉鷹山、二宮尊徳、中江藤樹、日蓮上人の5人が代表的日本人として紹介されている。

　私は、この5人の生き方のなかに、人生の普遍的な価値が示されていると思っている。この5人の日本を代表する偉人の方々の生き方を学ぶなら、必ず人間のあるべき姿について多くの示唆が得られるはずである。彼らの生き方と自分の生き方を常に照らし合わしていけば、きっと意義深い人生が送れるはずだ。

　私たちは、21世紀を目前にしたいま、いつまでも迷いつづけているわけには行かない。確固たる人生観を持ち、意義ある毎日を送るべきなのである。そのためにも、私はこの『代表的日本人』は一読の価値があると思っている。

　幸い、今回、講談社インターナショナルの協力を得て、英文の原書をよりわかりやすい日本語に翻訳し、出版することができた。広く多くの方々が、英語原文に新訳を添えた、この『代表的日本人』を通じ、本当の人生のあり方を学ばれることを、監訳者として心より願っている。

稲 盛 和 夫

1999年2月2日

Western people to know that "there are such remarkable figures among my countrymen." His choices: Saigō Takamori, Uesugi Yōzan, Ninomiya Sontok, Nakae Tōju, and Saint Nichiren.

I believe their lives represent a certain set of universal human values. Learning about the lives of these five great men is one way to discover what it should mean to be truly human. Compare their lives with your own, and you may be able to live a more meaningful life.

At the dawn of the new millennium, there is no more time for blind wandering. A clear philosophy is needed to make our lives more meaningful. Here, I believe, *Representative Men of Japan* will prove most useful.

Fortunately, I have had this opportunity, thanks to Kodansha International Ltd., to supervise the translation of this important book into readable Japanese and reintroduce it to people in both East and West. I sincerely hope this new edition of *Representative Men of Japan*, which features the original English text along with a modern Japanese translation, will encourage today's people to rediscover this classic, and to think about some of the deeper truths of human life.

Kazuo Inamori

February 2, 1999

## 改訂版はしがき

本著は、日清戦争[訳注1]さなかの13年前に上梓した拙著『日本及び日本人』(*Japan and the Japanese*) の主要部分の再版である。原著にあった誤りは、ある友人が訂正してくれた。若き日の熱い愛国心はとうに冷めてしまったが、それでも日本人のもつ素晴らしい特性に目をつぶってはいられない。それに、日本が私の祖国であることに変わりはない。日本は、私が「わが祈り、わが希望、わが無償の奉仕」を捧げる唯一の国だ。わが同胞のよき特性——しばしば日本人に帰せられる盲目的忠誠や血塗られた愛国心とは別な特性——を、外なる世界に伝える一助となること。それが本書の目的である。おそらく、私が外国語で本を出すのはこれが最後[訳注2]であろう。

内 村 鑑 三

東京近郊柏木にて
1908年1月8日

# PREFATORY NOTE TO THE REVISED EDITION

This little book is a reprint, with many corrections by a friendly hand, of the main portion of what appeared under the title of "Japan and the Japanese," during the war with China, thirteen years ago. With all the cooling of my youthful love for my country, I cannot yet be blind to many fine qualities of her people; and she is still the land, the only land, to whom I give "my prayers, my hopes, my service, free." That I may still help to make the good qualities of my countrymen known to the outside world,—the qualities *other* than blind loyalty and bloody patriotism usually attributed to us—is the aim of this, I presume, my last attempt in a foreign language.

Kanzō Uchimura

Kashiwagi, near Tokyo
January 8, 1908

# 目 次

# CONTENTS

1827–77（文政10年〜明治10年）

# 西郷隆盛

## 新日本の創設者

---

# SAIGŌ TAKAMORI

## A Founder of New Japan

## I – 1868年の日本の維新

日本は、天の意志によって紺碧（こんぺき）の大海原より姿を現したときに、「日本よ、門のうちにとどまれ。召すまでは世界と交わるな」と命じられた。日本は2千余年にわたってこれを守ったから、その海を外国の艦隊が波を切って進むことはなく、海岸が侵されることもなかった。

長く国を閉ざしていたと日本を非難するのは、まったく道理を外れた批判である。日本が国を閉ざしたのは天命であり、それは日本にとっても、世界にとっても、かえって良かったのであり、今でもそれは変わらない。世界から遠いことは、一国にとって必ずしも不幸ではない。いわゆる「文明開化」に浴させるためとはいえ、幼いわが子を外の世界に放り出す父親はいないだろう。世界との距離がもっと近かったインドは、やすやすとヨーロッパの利己主義の餌食（えじき）になった。インカ帝国やモンテスマの平和な国に、世界は何をしたか。私たちが鎖国を非難されて、その門戸を開けば、とたんにクライブやコルテスのような輩（やから）がこの国に襲いかかってくることになるのだ。戸締まり厳重な家に押し入る強盗は、そういう機会を狙っているものだ。

したがって、日本の四方を囲む海と大陸が、世界に

# I– The Japanese Revolution of 1868

When Nippon first, at Heaven's command, arose from the azure main, this was the charge to the land: "Niphonia, keep within thy gates. Mingle not with the world till I call thee forth." So she remained for two thousand years and more, her seas unplowed by the fleets of the nations, and her shores free from their defilement.

That is a most unphilosophical criticism that condemns Japan for her long seclusion from the world. Wisdom higher than all wisdoms has ordered it so, and the country was better for having remained so, and the world was, and is, to be better for her having been kept so. Inaccessibility to the world is not always a curse to a nation. What benignant father would have his children prematurely thrown into the world that they might come under its so-called "civilizing influences"? India with her comparative accessibility to the world became an easy prey to European selfishness. What did the world with Inca's empire and Montezuma's's[*1] peaceful land? They condemn us for our seclusion. We open our gates, and Clives and Corteses[*2] are let loose upon us. Do not armed burglars do the same when they break into a well-locked house?

Providence was kind therefore in locking us up from the

対する戸締まりの用を果たしていたことは天の恵みだった。定められた時がくる前にも、欲にかられた者たちがわが国に侵入を試みることがあったが、私たちは自己防衛の本能に従って、門戸を開くことを拒んだ。私たちが開国したとたんに世界に呑み込まれ、明確な形のない、自分らしさを失った存在にならないように、前もって自分たちの国民性を完全な形につくりあげる必要があった。また世界の方も、日本を仲間に迎える前に、もっと洗練される必要があった。思うに、1868年の日本の維新は、二つの異質な文明を代表する二つの民族が互いの名に恥じない名誉を重んじる交際に入る、世界史上の重要な転機となり、「進歩的な西洋」は無秩序な進歩に歯止めをかけられ、「保守的な東洋」は安寧のまどろみから目を覚まされた。そしてそれからは西洋も東洋もなく、人道と正義のもと、世界は一つになった。日本が目覚める前は、東洋と西洋は互いに背を向けていた。日本により、日本を通じて、両者は互いに向き合うようになったのである。ヨーロッパとアジアの好ましい関係を模索するのは日本の務めであり、今もその努力は続けられている。

　このように、わが国の長い鎖国は終わりに近づいていたが、それを完全に終わらせるには、しかるべき人物と機会が必要であった。この頃、太平洋の両岸に位置する中国とカリフォルニアの門戸が開放され、世界の両端を結びつけるためにも日本の開国が必要になった。これが外的な機会である。一方、国内では最後にして最強の封建領主［徳川幕府］が弱体化し、藩ごとに分断され反目し合うことに倦み疲れていた日本人は、史上初めて国家統一の重要性を感じ、望むようになっ

world with seas and continents on all sides; and when greed more than once tried to force its way into us before our appointed time came, it was our genuine instinct of self-defence that refused to open our gates to the world. Our national character was to be fully formed that the world might not swallow us up when we come in contact with it, and make of us an amorphous something without anything special to call our own. Then the world too needed further refinement, before it could receive us into its membership. I think the Japanese Revolution of 1868 signifies a point in the world's history when two races of mankind representing two distinct forms of civilization were brought to *honorable* intercourse one with the other, when the Prospective West was given a check in its anarchic progress, and the Retrospective East was wakened from its stagnant slumber. From that time on, there were to be neither Occidents nor Orients, but all to be one in humanity and righteousness. Before Japan awoke, one part of the world turned its back to the other. By her and through her, the two were brought face to face. Japan is to solve, and is solving, the question of the *right relation* of Europe with Asia.

So our long seclusion was to end, and men and opportunities were needed to bring it to an end. China and California on the opposite banks of the Pacific opened at about the same time, there came a necessity for opening Japan to bring the two ends of the world together. This was an external opportunity. Internally, the last and greatest of the feudal dynasties was losing its power, and the nation, tired of separation and mutual animosities within, felt, for the first time in its history, the importance and desirability of union. But man makes and uses opportunities. I consider

ていた。だが、機会を生み出すのも利用するのも人間である。思うに、米国のマシュー・カルブレイス・ペリー提督[脚注6]は、世界史から見ても、最高に人道を重んじる人物だった（脚注・ペリー提督『日本遠征記』を参照のこと）。提督の日記を読むと、彼が日本の国土に大砲ではなく、神を称える歌で衝撃を与えようとしたことがわかる。ペリーに課せられた任務は、隠者の国の尊厳を傷つけず、しかし生まれながらの誇りは押しとどめ、日本を目覚めさせなければならないという微妙なものだった。これは世界を支配する神に何度も祈りを捧げ、神の慈悲深い助けがあってこそできる、真の宣教師の仕事だった。日本にキリスト教徒の提督が開国を求めに訪れたことは天恵であった。そして外から扉を叩いたキリスト教徒の提督に、内から応えたのが「敬天愛人」を奉ずる、勇敢で正直な将軍であった。この二人は生涯顔を合わせることはなく、互いに相手を褒め称えたという記録もない。しかし二人の生涯をたどると、外見こそ違え、二人の心は一つであったことがわかる。二人は知らないうちに協力していた。一方が始めた仕事を、他方がやり遂げたのである。凡人の曇った眼には見えなくとも、思慮深い歴史家の眼には「神」が「神意」の衣を織りあげていく様がはっきりと見える。

　このように、1868年の日本の維新は、永続する健全な革命がみなそうであるように、正義と神意による必然から起きたものである。貪欲さには頑なに扉を閉ざしてきた国が、正義と公正に対しては惜しげなく国を開いた。魂の奥底から発せられる声に従った稀有な犠牲的精神が、日本の扉を世界へと開かせたのだ。ゆえに、この国で自己の権力の拡大を求める者は天の高みにおわす神に対して罪を犯すことになり、また、この国の崇高な使命を見

Matthew Calbraith Perry of the United States Navy to be one of the greatest friends of humanity the world has ever seen. In his diaries we read that he bombarded the shores of Japan with doxologies, and not with ordnance*. His mission was a delicate one of waking up a hermit nation without doing injury to its dignity, yet keeping its native pride at bay. His was the task of a true missionary, done with Heaven's gracious help, with many an invocation to the Ruler of nations. Thrice blessed is the land that had a Christian commodore sent to it to open it to the world.——To a Christian admiral knocking from outside, there responded a brave upright general, a "reverer of Heaven and lover of mankind" from within. The two never saw each other in their lives, and we never hear of one complimenting the other. Yet we their biographers do know that despite all the differences in their outward garments, the souls that dwelt in both were of kindred stuff. Unwittingly they worked in concert, one executing what the other had initiated. So does the World-Spirit weave his garment of Destiny, underneath the vision of purblind mortals, yet wonderful to the eye of the thoughtful historian.

Thus we see that the Japanese Revolution of 1868, like all healthful and permanent revolutions, had its origin in righteousness and God-made necessity. The land that had been obstinately closed against greed, opened itself freely toward justice and equity. Self-sacrifice of the rarest kind, based upon a voice from the innermost

---

* See *Narrative of Expedition of the American Squadron to the Chinese Seas and Japan* by Commodore Matthew C. Perry.

誤り、俗世の拝金主義がこの国を蹂躙するのを許す者も同罪である。


# II– 出生、教育、啓示

　その偉大さゆえ、また弟［従道］と区別するために、「大西郷」と呼ばれたその人物は、文政10（1827）年、鹿児島の町に生まれた。その生誕の地には小さな石碑が建っており、2年後に生まれた秀抜な同志大久保［利通］の生誕の碑も、そこから遠くないところに建っている。西郷の家は誇れるほどの名門ではなく、薩摩という大藩の「中の下」の家柄にすぎなかった。西郷は男4人、女2人の6人兄弟の長子だった。少年時代はあまり目立たず、おっとりとして無口で、友人たちにはバカ呼ばわりされていた。その彼が初めて義務の意識に目覚めたのは、遠縁の者の切腹を目の当たりにした時だったと言われている。その男はまさに腹に刀を突き刺す寸前、命は主君と国に捧げるものだと、この若者に語った。若者は泣いた。そしてその時の強い印象は生涯消えなかった。

　若者はどんぐり眼と広い肩が際立つ、太った大男に成長した。目玉が大きいため「うど目」というあだ名がついた。力持ちで、相撲をとるのが大好きだった。また、山歩きが好きで、この習慣は生涯変わらなかった。若くして王陽明の著作に惹かれた。陽明学は数ある中国思想のなかでも、善悪の観念と寛容ながらも厳

depth of soul, did fling open its doors to the world. They therefore sin against the height of the heavens who seek self-aggrandizement in this nation, as do they also who mistake its high-calling, and allow it to be trampled by the mammon of this world.

## II– Birth, Education, and Inspiration

"The Great Saigō," as he is usually called, both for his greatness and to distinguish him from the younger Saigō, his brother, was born in the 10th year of Bunsei (1827) in the city of Kagoshima. A stone-monument now marks the spot where he first saw light, not far from the place where his illustrious colleague, Ōkubo, was born two years later, which is also so marked. His family had no hereditary fame to boast of; only "below middle" in the large *han* of Satsuma.[*3] He was the eldest of six children,—four brothers and two sisters. In his boyhood there was nothing remarkable about him. He was a slow, silent boy, and even passed for an idiot among his comrades. It is said that his soul was first roused to consciousness of duty by witnessing one of his distant relatives committing *harakiri* in his presence, who told the lad just before he plunged a dagger into his belly, of the life that should be devoted to the cause of his master and country. The boy wept, and the impression never left him through his life.

He grew up to be a big fat man, with large eyes and broad shoulders very characteristic of him. "Udo," the big-eyed, was the nickname they gave him. He rejoiced in his muscular strength; wrestling was the favorite sport with him, and he liked to roam in the mountains much of his time, a propensity which never left him till the very end of his life. His attention was early called to the

格な天の法を説く崇高な教えという点で、同じアジアから生まれたかの威厳ある信仰［キリスト教］に最も近い。西郷の残した文章には、この影響が色濃く反映されている。そこに見られるキリスト教的な感情はすべて、その偉大な中国人［王陽明］の思想の明解さの証（あかし）であり、またそれらをすべて吸収して、あれほど実際的な人物となった西郷の偉大な天性の証でもある。彼はまた禁欲的な仏教の一派である禅も探求していた。のちに友人に打ち明けるように、これは「情のもろさを抑えるため」であった。いわゆるヨーロッパ文化の素養は、彼にはまったくなかった。日本人としては格段に心が広く、進歩的であった人物の受けた教育は、すべて東洋のものだったのである。

　では、西郷が生涯を通じて抱き続けた二つの顕著な思想——(1) 帝国の統一、(2) 東アジアの統合——は、いったいどこから生まれたのだろうか。陽明学を論理的に突き詰めれば、そのような考えに行き着くとも考えられる。旧政府［徳川幕府］が体制維持のために奨励した保守的な朱子学とは違い、陽明学は進歩的で前向きで、可能性に富んだ思想であった。キリスト教との類似性がこれまでも何度か言われ、日本ではなにかと理由をつけて禁止同然の扱いを受けていた。「これは陽明学と似ている。帝国の崩壊はここから始まるだろう」と、維新で名を挙げた長州の戦略家、高杉晋作は長崎で初めて聖書を目にした時、こう叫んでいる。キリスト教に似た思想が日本の再建に欠かせないものであったことは、日本のこの時代において特記すべき事実である。

　西郷の置かれた状況や環境も、命を賭した偉大な計画を立てる役に立ったにちがいない。日本列島の南西

writings of Wang Yang Ming, who of all Chinese philosophers, came nearest to that most august faith, also of Asiatic origin, in his great doctrines of conscience and benign but inexorable heavenly laws. Our hero's subsequent writings show this influence to a very marked degree, all the Christianly sentiments therein contained testifying to the majestic simplicity of the great Chinese, as well as to the greatness of the nature that could take in all that, and weave out a character so practical as his. He also delved a little into the Zen philosophy, a stoic form of Buddhism, "to kill my too keen sensibilities," as he told his friends afterward. So-called European culture he had absolutely none. The broadest and most progressive of Japanese, his education was wholly Oriental.

But whence came the two dominant ideas of his life, which were (1) the united empire, and (2) reduction[*4] of Eastern Asia? That Yang Ming philosophy, if logically followed out, would lead to some such ideas is not difficult to surmise. So unlike the conservative Chu philosophy fostered by the old government for its own preservation, it (Yang Ming philosophy) was progressive, prospective, and full of promise. Its similarity to Christianity has been recognized more than once, and it was practically interdicted in the country on that and other accounts. "This resembles Yang-Ming-ism; disintegration of the empire will begin with this." So exclaimed Takasugi Shinsaku, a Chōshū strategist of Revolutionary fame, when he first examined the Christian Bible in Nagasaki. That something like Christianity was a component force in the reconstruction of Japan is a singular fact in this part of its history.

His situations and surroundings too must have helped him in forming his great projects of life. Situated in the south-western

の端に位置する薩摩藩は、当時はもっぱら南から来ていたヨーロッパの影響を一番受けやすかったといえる。長崎に近いことも、この点では非常に有利だった。薩摩藩に属する小島<sup>訳注7</sup>では、中央政府から正式な許可が下りるずっと前から、外国との交易が行われていたという。

しかし、西郷が外から受けた影響では、同時代の二人の人物の影響がもっとも大きかった。薩摩藩主の島津斉彬（なりあきら）と、水戸藩の藤田東湖である。斉彬は、誰が見ても非凡な人物だった。冷静で先見の明があり、やがてこの国に訪れる避けがたい変化に、いち早く気づき、迫りくる危機に備えて領内の改革に乗り出していた。彼は鹿児島の町の防御も固め、そのため1863年に攻撃をしてきたイギリス艦隊は、大いに苦しめられた。斉彬は強い攘夷思想を抱いていたにもかかわらず、うるさく反対する家臣を押え込んで、領内に上陸したフランス人を丁重に迎えた。「必要とあらば、あえて戦争も辞さない平和の士」と評された藩主は、西郷が心から好きな人物だった。西郷は家臣として、この偉大な先見の明のある藩主に忠節を尽くした。二人は親友同士のような間柄だった。国の将来に対する意見も非常に似ていた。

だが、最も重要で大きな感化は、この時代の精神的指導者であった人物から受けている。水戸の藤田東湖は「大和魂（やまと）の塊」のような人だった。日本の精神がその魂に宿ったような人物で、鋭い容貌と角張った体つきは火を噴く富士を思わせたが、内にはまことに誠実な魂を持っていた。正義を熱烈に愛し、野蛮な西洋人

corner of the country, Satzuma stood nearest to the European influence, then coming all from that direction. Its proximity to Nagasaki was a great advantage in this respect, and we are told of foreign commerce actually carried on on some of its dependent islands, long before formal permission was given thereto by the central government.

But of all outward influences, two living men had most to do with Saigō. One was his own feudal master, Shimazu Nariakira of Satzuma, and the other was Fujita Tōko of the Mito *han*. That the former was no common character, no one can doubt. Self-possessed and far-sighted, he early saw the inevitable changes that were coming upon his country, and introduced reforms into his dominion to prepare for the crises that were near at hand. It was he who fortified his own city of Kagoshima, which cost so much for the English fleet to break down in 1863. It was also he, who, notwithstanding his strong anti-foreign sentiments, received with great respect Frenchmen who visited his shore, against the remonstrance of his turbulent subjects to the contrary. "A pacific gentleman who avoided not war if necessary," he was a man after Saigō's own heart, and the subject ceased not in after years to express his dues to his great and farseeing master. The relation between the two was that of two intimate friends, so near came they to each other in their views as to the future of their country.

But the chief and greatest inspiration came from the master spirit of the time. In Fujita Tōko of Mito, "the spirit of Yamato had concentrated itself." He was Japan etherialized into a soul. Sharp in outlines and acutely angled, the form was that of the volcanic Fuji, with the soul in it of all sincerity. An intense lover of righteousness, and an intense hater of the Western Barbarians, he

を徹底的に憎む彼のまわりには、おのずと次の日本を
担う若者たちが集まってきた。そして、遥か離れた地
で彼の評判を耳にした西郷は、藩主に従って江戸へ入
ったときに、東湖に会って、その人柄にじかに触れる
機会を逃さなかった。二人は意気投合した。「私が今胸
に抱いている志を後に伝えてくれるのはあの若者をお
いてない」と師は語り、「天下に畏るべき人物はただ一
人、それは東湖先生です」と弟子は言った。帝国の統
一、その国が「ヨーロッパと肩を並べる国になるため」
の大陸への領土拡大、これを実現するための具体策は、
東湖から受けた新たな感化によって、西郷の頭のなか
で形を結んでいったようだ。西郷は、こうして自分が
実現すべき理想をしっかりとつかむと、あとはひたす
らに目標にむかって一直線に進んでいった。維新の思
想は、東湖の激しい精神のなかに種を蒔かれたものの、
それが実現するには西郷のような穏やかな魂の中に植
え替えられる必要があった。東湖は1855年の地震で55
歳で世を去り、その精神に芽生えた理想の実現は、優
秀な弟子に委ねられた。

　西郷は、大好きな山歩きを、ときに何昼夜も通して
続けている間に、天の輝きから声が聞こえてこなかっ
ただろうか。杉林の静寂の中で「静かにささやく声」
が、彼は使命を背負ってこの世に遣わされたのであり、
その使命を果たすことはこの国と世界にとって非常に
重要なのだ、と彼に語りかけなかったか。そういうこ
とがあったからこそ、彼の文章や会話には幾度となく
天という言葉が登場するのではないか。おっとりして
無口で無邪気な西郷は、思索に耽りながら一人で過ご
すことが多かったようである。その心は、彼自身や全

drew around him the rising generation; and Saigō, hearing of his fame at a distance, lost no opportunity of seeing and feeling the man when he was in Yedo with his lord. No two more congenial souls ever met together. "Only that young man shall carry to posterity the plans that I now store in my bosom," said the master of the pupil. "There is none to be feared under heaven except one, and that one is Master Tōko," said the pupil of the master. The united empire, and the extension of its dominion over the continent "so as to enable the land to stand on equal terms with Europe," and the practical ways of leading the nation thereto, seem to have taken final shapes in Saigō's mind by the new influence he came under. He had now distinct ideals to live up to, and his life since then was *one direct march* toward the mark thus laid before him. The Revolution had its seed-thought sown in Tōko's vehement mind; but this needed transplanting to a less intense and more equable soul like Saigō's, that it might bring forth an actual revolution. Tōko died in the earthquake of 1855 at the age of fifty, leaving his illustrious pupil to carry out the ideals first conceived in his mind.

Shall we also deny to our hero a voice direct from Heaven's splendor, as he roamed over his favorite mountains, oftentimes for days and nights in succession? Did not a "still small voice" often tell him in the silence of cryptomeria forest, that he was sent to this earth with a mission, the fulfillment of which was to be of great consequence to his country and the world? Why did he mention Heaven so many times in his writings and conversations if he had not such visitations? A slow, silent, childlike man, he seems to have been mostly alone with his own heart, where we believe he found One greater than himself and all the universe,

宇宙よりも大きな存在が彼に、密かに語りかけてくるのに気づいたにちがいない。現代のパリサイ人が西郷を異教徒と呼び、来世での魂の在処（ありか）を取り沙汰しても、彼にはどうでもいいことだ。「道を行う者は、天下こぞってそしるも足らざるとせず、天下こぞって誉むるも足れりとせず」。「人を相手にせず、天を相手にせよ。天を相手にして、己を尽して人をとがめず、わが誠の足らざるを尋ぬべし」。「道は天地自然の道なるゆえ、講学の道は敬天愛人を目的とし、身を修するに克己を以て終始せよ。……天は人も我も同一に愛し給うゆえ、我を愛する心を以て人を愛するなり」訳注9。西郷はここに引いた言葉以外にも、似たような言葉を数多く残している。これらはすべて、彼が天から直接聞いた言葉だと、私は信じている。


## Ⅲ− 維新革命における役割

維新革命における西郷の役割をすべて記すことは、革命の全史を記すことに等しいだろう。思うに、ある意味で1868年の日本の維新革命は西郷の革命であったと言えるのではないか。もちろん、一国の再建は一人の力ではできない。新しい日本を西郷の日本とは呼べない。それでは維新革命に参画した大勢の他の優秀な男たちに対して不公平である。実際、西郷の同志のなかには、多くの点でもっと優れた人物がいた。経済改革に関しては、西郷ほど不向きな人間もいなかっただろう。内政については木戸［孝允（たかよし）］や大久保のほうが精通していたし、維新革命後の国家を平和裏に治める

holding secret conversations with him. What cares he if the modern Pharisees call him a heathen, and dispute as to the whereabouts of his soul in the future existence! "He that follows the heavenly way abases not himself even though the whole world speaks evil of him; neither thinks he himself sufficient even though they in unison praise his name." "Deal with Heaven, and never with men. Do all things for Heaven's sake. Blame not others; only search into the lack of sincerity in us." "The law is of the universe and is natural. Hence he only can keep it who makes it his aim to fear and serve Heaven.... Heaven loves all men alike. So we must love others with the love with which we love ourselves." (我を愛する心を以て人を愛すべし。) Saigō said these things and much else like them, and I believe he heard all these directly from Heaven.

## III– His Part in the Revolution

To write out in full Saigō's part in the Revolution would be to write the whole history of the same. In one sense we may say, I think, that the Japanese Revolution of 1868 was Saigō's revolution. Of course no one man can rebuild a nation. We will not call New Japan Saigō's Japan. That certainly is doing great injustice to many other great men who took part in this work. Indeed, in many respects, Saigō had his superiors among his colleagues. As for matters of economic rearrangement, Saigō was perhaps the least competent. He was not for the details of internal administration as Kido and Ōkubo were, and Sanjō and Iwakura were far his superiors in the work of the pacific settlement of the revolutionized

ことにかけては三条［実美］や岩倉［具視］らのほうが有
能だった。新しい帝国は、これらの人々がすべてそろ
わなければ、現在のような形にならなかったのである。
　だが、西郷なくして維新革命が可能であったかとい
うと、それは疑問だ。木戸や三条のような人物を欠い
ても、少しは手間取ったかもしれないが、維新革命は
おそらく成就していただろう。維新の運動が始まるに
は原動力が必要であった。その運動に形を与え、天の
全能の法が導く方向へ進ませる人物が必要だった。運
動はいったん始まって、進む方向さえ決まれば、あと
は比較的簡単な仕事だ。その多くは、西郷のような度
量がなくても行える、単調な骨折り仕事である。我々
が西郷の名を「新日本帝国」と深く結びつけるのは、
彼の大きな心のなかに生まれた力、のちに世の出来事
に作用して彼の時代の社会を動かした力を、始動させ、
方向づけたのは西郷その人だと信じるからだ。
　東湖と有意義な面談を果たし、将軍のいる江戸から
故郷へ戻った西郷は、当時西日本で台頭していた反徳
川幕府の勢力に加わった。月照という熱烈な尊皇主義
の学僧と関わった事件を機に、西郷の志は広く世間に
知れ渡ることとなる。徳川方から厳しく追われていた
月照を匿うことになった西郷は、僧を守りきれないと
観念し、共に死に就く同意を得る。二人の愛国者は月
が照らす夜の海に舟で漕ぎ出て、「秋の光景にひとしお
心慰められ」、互いに手をとり（相抱いて）身を投じた。
その水音で眠っていた藩吏が目を覚まし、すぐに捜索
が始まった。二人の身体は引き上げられた。西郷は息
を吹き返したが、月照は帰らぬ人となった。新帝国を
双肩に担う男は、友人に対する友情ともてなしの証と

country. The New Empire as we have it now, would not have been, were it not for *all* these men.

But we doubt whether the Revolution was possible *without* Saigō. A Kido or a Sanjō we might not have had, and yet the Revolution we would have had, though perhaps not so successfully. A need there was of a primal force that could give a start to the whole movement, a soul that could give a shape to it, and drive it in the direction ordered by Heaven's omnipotent laws. Once started and directed, the rest was comparatively an easy work, much of it mere drudgeries, that could be done by smaller men than he. And when we connect the name of Saigō so intimately with the New Japanese Empire, it is because we believe him to be the starter and director of a force generated in his big mind, and afterward applied to the course of events then running in the society of his time.

Soon after his return from the Shōgun's capital, after the all-important meeting with Tōko, Saigō identified himself with the anti-Tokugawa party then gaining force in the western part of the country. His episode with Gesshō, a learned Buddhist priest and a warm advocate of the imperial cause, marks the point in his career when his avowed aim began to be known to the public. Unable to shelter the fugitive priest, with whose custody he was entrusted, from the hot pursuit of Tokugawa men, Saigō proposed death to his guest and was accepted. They two went to the sea on a moonlit night, "drew maximum consolation from the autumnal view," and then hand in hand, the two patriots plunged into the sea. The splash called the attention of the attendants then asleep, and search for the lost began at once. Their bodies were secured,

して自分の命さえ惜しみはしなかったのである！　この弱さ──禅の修行で「抑え」ようとした「情のもろさ」──こそ、のちに述べるように、彼に身の破滅をもたらすものであった。


　このほかにも倒幕運動に連座したかどで、西郷は二度、南の島に流されている。1863年のイギリス艦隊による砲撃後に鹿児島へ戻ると、すぐに運動に復帰したが、今度はもっと慎重になっていた。西郷の仲介で長州と徳川幕府の間に和平協定が結ばれた。しかし1年後、幕府は長州に無理難題を押しつけ、長州がこれを断固拒否したため、いわゆる長州征伐に発展した。薩摩藩は西郷の指示により、割り当てられた兵力を長州征伐に送ることを拒んだ。薩摩のこの政策は、のちに維新の歴史において重要な意義を持つことになる、有名な「薩長連合」の始まりであった。長州征伐軍の完全な敗北と、外交政策における大失態で、旧政権の終焉は予想外に早く訪れた。ぐらつき始めた政権を倒す許可を与えた詔書を薩長連合が手に入れたまさにその日、将軍はみずから進んで300年続いた政権を放棄し、正当な主権者はなんの抵抗も受けずに復権したのである（1867年11月14日）。薩長連合とその同盟軍による京都の町の制圧、「12月9日の王政復古の大号令」、将軍の二条城からの撤退があいついで行われた。1868年1月3日、伏見の戦いを機に戦争が始まった。官軍は全面的勝利を収め、当時「賊軍」と呼ばれた徳川方は東へ退却していった。大軍が二方からこれを追い、西郷は東海道軍を[参謀として]指揮した。なんの抵抗もなく、4月4日には

Saigō revived, but Gesshō did not. The man who had a new empire upon his shoulders thought not his life to be too precious to be given away for his friend as a pledge of his affection and hospitality! It was this weakness,—the weakness of "too keen sensibility" which he tried "to kill" by his Zen Philosophy,—that brought upon his final destruction, as we shall see afterward.

For this and other complicities in anti-Tokugawa movements, he was twice exiled to south-sea islands. Returning to Kagoshima after its bombardment by the British fleet in 1863, he at once resumed his old course, though this time more cautiously than before. By his advice a pacific settlement was made between Chōshū and the Tokugawa Government; but a year later, when the latter forced unreasonable demands upon the former, and their flat refusals called forth the so-called Chōshū Invasion, Satsuma under Saigō's direction declined to send its quota of troops to join the expedition. This policy of Satsuma was the beginning of the famous coalition effected between it and Chōshū, of so momentous import in the history of the Revolution. The total discomfiture of the invading force, and the evident imbecility of the old government in its dealings with foreign affairs, precipitated its downfall much earlier than was expected; and on the same day when the coalition secured an imperial decree for the upsetting of the tottering dynasty, the Shōgun out of his own free-will, laid down his authority of three centuries' standing, and the rightful sovereign was reinstated in power seemingly without any opposition (Nov. 14, 1867). The occupation of the city of Kyōto by the army of the coalition and its allies, "the Grand Proclamation of the Ninth Day of December," and the evacuation of the Nijō castle by the Shōgun followed in rapid succession. On the 3rd of

江戸城は官軍に差し出された。その後の多大な影響を<sup>訳注11</sup>思えば、これは史上もっとも安く上がった革命と言える。

維新革命がこれほど少ない代償で、かつ効果的に成し遂げられたのは西郷のおかげである。安上がりと効果的という矛盾する二つの面こそ、西郷の偉大さをもっとも顕著に証明している。旧体制を一掃した効果の点から見れば、「12月9日の王政復古の大号令」に比肩しうるのは、1790年7月14日にフランスの首都でなされた宣言だけである。西郷の冷静さは伏見の戦いが始まったときから官軍の柱であった。戦場から伝令がきて「援軍を出してください。我々は一連隊だけで、敵の砲火にさらされています」と言ったとき、西郷は「よかろう。諸君が全員戦死したら出そう」と答えた。伝令は戦場に戻り、敵軍は打ち破られた。このような将を持つ側が負けるはずがない。東海道軍は品川へ進駐し、西郷は旧友の勝海舟に会った。勝は徳川方にあってただ一人、避けがたい幕府の最期を見越し、国の存続のためには主家の最高権力さえ犠牲にする覚悟ができていた。「このたびはさぞお困りでしょう」と、官軍の将である西郷は旧政府の使者の勝に言った。「私の立場に身を置かれてこそ、私の心中もご理解いただけましょう」と友は答えた。西郷はそこで笑い出した。友の苦境を目の当たりにしてなお、朗らかであるとは！ 彼の心は今や和平に傾いた。京都へ帰り、非常な抵抗に

January 1868, the war began with the battle of Fushimi. The imperialists were entirely successful, and the rebels, as the Tokugawa party was called from that time, retired toward the east. Two grand armies followed the latter, Saigō commanding the Tōkaidō branch. No opposition was met, and on the 4th of April the castle of Yedo was tendered to the imperialists. The Revolution, considering its tremendous after-effects, was the cheapest ever bought.

And it was Saigō who bought it so cheaply and made it so effective, his real greatness showing itself most conspicuously in these two contrary aspects of our revolution. "The Grand Proclamation of the Ninth Day of December" is comparable only to the similar proclamation of the Fourteenth of July 1790 in the French capital, in its sweeping effect upon old institutions. His self-possession was the stay of the imperialists when the first battle was opened at Fushimi. A messenger came to him from the field and said, "Pray send us a reinforcement. We are only one regiment, and the enemy's fire is hot upon us." "I will," said General Saigō, "when every one of you is dead upon the field." The messenger returned, and the enemy was repulsed. The side that had such a general could not but win. This Tōkaidō army marched up to Shinagawa, and the general was met by an old friend of his, Katsu[*5] by name, who alone among the Tokugawa men saw its inevitable end, and would resign himself to sacrifice the supremacy of his master's house that his country might live thereby. "I believe my friend is at wit's end by this time," said the commander of the imperial army to the messenger from the old government. "Only by placing yourself in my position you can understand where I am," responds the latter. The general bursts into a peal of laughter; he is amused at seeing his friend in distress! His mind is now inclined

あいながらも、将軍やその追従者に対する恩赦を主張し続けた。そして、包囲された側が受け入れやすい条件を江戸に持ち帰った。西郷が和睦を結ぼうと決心する数日前、勝は西郷を愛宕山へ散歩に誘ったと言われている。眼下に広がる「壮大な都市」を目にして、西郷は強く心を打たれた。旧友に向かい「もし我々が一戦交えれば、この罪もない人々が我々のせいで苦しむことになる」と言ったきり、しばらく押し黙っていた。西郷の「情」が頭をもたげてきたのである。罪もない人々のために和平を実現しなければならない。「強者は弱者に足を取られぬときが最も強い」。西郷の強さの奥には女性的な優しさが多分に潜んでいた。江戸の町は残され、和平が結ばれ、将軍は武器を捨てて江戸城を天皇に明け渡した。

天皇は正当な地位に復し、国は正当な主権のもとに統一され、新政府は西郷の意図した方向へ動き出した。西郷は即、一線から退いて故郷の薩摩に戻り、数年間はそこで歩兵大隊の訓練に明け暮れた。他の同国人とは異なり、西郷にとっての戦いはまだ終わっていなかった。これから導入されるべき社会の大改革には軍事力が必要だったし、もう一つの目標（そのためには国家の統一も一つのステップにすぎなかった）のためにも軍事力が必要だった。首都に呼ばれた西郷は、維新革命の他の功労者とともに「参議」という要職に就いた。しかし、同僚たちが彼について行けなくなるときがきた。今までは共通の目的のために行動をともにしてきたのだが、同僚らが終点と考えるところを西郷は出発点として先に進もうとし、ついには袂を分かつことになったのだ。

toward peace. He goes back to Kyōto, and maintains against all oppositions amnesty toward the Shōgun and his followers, and returns to Yedo with terms very favorable to the beleagured party. It is said that a few days before he finally made up his mind for peace, Katzu took him up to the Atago Hill for a friendly walk. Seeing "the city of magnificent dimensions" under his feet, the general's heart was deeply touched. He turned to his friend and said, "In case we exchange arms, I believe these innocent peoples will have to suffer on our account," and was silent for some moment. His "sensibility" moved in him; he must have peace for those innocent ones' sake. "The strong man is most powerful when unimpeded by the weak." Saigō's strength had considerable of womanly pity in it. The city was spared, peace was concluded, and the Shōgun was made to lay down his arms and tender his castle to the Emperor.

The Emperor reinstated in his rightful position, the country united under its rightful sovereign, and the government set moving in the direction he had aimed at, Saigō retired at once to his home in Satzuma, and there for several years occupied himself mostly in drilling a few battalions of soldiers. To him the war did not end, as it did to others of his countrymen. Great social reforms that were yet to be introduced into the country needed force, as also for that other purpose for which in his eye the united empire was only a step. Called up to the capital, he filled the all-important office of *Sangi* (Chief Councillor) with other men of revolutionary fame. But time came when his associates could follow him no longer. Hitherto they had come together because they had an aim in common; but where they wanted to stop, he wanted to begin, and rupture came at last.

# IV - 朝鮮問題 <sup>訳注13</sup>

た だ征服だけを目的として戦争を起こすことは、西郷の良心に反した。東アジア統合の目的も、当時の世界情勢に関する彼の見解から必然的に出てきたものであった。日本がヨーロッパの「列強」と並ぶためには領土を相当に拡大する必要があり、国民の士気を高めるに足る、攻めの姿勢が必要であった。しかも彼には、日本を東アジアのリーダーにするという大きな使命感があったようだ。弱い者いじめは彼には似合わない。弱者を率いて強者に立ち向かい、奢れる者を叩きのめすことこそ彼の本領であった。西郷の理想とする英雄はジョージ・ワシントン<sup>訳注14</sup>だったと伝えられているし、ナポレオンのような輩には露骨な嫌悪感を示していたことからも、彼が低次元の野望に踊らされていたのでないことは明らかである。

自国の使命についてこれだけの自覚を持っていても、彼は十分な理由なしに戦争をしかける男ではなかった。そうしたことは、自身の重んずる「天」の法に反することになる。だが思いがけず機会が訪れると、西郷はそれを、日本がこの世の始まりから託されていた使命を遂行するために「天」が与えた機会と受け止めた。大陸の隣国である朝鮮が、日本の新政府の派遣した使節に対して無礼な態度を取ったのである。それだけでなく、朝鮮は同地に在住する邦人に露骨な敵意を示し、友好的な隣国の尊厳を著しく傷つける布告を国民に向かって発したのだ。このようなことを放っておいてよいのか？　西郷と彼の同志は主張した。非礼を理由に戦争を始めるわけにはいかない。だが数人の高官から

# IV – The Corean*6 Affair

Saigō was too much of a moralist to go to war merely for conquest's sake. His object of the reduction of Eastern Asia came necessarily out of his views of the then state of the world. That Japan might be a compeer with the Great Powers of Europe, she needed a considerable extension of her territorial possessions, and enough aggressiveness to keep up the spirit of her people. Then too, we believe he had somehow an idea of the great mission of his country as the leader of Eastern Asia. To crush the weak was never in him; but to lead them against the strong and so crush the proud, was his whole soul and endeavor. The single fact that his ideal hero was said to be George Washington, and that he showed intense dislike toward Napoleon and men of his type, should be enough evidence that Saigō was never a slave of low ambitions.

Yet with all his high notions of his country's mission, he would not go to war without sufficient cause for it. To do so would be against Heaven's law that he made so much of. But when an opportunity presented itself without his own making, it was very natural that he took it as a heaven-sent one for his country to enter upon a career assigned her from the beginning of the world. Corea, her nearest continental neighbor, proved herself insolent to several of the Japanese envoys sent out by the new government. Moreover, she showed distinct enmity against the Japanese residents there, and made a public proclamation to her people highly derogatory to the dignity of her friendly neighbor. Should such go unheeded? argued Saigō and men of his inclination. The insolence was not yet sufficient to precipitate war. But let an embassy consisting of a

なる外交使節を朝鮮の宮廷に派遣し、非礼を改めるよう求め、それでもなお朝鮮側が横柄な態度を取り続け、わが国の使節に対して侮辱を重ね、肉体的に危害を加えたりするならば、そのときこそ大陸へ軍を派遣すべき合図とみなし、「天」が許す限りにおいて彼の地を征服すべきだ。この使節には重責と身の危険がともなうので、西郷自身が使者の役を買って出た。同胞に征服への道を開くため、征服者自らが命を投げ出そうと言うのだ！ 歴史上、このような征服のやり方は他に例をみない。

　おっとりして無口の西郷が、閣議で朝鮮問題が論じられる段になると、やおら熱気を帯びて積極的に発言した。自分を遣韓大使に任命するよう同僚に懇願し、その希望がかなったときの喜びようは、念願の物を手に入れて嬉々として飛び跳ねる子供のようであった。西郷が、友人の板垣［退助］（現在は伯爵）に宛てた手紙がある。西郷の任命が閣議で決まったのは、板垣が裏で密かに働きかけたからだった。


　「板垣様

　　昨日、参上つかまりましたが、お留守でしたのでお礼も述べずに引き返して参りました。私の宿願が叶えられましたのは、ひとえに先生のご尽力の賜物でございます。病もたちまち全快いたしました。喜びのあまり三条大臣家から貴邸に飛んでまいりましたが、軽い足どりでございました。もはや『横槍』の入る心配はないと存じます。生涯の愉快とはこのことでございます。目的が叶えられましたので、再び青山の拙宅にこもります。と

few men of the highest rank be sent to the Peninsular Court to demand justice for her insolence; and should she still insist in her haughty attitude, and add insult, and very possibly, personal injury, to the new embassy, let that be the signal to the nation to dispatch its troops into the continent, and extend its conquest as far as Heaven would permit. And since great responsibility and utmost danger would attend such an embassy, he (Saigō) himself would like to be appointed to that office. The conqueror will first lay down his life to open a way of conquest to his countrymen! Never in History was conquest undertaken in this fashion.

The slow, silent Saigō was all fire and activity when the question of the Corean embassy was discussed in the cabinet. He *implored* his colleagues to appoint him as the chief envoy, and when it was fairly settled that his request would be granted, his gladness was that of a child leaping for joy possessed with the object of its heart's desire. Here is a letter which he wrote to his friend Itagaki (now count) by whose special endeavor the appointment was privily settled in the court.

"Itagaki Sama,

I called upon you yesterday, but you were absent, and I was sent back without expressing my thanks to you. By your effort I am to have *all* I wished. My illness is all gone now. Transported with gladness, I flew through the air from Minister Sanjō's to your mansion; my feet were so light. No more fear of 'side thrust' I suppose. Now that my aim is secured, I may retire to my residence in Aoyama and wait for the happy issue. This is only to convey my gratitude to you.

Saigō."

りあえず書面にてお礼を申し上げます。

西郷拝」


　ちょうどこのとき、岩倉が大久保や木戸とともに世界巡察の旅から帰国した。彼らは文明をその中心地で視察し、文明がもたらす快適さと幸せを目の当たりにしてきた。西郷にとってパリやウィーンの人々の暮らしが想像を絶するものであったのと同じくらい、彼らにとっては外国との戦争など言語道断の選択であった。そこで岩倉らはあらゆる権謀術策をめぐらし、自分たちの留守中に成った閣議決定を覆すことに全力を傾けた。そして、ついに三条大臣の病気を理由に、彼らの思惑を押し通すことに成功したのである。1873年11月28日、遣韓大使派遣の決議は撤回された。それまで人前では怒りをみせたことのなかった西郷だが、彼が「長袖者流」と呼んでいた卑劣な公卿の手口には激昂した。西郷を最も怒らせたのは、決議が撤回されたことではなく、撤回させたやり方だった。また、そこに至った動機が、彼には我慢の限界をこえるほど不快だった。西郷は腐敗した政府とは縁を切ろうと決心し、閣議の席で辞表を叩きつけ、東京の住まいを引き払って、ただちに故郷の薩摩に引退し、自分が粉骨砕身して築いてきた政府には二度と加わらなかった。

　征韓論を抑えたことにより、政府の侵略策はすべて消え、その後の政策はすべて「内治改良」とその支持者たちが呼ぶ路線に沿って立てられた。そして、岩倉と彼が率いる「平和派」の思惑通り、国はいわゆる文明開化を謳歌した。それと引き替えに、優柔不断、決断の回避、正義をも犠牲にする平和への固執といった、

At this juncture, Iwakura returned with Ōkubo and Kido from their tour around the world. They saw civilization in its center, its comfort and happiness. They no more thought of foreign war than Saigō did of Parisian or Viennese ways of living. So, resorting themselves to duplicities and ambiguities of all kinds, they in concert did all in their power to overthrow the decision reached in the cabinet council during their absence, and taking advantages of Minister Sanjō's illness, they succeeded at last in carrying their ways through. The Corean Embassy Act was repealed, Nov. 28, 1873. Saigō, who to all outward appearances had known no anger thus far, was now wild over the measures of the "long-sleeved," as he called the coward courtiers. That the act was repealed was not what offended him most; but the way in which it was rescinded, and the motives that led thereto, were objectionable to him beyond his power of forbearance. He made up his mind that he would do nothing with the rotten government, threw his written resignation upon the cabinet-table, gave up his residence in Tokio,[*7] and retired at once to his home in Satzuma, never again to join the government that was set up mostly through his endeavor.

With the suppression of the Corean Affair ceased all the aggressive measures of the government, and its whole policies since then have been directed toward what its supporters called "internal development." And agreeably to the heart's wish of Iwakura and his "peace-party," the country has had much of what they called civilization. Yet withal also came much effeminacy, fear of

真のサムライが嘆くような状況が見られるようになった。「文明とは道のあまねく行わるるを賛称せる言にして、宮室の壮厳、衣服の美麗、外観の浮華を言うにはあらず」。これが西郷の文明の定義である。彼の言う意味での文明には、この時代以降、あまり進歩が見られないように思える。

# V – 謀反人としての西郷

西郷の生涯で最も痛ましい晩年については、多くを語る必要もないだろう。彼が謀反人として時の政府に刃向かったのは事実である。西郷がなぜそこまでする気になったかについては様々な憶測が言われてきた。反逆者と結んだ主な理由を、彼の生来の弱点である「情のもろさ」だとする見方は、それなりの説得力がある。西郷を世界でただ一人の真の男と崇拝する5千人もの若者が、公然と政府に反乱を起こしたのだが、どうも西郷は何も知らなかったようで、彼の意志にも反していたらしい。反乱の成否はひとえに、運動に西郷の名を冠して影響を与えられるかどうかに尽きていた。強さにかけては誰にも引けを取らない西郷も、切羽詰まった人々の嘆願にはほとんど無力だった。20年前、客人を歓待する証として、命も差し出すと誓ったことがあった。そして今ふたたび、自分を敬う弟子たちへの友愛の証として、命も名誉もすべて捧げる覚悟を決めたのかもしれない。西郷を最もよく知る人々はそう考えているようだ。

西郷が、当時の政府に強い不満を抱いていたことについては論駁の余地がない。しかし、彼ほどの冷静な

decisive actions, love of peace at the cost of plain justice, and much
else that the true samurai laments. "What is civilization but an effectual working of righteousness, and *not* magnificence of houses,
beauty of dresses, and ornamentation of outward appearance."
This was Saigō's definition of civilization, and we are afraid civilization in *his* sense has not made much progress since his time.

## V – Saigō as a Rebel

We need say but very little about this last and most lamentable part of Saigō's life. That he turned a rebel against
the government of his time was a fact. What motive led him to
take that position has been conjectured in many ways. That his
old weakness, "too keen sensibility," was the main cause of his
uniting with the rebels seems quite plausible. Some five thousand
young men who worshipped him as the only man in the world,
went into an open rebellion against the government, seemingly
without his knowledge, and much against his will. Their success
depended wholly upon his lending his name and influence to their
cause. A strongest of men, he was almost helpless before the suppliant entreaty of the needy. Twenty years ago he had promised
his life to his guest as a pledge of his hospitality; and now again he
might have been induced to sacrifice his life, his honor, his all, as
a pledge of his friendship to his admiring pupils. This view of
things is taken by many who knew him best.

That he was strongly disaffected with the government of his
time needs no controversy; but that he a level-headed man

人間が、ただ恨みだけで戦争を始めるとは到底考えられない。少なくとも西郷にとっては、反乱は人生の大きな目的が挫折した失望の結果だったと考えたいのだが、これは間違っているだろうか。1868年の維新革命が、西郷の理想に反する結果となったため、それは彼が直接招いた事態ではないにせよ、彼の心の中に言い知れぬ苦悩となって残っていたのである。もし反乱が成功するなら、生涯追い続けてきた大きな夢が実現する可能性も出てくるのではないか。疑念を抱きながらもわずかの希望を託して、彼は反乱者たちと結び、本能的に予感していたと思われる運命をともにした。だが、西郷の生涯のこの時期を歴史が解明するまでには、あと100年かかるだろう。

　西郷は戦いのあいだ、終始口出しもせず、作戦については一切桐野［利秋］や他の者たちに任せていた。彼らは1877年の2月から9月まで戦った。そして希望がことごとく打ち砕かれるや、「父祖の墓」に葬られるため、辛うじて鹿児島に戻った。城山に追い詰められ、麓を政府軍に包囲されていたとき、西郷は碁に興じていた。そして側にいた従者の一人に向かって言った。「あれはお前ではなかったか、野良仕事の帰りに荷馬をひいて通りかかった私に、下駄の鼻緒をすげさせたのは」。男はその時のことを思い出し、無礼を詫び、恐縮して許しを請うた。それに対し、「気にするな。退屈なのでちょっとからかっただけだ」と西郷は応えたという。この総大将が、二人の若者の横柄な要求に従ったことがあるのは事実だった。薩摩では、武士は農夫と道で行き交えば、下駄の鼻緒をすげさせることが慣例となっていた。そのときは、たまたま通りかかった農夫とい

should go to war for the mere sake of enmity is hard to conjecture. Are we mistaken when we maintain that, in his case at least, the rebellion was a result of disappointment in the grand aims of his life? Though not directly caused by him, it found him in unspeakable anguish of soul, because the revolution of 1868 produced the result so contrary to his ideal. Should the rebellion chance to be a success, might he not realize yet the great dreams of his life? Doubtingly, yet not entirely without some hope, he united with the rebels and shared with them the fate he seemed to have instinctively foreseen. But history may wait a hundred years more before it can settle this part of his life.

He remained a passive figure all through the war, Kirino and others looking after all the maneuvers in the field. They fought from February to September, 1877, and when their hopes were all shattered, they forced their way back to Kagoshima, there to be buried in their "fathers' grave-yard." There beleaguered in the Castle Hill, all the government forces gathered at its foot, our hero was playing *go* in the best of spirit. Turning to one of his attendants he said, "Aren't you the one the latchet of whose wooden shoes I mended one day, as I was returning from my farm, drawing my packhorse behind me?" The man remembered the occasion, confessed his insolence, and sincerely asked for forgiveness. "Nothing!" replied Saigō, "Too much leisure made me to poke you a little." The fact was, the General did yield once to the impudent demands of two youths, who, as was the custom in Satsuma, used the right of the samurai to have his wooden-shoes mended by any farmer he happened to meet. The farmer in this

うのが大西郷だったのである。彼は一言も不平を言わずに卑しい仕事をやり、控えめな態度で立ち去ったという。終焉の地で西郷に仕えていた人間が、このような西郷の思い出話を残しているのはうれしいかぎりだ。アクィナスでも我らが西郷ほど控えめではなかった。

　1877年9月24日の朝、政府軍による城山への総攻撃が行われた。西郷はまさに敵軍を迎え撃とうと同志とともに立ち上がったとき、腰に弾丸を受けた。まもなく少数の味方は全滅し、西郷の遺体は敵方の手に落ちた。敵将の一人が「無礼の挙動があってはならぬぞ」と叫び、もう一人は「ああ、お顔は温厚でいらせられる」と言った。西郷を討った側の人間も皆、その死を悼んだ。涙ながらに彼の遺体は埋葬され、今日も涙にくれて墓参をする人はあとを絶たない。こうして最も偉大な人物がこの世を去り、最後のサムライも消えたのである。


# VI − 西郷の生活と人生観

西郷の国家に対する貢献を、歴史が正しく評価するにはまだ時を待たなければならない。しかし、彼の人物像を正しく描けるだけの資料は十分にある。そして、西郷の後半生の生き方が、前半生の説明にもなると思われるので、少し西郷の私生活と持論を見ていきたいと思う。

　まず、西郷ほど無欲で生きた人はいなかった。帝国陸軍元帥と近衛都督を兼任し、閣僚のなかの最有力者でありながら、外見は普通の兵士と同じだった。月収が数百円あっても、生活は15円で優にまかない、残りは困窮している友人に気前よく与えていた。東京の番

case happened to be the great Saigō, who without a word of complaint, did the menial service, and went away in all humility. We are exceedingly thankful for this piece of reminiscence given of him by the very man who attended upon him in his last hours. Saint Aquinas was not more humble than this our Saigō.

On the morning of 24th of September 1877, general assault was made upon the Castle Hill by the government force. Saigō was on the point of rising with his comrades to meet the enemy, when a bullet struck his hip. Soon the little party was annihilated, and Saigō's remains fell into his enemy's hand. "See that no rudeness is done to them," cried one of the enemy's generals. "What a mildness in his countenance!" said another. They that killed him were all in mourning. In tears they buried him, and with tears his tomb is visited by all to this day. So passed away the greatest, and we are afraid, the last of the samurai.

## VI – His Ways of Living and Views of Life

History has yet to wait for the just estimate of Saigō's public service to his country; but it has enough materials at its command for forming right views of the kind of man he really was. And if the latter aspect of his life will help much to clear up the former, I believe my readers will pardon me for dwelling at some length upon his private life and opinions.

First of all, we know of no man who had fewer wants in life than he. The commander-in-chief of the Japanese army, the generalissimo of the Imperial Bodyguard, and the most influential of the cabinet-members, his outward appearance was that of the commonest soldier. When his monthly income was several hundred

町にあった住居は、見るからにみすぼらしい造りで、1ヵ月の家賃は3円だった。普段着は、薩摩絣の短衣に幅広の兵子帯で、大きな下駄をはいていた。この身なりのまま、宮中晩餐会でもどこへでも出かけた。出された食べ物は何でも食べた。ある人が西郷の家を訪ねると、ちょうど西郷が数人の兵士や従者と、大きな木製の鉢を囲んで、冷たい蕎麦を食べているところだった。純真素朴な大きな子供のようだった西郷にとって、若者たちと一緒に食事をすることが、お気に入りの宴会だったようだ。


　西郷は自分のことだけでなく、財産にも無関心だった。東京の一等地に所有していた広い土地を、設立されて間もない国立銀行に譲り渡したときには、売値を聞かれても、頑として自分から言おうとはしなかった。その土地は今でもその銀行が持っており、数十万ドルの価値がある。西郷の多額の年金は、ほとんどが鹿児島に創設した私学校の維持費に充てられた。西郷が詠んだ漢詩に、次のようなものがある。

　　　わが家の遺法、人知るや否や
　　　児孫のために、美田を買わず

　この詩のように、西郷は妻子に何も遺さなかったが、謀反人として死んだにもかかわらず、国家が遺族の面倒をみた。西郷のこのような「無関心」は、近代経済学からすると、とんでもない話だろう。

yen, he had enough for his wants with fifteen, and every one of his needy friends was welcome to the rest. His residence in Banchō, Tokio, was a shabby-looking structure *the rent three yen a month*. His usual costume was Satzuma-spun cotton stuff, girdled with a broad calico *obi*, and large wooden clogs on his feet. In this attire he was ready to appear at any place, at the Imperial dinner-table, as anywhere else. For food he would take whatsoever was placed before him. Once a visitor found him in his residence, he and several of his soldiers and attendants surrounding a large wooden bowl, and helping themselves to buck-wheat macaroni cooled in the receptacle. That seemed to be his favorite banquet, eating with young fellows, himself a big child of the simplest nature.

Careless about his body, he was also careless about his possessions. He gave up a fine lot of land in his possession in the most prosperous section of the city of Tokio to a national bank just then started, and when asked its price, he refused to mention it; and so it remains to this day in the possession of the said corporation, worth several hundred thousand dollars. A large income from his pension was spent wholly for the support of a school which he started in Kagoshima. One of his Chinese poems reads,

> "Does the world know our family law?
> We leave not substance to our children."

And so he left nothing to his widow and children; but the nation took care of them, though he died a rebel. Modern Economic Science may have much to say against this "carelessness" of his.

西郷の唯一の趣味は犬だった。届け物は、贈り物と見なして一切受け取らなかったが、犬に関するものは、厚く感謝して受け取った。犬の多色石版画、石版画、鉛筆によるスケッチ画には大層喜んだ。西郷が東京の家を譲り渡したときには、大きな箱一杯の犬の絵があったと言われている。大山〔巌〕元帥に送った手紙の一通から、西郷がいかに犬の首輪の好みにうるさかったかがうかがえる。「犬の首輪の見本をわざわざお送りくださいましたことを、深く感謝申し上げます。舶来品よりもすぐれていると存じます。緒をあと3寸ほど長くして、4、5個作製して下さいますよう、心からお願い申し上げます。さらに一つ、少し幅を広くし、5寸ほど長いものもぜひお願い申し上げます。云々」。西郷は生涯、犬を友とした。犬を伴って、昼も夜も山中で過ごすことが多かった。誰にもまして孤独の人であった西郷は、犬をもの言わぬ友として孤独を分かち合っていたのだ。

　西郷は口論することが大嫌いだったので、できる限りそれを避けていた。あるとき、宮中の宴会に招かれ、いつもの簡素な着物姿で出席した。そして退出しようとすると、入り口で脱いだはずの下駄が見つからない。だが、そのようなことで人を煩わせたくなかったので、裸足のまま、しかも小雨のなかを歩き出した。城門までやってくると、門衛に呼び止められ、身分を訊かれた。ごく平凡な身なりだったので怪しまれたのだ。西郷は、「西郷大将〔参議〕」と答えた。しかし門衛はその言葉を信用せず、門の通過を許さなかった。西郷は雨に濡れて立ち尽くし、自分の身分を門衛に証明してくれる人が来るのを待った。間もなく岩倉大臣〔公〕を乗せた馬車がやってきた。裸足の男は大将〔参議〕だと証

He had one hobby, and that was the dog-kind. Though he accepted nothing else that was taken as a present to him, anything that related to dogs he received with all thankfulness. Chromos, lithographs, pencil-sketches of the canine tribe were always very pleasing to him. It is said that when he gave up his house in Tokio, he had a large boxful of pictures of dogs. One of his letters to General Ōyama was very particular about collars for his hounds: "Many thanks for the specimens of the dog-collars you kindly sent me," he writes. "I think they are superior to imported articles. Only if you could make them three inches longer, they would fit my purpose exactly. Make four or five of them, I beseech you. And one more, a little broader and five inches longer, I pray, etc." His dogs were his friends all through his life. He often spent days and nights with them in the mountains. The loneliest of men, he had dumb brutes to share his loneliness.

He disliked disputings, and he avoided them by all possible means. Once he was invited to an Imperial feast, at which he appeared in his usual plain costume. As he retired, he missed his clogs left at the palace-entrance, and as he would not trouble anybody about them, he walked out barefooted; and that in a drizzling rain. When he came to the castle-gate, the sentinel called him to halt, and demanded of him an explanation of his person,—a doubtful figure he appeared in his commonest garb. "General Saigō," he replied. But they believed not his words, and allowed him not to pass the gate. So he stood there in the rain waiting for somebody who might identify him to the sentinel. Soon a carriage approached with Minister Iwakura in it. The barefooted man was proved to be the general, was taken into the minister's coach, and

明され、岩倉大臣［公］の馬車に同乗して立ち去った。
西郷には、熊吉という名の下男がいたが、長年西郷の
つつましい家に仕え、親しまれた人物だった。ところ
が、ある時、解雇されても当然の重大な過ちを犯した。
だが、寛大な主人は、解雇された場合の下男の行く末
を案じた。そこで、西郷は熊吉をそのまま家に留め置
いた。だが、その後長い間決して用事を言い付けなか
った。熊吉は主人の死後も、長く生きながらえ、誰よ
りも不運な英雄を慕い悲しむ一人となった。

　ある人は、西郷の私生活について次のように伝えて
いる。「私は13年間西郷と一緒に暮らしましたが、下男
を叱る姿は一度も見たことがありません。ふとんの上
げ下ろし、戸の開け閉め、その他身の回りのことは、
ほとんど自分でしていました。でも、他の者が西郷の
ためにしようとするのを遮ることはありませんでした。
手伝おうという申し出を断ることもありませんでした。
無頓着で無邪気な様子は、子供そのものでした」

　実際、西郷は人の平穏な暮らしをかき乱すことをひ
どく嫌い、しばしば他人の家を訪ねることはあっても、
家の中に入って声をかけることはせず、玄関に立った
まま、家の人がたまたま出てきて彼に気づくまで、じ
っと待っていたのである！

　西郷の生活は、このように地味で簡素だったが、そ
の思想は、これまで紹介してきたように、聖者か哲学
者の思想だった。

　「敬天愛人」の言葉が西郷の人生観をすべて要約して
いる。すべての知恵はこの教えにあり、すべての無知
は、自分だけを愛する利己心にある。西郷が「天」を
どのようなものとして受けとめていたか、それを「力」

so carried away.——He had a servant, Kuma by name, a well-known figure in his modest household for many years. The latter, however, once committed an offence grave enough to have his position forfeited. But the indulgent master was solicitous about his servant's future if discharged from his service. So he simply kept him in his house; but for many years he gave him not a single order to be executed. Kuma survived his master many years, and was one of the deepest mourners for the ill-fated hero.

A witness has this to say of Saigō's private life: "I lived with him thirteen years; and never have I seen him scolding his servants. He himself looked to the making and unmaking of his bed, to the opening and shutting of his room-windows, and to most other things that pertained to his person. But in cases others were doing them for him, he never interfered; neither did he decline help when offered. His carelessness and entire artlessness were those of a child."

*Indeed he was so loath to disturb the peace of others that he often made visits upon their houses, but dared not to call for notice from inside; but stood in the entrance thereof and there waited till somebody happened to come out and find him!*

Such was his living; so lowly and so simple; but his thinking was that of a saint and a philosopher, as we have had already some occasions to show.

"Revere Heaven; love people," summed up all his views of life. All wisdom was there; and all *un*-wisdom, in love of self. What conceptions he had of Heaven; whether he took it to be a Force or a Person, and how he worshipped it except in his own

と見ていたか「人格」と見ていたか、彼独自の実践的方法以外には、「天」をどのように崇拝していたか確認する方法はない。しかし、西郷が「天」は全能であり、不変であり、きわめて慈悲深い存在であり、その法は疑うことなく誰もが従うべき、きわめて恵み豊かなものとして理解していたことは、その言動が十分に証明している。「天」とその「法」に関する西郷の言葉は、すでにいくつか紹介してきた。そのことは西郷が繰り返し書いているので、ここで多く付け足す必要はないだろう。「天は人も我も同一に愛したまうゆえ、我を愛する心を以て人を愛するなり」という西郷の言葉には、律法と予言者の思想が込められており、西郷がそのような壮大な教えをどこから得たのか興味深いところである。

「天」を相手にするには真心を尽くさなければならない。さもなければ、その道について知ることはできない。西郷は人間の知恵を嫌い、すべての知恵は高潔な心と志から生まれるものだとした。心を清くして志を高く持てば、戦場でも議場でも、必要なときに道はすぐにも開ける。いつも策を練っている者は、危機が迫ったときは無策なのだ。西郷は「至誠の域は、まず慎独より手を下すべし。間居即慎独の場所なり」と言っている。不誠実とその落とし子である利己心は、人生の失敗の主な原因である。「総じて人は己に克つを以て成り、自ら愛するを以て敗るるぞ。…事業を創起する人その事たいてい十に七八まではよく成しうれども、残り二つを終るまで成しうる人の希れなるは…功立ち名顕るるにしたがい、いつしか自ら愛する心起り、恐懼戒慎の意ゆるみ、驕矜の気ようやく長じ、その成しえたる事業をたのみ、いやしくもわが事を仕遂げんと

practical way, we have no means of ascertaining. But that he knew it to be all-powerful, unchangeable, and *very* merciful, and its Laws to be all-binding, unassailable, and *very* beneficent, his words and actions abundantly testify. We have already given some of his expressions about Heaven and its Laws. His writings are full of them, and we need not multiply them here. When he said, "Heaven loveth all men alike; so we must love others with the love with which we love ourselves," he said all that is in the Law and Prophets, and some of us may be desirous to inquire whence he got that grand doctrine of his.

And this Heaven was to be approached with all sincerity; else the knowledge of its ways was unattainable. Human wisdoms he detested; but all wisdoms were to come from the sincerity of one's heart and purpose. Heart pure and motive high, ways are at hand as we need them, in the council-hall as on the battle-field. He that schemes always is he that has no schemes when crises are at hand. In his own words, "Sincerity's own realm is one's secret chamber. Strong there, a man is strong everywhere." Insincerity, and its great child, Selfishness, are the prime causes of our failures in life. Saigō says, "A man succeeds by overcoming himself, and fails by loving himself. Why is it that many have succeeded in eight and failed in the remaining two? Because when success attended them, love of self grew in them; and vigilance departing, and desire for ease returning, their work became onerous to them, and they failed." Hence we are to meet all the emergencies of life with our lives in our hands. "I have my life to offer," he often

してまずき仕事に陥り、ついに敗るるもの…なり」と西郷は言う。だから我々は命がけで、人生のあらゆる危機に立ち向かわなければならないのだ。「我が命を捧げる」とは、西郷が責任ある立場で、何かの行動を申し出た時によく口にした言葉だ。完全な自己否定の精神が、西郷の勇気の秘密であったことは、次の注目すべき言葉からも明らかである。「命もいらず、名もいらず、官位も金もいらぬ人は、仕末に困るものなり。この仕末に困る人ならでは、艱難を共にして国家の大業は成し得られぬなり」

　「天」を信じ、その法を信じ、またその時を信じた西郷は、自分のことも信じていた。「天」を信じることは、常に自分を信じることでもあったからだ。「断じて行えば鬼神もこれを避ける」と西郷は言った。また、「事の上にて、機会というべきもの二つあり。僥幸の機会あり、また設け起す機会あり。世人の唱うる機会とは、多くは僥幸の仕当てたるを言う。真の機会は、理を尽して行い、勢いをつまびらかにして動くというにあり。大事にのぞんではぜひ機会は引き起さずんばあるべからず」とも言っている。それで、西郷は「人」つまり有能な人材を何よりも重んじた。「なにほど制度方法を論ずるとも、その人にあらざれば行われがたし。人ありて後方法の行わるるものなれば、人は第一の宝にして、己その人になるの心がけ肝要なり」

　「天を敬う人」は、正義を尊重し、実行する人にならざるをえない。「正義のひろく行われること」が、西郷の文明の定義だった。西郷にとって、正義ほど天下に大事なものはなかったのだ。自分の命はもちろん、国家さえ正義よりも大事ではなかった。西郷はこう言って

uttered when he had some action to propose in his responsible position. That entire self-abnegation was the secret of his courage is evident from the following remarkable utterance of his: "A man that seeks neither life, nor name, nor rank, nor money, is the hardest man to manage. But with only such life's tribulations can be shared, and such only can bring great things to his country."

A believer in Heaven, its laws and its time, he was also a believer in himself, as one kind of faith always implies the other kind. "Be determined and do," he said, "and even gods will flee from before you." Again he said: "Of opportunities there are two kinds: those that come without our seeking and those that are of our own make. What the world calls opportunity is usually the former kind. But the true opportunity comes by acting in accordance with reason, in compliance with the need of the time. When crises are at hand, opportunities must be caused by us." A MAN therefore, a capable man, he prized above all things. "Whatever be the ways and institutions we speak about," were his words, "they are impotent unless there are men to work them. Man first; then the working of means. Man is the first treasure, and let every one of us try to be a man."

A "reverer of Heaven" cannot but be a reverer and observer of righteousness. "An effectual working of righteousness" was his definition of civilization. To him there was nothing under Heaven so precious as righteousness. His life, of course, and his country even, were not more precious than righteousness. He says:

いる。「正道を踏み国を以て斃るるの精神なくば、外国交際は全かるべからず。彼の強大に畏縮し、円滑を主として、曲げて彼の意に順従する時は、軽侮を招き、好親かえって破れ、ついに彼の制を受くるに至らん」。さらに続けて、「国の凌辱せらるるに当りては、たとえ国を以て斃るるとも、正道を踏み、義を尽すは政府の本務なり……戦の一字を恐れ、政府の本務を墜しなば、商法支配所と申すものにて、さらに政府にはあらざるなり」。そして、このような発言をした西郷を、当時首府に駐在していた外国の使節は、そろって尊敬した。誰よりも西郷を尊敬したのは、東洋的外交術に長け、長年にわたって我が国におけるイギリスの国益を巧みに守り通した、ビクトリア女王治世下のイギリス公使、ハリー・パークス卿であった。「正しくあれ、恐れるな」というのが、西郷の国政のやり方だったのだ。

　このように一貫した考えをもっていたので、当然ながら、西郷は自分の周囲で進行している運動の成り行きについても、はっきりとした見通しをもっていた。維新革命が達成されるはるか以前、志士たちの多くにとってさえ、新政府がいまだ白日夢であった頃、西郷にとってはそれは成就した現実だったのだ。長年にわたる追放が解かれ、西郷をかつての重要な役務に呼び戻すために、西郷の流されていた小島に使者がきたとき、西郷は砂浜に新国家の建設のために考えていた方

"Unless there is a spirit in us to walk in the ways of righteousness, and *fall with the country if for righteousness' sake*, no satisfactory relation with foreign powers can be expected. Afraid of their greatness and hankering after peace, and abjectly following their wishes, we soon invite their contemptuous estimate of ourselves. Friendly relations will thus begin to cease, and we shall be made to serve them at last." In a similar strain he says: "When a nation's honor is in any way injured, the plain duty of its government is to follow the ways of justice and righteousness *even though the nation's existence is jeopardized thereby....* A government that trembles at the word 'war,' and only makes it a business to buy slothful peace, should be called a commercial regulator, and it should not be called a government." And the man who uttered these words was the object of universal esteem by all the ambassadors of the foreign courts then represented in our capital. None esteemed him more than Sir Harry Parkes of her Britannic Majesty's Legation, who as an adept in the art of Oriental diplomacy, was for a long time a shrewd upholder of the British interests on our shores. "Be just and fear not" was Saigō's method of running a government.

With such a singleness of view, he was naturally very clear-sighted as to the outcome of the movements then going on around him. Long before the Revolution, when the new government was yet a day-dream even to many of its advocates, it was an accomplished reality to Saigō. It is said that, when, after many years of banishment, he was sent to in his isle of exile to call him back to his old position of responsibility, he told the messenger, with diagrams on the beach-sand, all the maneuvers he had framed in his mind for the upbuilding of the new empire; and so true to the

策のすべてを、図で示しながら語ったと伝えられている。そのとき西郷が語った予見は、あまりにも現実と合致しすぎていたため、話を聞いた使者は、西郷は人間ではなく神だと、あとで友人に語ったという。維新革命の最中の、西郷の見事な落ち着きぶりはすでに見てきたが、西郷の鋭い洞察力をもってすれば、当然の結果だといえる。維新革命がどうにか始まった頃、ほぼ10世紀もの間非常に不安定であった天皇の地位がどうなるのか、一部にはかなりの不安があった。著名な宮廷歌人、福羽［美静］は次のように西郷に尋ねた。

「維新が成就することは望んでいます。だが、新政府が樹立された場合、神聖なる天皇の地位はどのようになりますか」

それに対する西郷の答えは、次のように明快であった。

「新政府においては、天皇は本来あるべき地位についていただきます。それは親しく国政にあたることであり、それによって天皇は天から与えられた使命をまっとうすることになるのです」

この人物には、少しも回りくどいところがなかった。正義の道の常として、簡潔で、公明正大で、太陽の光のように澄み切っていたのだ。

西郷は1冊の著作も遺していない。だが、多くの詩と、数編の小文は遺した。折りにふれて書き残した詩文を通して、西郷の心の中を垣間見ることができ、それが彼の行動に投影されていたことがわかる。西郷の詩文には、知識をひけらかすようなところはない。西郷と同じくらい学識のある日本の学者と違い、西郷の言葉と比喩は、きわめて簡潔なものであった。たとえば、次にあげる詩ほど簡潔な詩を他に見つけることはできない。

situation was the prescience then offered that the listener told his friends afterward that, in his view, Saigō was not a man but a god. And we have seen his perfect self-possession during the Revolution,—a natural result of his clear vision. When it had fairly begun, there was much anxiety in some quarters as to the position of the Emperor in the new government, seeing that for well-nigh ten centuries his real situation had been a very undefinable one. Mr. Fukuba, a well-known court-poet, asked Saigō on this wise:

"The Revolution I desire to have; but when the new government is set up, where shall we place our holy Emperor?'"

To which Saigō's very explicit reply was as follows:
"In the new government we shall place the Emperor where he should be; that is make him personally see to the affairs of the state, and so fulfill his heaven-appointed mission."

No tortuosities in this man. Short, straight, clear as sunlight, as the ways of righteousness always are.

Saigō left us no books. But he left us many poems, and several essays. Through these occasional effusions of his, we catch glimpses of his internal state, and we find it to be the same as was reflected in all his actions. Pedantry there is not in all his writings. Unlike many Japanese scholars of his degree of attainment, his words and similes are the simplest that can be imagined. For instance, can anything be simpler than this:

我に千糸の髪あり
鬆々漆より黒し
我に一片の心あり
晧々として雪より白し
我が髪はなお断つべし
我が心は截るべからず

また、次のように西郷らしい詩もある。

一貫唯唯諾す
従来鉄石の肝
貧居傑士を生じ
勲業多難に顕わる
雪に耐えて梅花麗しく
霜を経て楓葉丹し
もしよく天意を識らば
あに敢て自ら安きを謀らん

次の、山を詠んだ短い詩は全く西郷そのものだ。

地古く、山高く
夜よりも静かなり
人語を聞かず
ただ天を看るのみ

「生財」と題された西郷の文章の一部を紹介しよう。

『左伝』にこう書かれている。「徳が源であり、財は

"Hair I have of thousand strings,
    Darker than the lac.
A heart I have an inch long,
    Whiter than the snow.
My hair may divided be,
My heart shall never be."

Or this, very characteristic of him:

"Only one way, 'Yea and Nay;'
    Heart ever of steel and iron.
Poverty makes great men;
    Deeds are born in distress.
Through snow, plums are white,
Through frosts, maples are red;
If but Heaven's will be known,
Who shall seek slothful ease!"

The following bit of a mountain-song of his is perfectly natural to
him:

"Land high, recesses deep,
    Quietness is that of night.
I hear not human voice,
    But look only at the skies."

We have space here only for a part of his essay entitled, "On
the Production of Wealth."

"In the book of 'Sa-den' it is written: 'Virtue is a source of

結果としてもたらされるもの」。徳が盛んなれば、財は
おのずと足る。徳が衰えれば、それに応じて財も少な
くなる。財とは、国家をうるおし、国民に安らぎを与
えることにより生じるものだからだ。小人は自分を利
することを目的とし、君子は民を利することを目的と
する。前者は利己心により身を滅ぼし、後者は公の精
神により栄える。生き方しだいで、盛衰、貧富、興廃、
生死がわかれる。慎むべきではないだろうか。

　世人は「取れば富み、与えれば失う」と言う。なん
という間違いだろう。農業にたとえよう。けちな農夫
は種を惜しんで蒔き、秋の採り入れを座して待つ。も
たらされるのは、飢餓だけである。よい農夫はよい種
を蒔き、その上、手入れを惜しまない。五穀は百倍も
の実りとなって増え、有り余るほどの収穫を得ること
になる。貯めることだけに執心する者は、収穫するこ
とを知っているだけで、植えることを知らない。だが、
仁政を行う者は植えることに精を出す。そのため収穫
は、求めずとも訪れるのだ。

＊　＊　＊

　徳に励む者には、財は求めなくてもおのずと生じる。
したがって、世人が損と呼ぶものは損ではなく、得と
呼ぶものは得ではない。いにしえの聖人は民に仁を施
し、恵みを与えることを益となし、民から取ることを
損とみた。今はその正反対だ。

＊　＊　＊

　ああ、賢の大道に背いて歩み、民のために財と豊か
さとを求めることは、賢明といえるのだろうか。損益

which wealth is an outcome.' Virtue prospers, and wealth comes by itself. Virtue declines, and in the same proportion wealth diminishes. For wealth is by replenishing the land and giving peace to the people. The small man aims at profiting himself; the great man, at profiting the people. One is selfishness, and it decays. The other is public-spiritedness, and it prospers. According as you use your substance, you have prosperity or decay, abundance or poverty, rise or fall, life or death. Should we not be on our guard therefore?

"The world says: 'Take and you shall have wealth, and give and you shall lose it.' Oh what an error! I seek a comparison in agriculture. The covetous farmer sparing of his seeds sows but niggardly; and then sits and waits for the harvest of autumn. The only thing he shall have is starvation. The good farmer sows good seeds, and gives all his cares thereto. The grains multiply hundredfold, and he shall have more than he can dispose of. He that is intent upon gathering knows only of harvesting, and not of planting. But the wise man is diligent in planting; therefore the harvest comes without his seeking.

\* \* \*

"To him who is diligent in virtue, wealth comes without his seeking it. Hence what the world calls loss is not loss, and what it calls gain is not gain. The wise man of old thought it as gain to bless and give to the people, and as loss to take from them. Quite otherwise at present."

\* \* \*

"Ah, can it be called wisdom to walk contrary to the ways of the sages, and yet seek wealth and abundance for the people?

の法（真理）に背いて歩み、国を富ませようとすることは、賢明ではないといえないのだろうか。君子は節約し民に恵みを与える。自分の困苦を気にせず、ただ、人々の難苦を憂うるだけである。それゆえに、財は泉から水が湧き出るように、聖人のもとに流れ込む。恩恵は降り注ぎ、万民はそれに浴する。これはみな、聖人が徳と財との本末の関係を認識し、その源を求め、結果を求めないからである。

今日の近代的なベンサム主義者なら、「古くさい経済学」だと言うかもしれない。しかし、これはソロモンの経済学であり、それはまたソロモンより偉大な存在から生まれた経済学であり、世界のこれまでの長い営みからすれば、決して古くはないのだ。「施し散らして、なお富を増す人があり、与えるべきものを惜しんで、かえって貧しくなる者がいる」。「何よりもまず神の国と神の義を求めなさい。そうすれば、それに加えて、これらのものはみな与えられる」。このような聖書の言葉を、西郷の文章は適切に解釈してはいないだろうか。

もし、我が国の歴史上、もっとも偉大な人物を二人あげるとするならば、私はためらいもなく太閤［豊臣秀吉］と西郷をあげる。二人とも大陸に野望を持ち、全世界を自分の活躍の場とみていた。ともに同じ国の人間とは比べものにならないほど偉大だったが、二人の偉大さはまったく違っていた。太閤の偉大さは、ナポレオン的だったと思われる。太閤には、ナポレオンに顕著にみられる大ぼらふきの面が、彼ほどではないにしても、かなりあった。太閤の偉大さは、天才的な、生来の精神力によるもので、偉大になろうとしなくても偉大であった。だが、西郷の偉大さは違った。西郷の

Should it not be called unwisdom to walk contrary to the law (true) of gain and loss, and yet devise means to enrich the land? The wise man economizes to give in charity. His own distress troubles him not; only that of his people does. Hence wealth flows to him as water gushes from the spring. Blessings are rained down, and the people bathe in them. All this comes, because he knows the right relation of wealth to virtue, and seeks the source, and not the outcome."

"An old-school economy," I hear our modern Benthamites say. But it was the economy of Solomon, and of One greater than Solomon, and it can never be old so long as the universe stands as it did all these centuries. "There is that scattereth, and yet increaseth; and there is that withholdeth more than is meet, but it tendeth to poverty." "Seek ye first the kingdom of God and its righteousness; and all these things shall be added unto you." Is not Saigō's essay a fit commentary on these divine words?

If I am to mention the two greatest names in our history, I unhesitatingly name Taikō and Saigō. Both had continental ambitions, and the whole world as their field of action. Incomprehensively great above all their countrymen both of them were, but of two entirely different kinds of greatness. Taikō's greatness, I imagine, was somewhat Napoleonic. In him there was much of the charlatan element so conspicuous in his European representative, though I am sure in very much smaller proportion. His was the greatness of genius, of inborn capacity of mind, great without attempting to be great. But not so Saigō's. His was Cromwellian, and only for the lack of Puritanism, he was not a Puritan, I think.

偉大さは、クロムウエル的であり、ただピューリタニ訳注25
ズムを奉じていないためにピューリタンと呼べないだ
けである。西郷の場合、純粋な意志の力が大いに働い
ていた。つまり、最高に偉大な、道徳的偉大さだった
のである。西郷は、健全な道徳を基盤にして国を再建
しようとしたが、その偉業の一部は成功をみたのである。

Sheer will-power had very much to do in his case,—the greatness of moral kind, the best kind of greatness. He tried to rebuild his nation upon a sound moral basis, in which work he partially succeeded.

1751–1822（宝暦元年〜文政5年）

# 上杉鷹山

## 封建領主

---

# UESUGI YŌZAN

## A Feudal Lord

# I— 封建制

「天の王国」は、この貧しき地上には実現しないものなのだろうか。人間は、かなわぬこととは思わずに、王国を切望してきた。人間の歴史はその始まりから、地上に「天の王国」を実現しようとする飽くなき試みの繰り返しであったように思われる。キリスト教徒は、ヘブライの預言者たちにならい、キリスト<sup>訳注26</sup>の生誕から19もの世紀にわたって、王国の到来を祈り続けてきた。時には、待ちきれずに人間の力で達成できると考える人も出た。歴史上、アダムの堕落した子孫のなかに、本当に王国を実現しようとした大胆な試みほど、神聖な勇気と高貴な自己犠牲を示した例はない。サボナローラのフィレンツェ共和国、クロムウェルのイギリス共和国、デラウェア河畔におけるペンの<sup>訳注27</sup>「聖なる実験」は、そのような数少ない試みであり、最も高潔な人間の勇気が地上で行われた例である。しかし、そこでも理想は実現に近づいただけに過ぎない。政治の機構は改善されたが、天国がいまだに遠いことは、10世紀前の祖先の時代と変わりがない。事実、実情は少しも変わっていないので、人類は一つの方向、それも堕落へ向かっている、と警鐘を鳴らす賢人さえいる。

# I– The Feudal Form of Government

Is the "Kingdom of Heaven" an impossibility in this poor earth of ours? Mankind has yearned after it as a thing not wholly unattainable, and History from its very beginning seems to be a succession of some undefinable attempts for the realization of such a kingdom upon this earth. Christians have taken up the echo of the Hebrew prophets, and for the nineteen Christian centuries they ceased not to pray for the coming of such a kingdom among men. Indeed some impatient souls among us imagined that such was possible, and History knows of no higher examples of holy courage and noble self-sacrifice than a few bold attempts of making such a kingdom a practicability among the fallen sons of Adam. Savonarola's Florentine Republic, Cromwell's English Commonwealth, and Penn's "Holy Experiment" upon the banks of the Delaware, were a few such attempts,—the noblest pieces of human valor ever enacted upon the face of the globe. Yet the ideal was only approximately realized. With all our improved machineries of governments, we ourselves seem to be as far removed from the haven as our ancestors were ten centuries ago. Indeed, so stationary appears our real situation that a wise man among us startles us by stating that the human species has progressed in only one direction, and that is *downward*.

もちろん、どのような圧政も我々は嫌悪する。いまや専制政治は熱帯地方にだけみられ、それもやがて廃止されるだろう。しかし、圧政が投票箱に入り込めるはずはないと考えるのは愚かである。圧政は我々が悪魔と結託しているあいだはなくならず、悪魔が我々のなかから完全に追い出されるまでは存在し続けるだろう。したがって、人類は2種類の圧政、すなわち専制的な政治と、投票箱による政治に苦しめられてきた。後者は、前者より少しましというだけのことだ。それでも、もっとすぐれた最善のものが到来するはずだが、いつ、どのようにして実現するかは軽々しく口にすべきではない。

　しかし、徳に代わる制度はないと固く信じようではないか。いや、徳がありさえすれば、制度は助けになるどころか、むしろ妨げとなるのだ。「改善された政治機構」は、聖人を助けるよりは、泥棒を捕まえることを目的としている。代議制は改善された警察機構のようなものだ。ごろつきやならず者はそれで充分に抑えられるが、警察官がどんなに大勢集まっても、一人の聖人、一人の英雄に代わることはできない。「それほど悪くもなければ、良くもない」というのが、この制度について言えることだ。

　封建制度にも欠陥はあった。その欠陥のため、わが国は立憲制へ移行した。しかし、鼠を追い出すためにつけた火が、納屋をも焼き払うことになり、封建制の終焉とともに、それと結びついていた忠義や武士道が失われ、勇気や人情もかなり薄れてしまったのではないかと案じられる。真の忠義というものは、君主と家臣がじかに接してこそ生まれるものだ。その両者の間

Of course, tyrannies of all kinds we hate and detest. Despotic tyranny is now known only under the Tropics, and even there it will be soon done away with. But it is a foolishness to imagine that tyranny of any sort can make no entrance into ballot-boxes. Tyranny is among us so long as we are in league with devils, and it will not cease to exist among us till the last-named gentlemen are driven out entirely from our midst. Hence we say, of the two kinds of tyranny mankind has suffered from, namely the despotic kind and the ballot-box kind, the latter is only the lesser of two evils, and no more. The better or the best is yet to come, though when and how we are cautioned not to utter.

But let us all believe, and that unflinchingly, that no system can take the place of virtue. Yea more, when virtue *does* exist, systems are hindrance rather than helps. "The improved machineries" are intended more for binding robbers than for helping saints. We consider the representative system of government to be a sort of improved police system. Rogues and rascals are well kept down thereby, but no hosts of policemen can take the place of a saint or a hero. "Neither very bad nor very good," must be said of this system.

Feudalism has had its defects, and for those defects' sake, we had it exchanged for constitutionalism. But we fear the fire that was intended to burn rats burned the barn also, and together with feudalism has gone away from us loyalty, chivalry, and much of manliness and humaneness connected with it. Loyalty in its genuine sense is possible only when the master and the subject are in direct contact with each other. You bring a "system" between the

に「制度」を持ち込むと、君主はただの治者になり、家臣はただの人民となって、もはや忠義はありえない。憲法で定められた権利を求めて争いが生じ、争いを収めるのに文書に頼ろうとする。昔のように心に頼ろうとはしない。献身とその美点は、仕えるべきわが君主がいて、慈しむべきわが家臣があるところに生まれる。封建制の強みは、治める者と治められる者の関係が、このように人間的な性質をもっていた点だ。本質において、国は大きな家族だった。したがって、いかなる法律や憲法も「愛の律法」には及ばないように、封建制が完璧な形態をとれば、これ以上理想的な政治形態はない。聖書には、やがて来る約束された王国で、我々は「わたしの民」と呼ばれ、「あなたの鞭、あなたの杖」が我々を力づけると、書かれているではないか。ゆえに、我々は封建制が永遠に姿を消してほしくないと思っている。政体をめぐる論争が何百年いや何千年かたたかわされたのち、人は皆、同じ父の子であり、兄弟であると知る日が訪れ、そのときこそ封建制は完璧な、賛美されるかたちでよみがえり、真のサムライが復権して「敗者をいたわり、奢る者を砕き」、「平和の律法を築く」ことを願ってやまない。

　だが、そのような王国の到来を待つ間、それとよく似た王国が、この水と陸から成る地球上の、それも異教の国、日本にかつて実現した話を振り返り、元気をつけようではないか。西洋の知恵がもたらされる前に、この国はすでに和の道を知っており、独自に「人の道」が実践され、「死を恐れぬ勇者」がいたのである。

two, and loyalty is not, as the master is now no more a master but a governor, and the subject no more a subject but a people. Then come wranglings for constitutional rights, and men go to parchments for settling their disputes and not to hearts, as they used to in days of old. Self-sacrifice and all its beauty come when I have *my* master to serve, or *my* subject to care for. The strength of feudalism lies in this *personal* nature of the relation between the governor and the governed. In its essence it is really the family system applied to a nation. In its perfected form, therefore, it can be no other than the ideal form of government, as no law or constitution is better or higher than the Law of Love. Do we not read in the best of books that in the promised kingdom of the future, we shall be called "*My* people," that "*Thy* rod and *Thy* staff" shall comfort us? So we sincerely hope that feudalism is gone from us not for ever. After a few more hundred or thousand years of constitutional wranglings, when men shall have learnt that they are all children of one Father and hence are brothers, we do sincerely hope that feudalism will return to us once more, this time in its perfect and glorified shape, and the *true* samurai shall be installed once more in power "to spare the vanquished, and to crush the proud," and "the law of peace to found."

But while we are waiting for the coming of such a kingdom, let us refresh ourselves by an account of something very much like it, once enacted upon this terraqueous globe, and that in heathen Japan. Yes, before wisdom came from the West, the land did know the ways of peace, and in its own secluded manner, "the ways of man" were walked in, and "death was encountered with a hero's resolve."

## II- 人と事業

鷹山が、今の羽前の国にあたる米沢藩の家督を相 [訳注28] 続したのは、弱冠17歳のときであった。九州の小大名である秋月家に生まれた鷹山は、自分の家より [訳注29] も格が上で、領地も大きい上杉家の養子となった。しかし、養子となったのは、鷹山にすれば有難迷惑だった。全国でも例がないほどの重責を担わされることになったからである。この少年は「物静かで思慮深く、孝行心厚い性格」であると、先代の米沢藩主に対して叔母がほめている。鷹山は他の身分の高い家柄の子弟とは異なり、師の言うことを素直によく聞く生徒だった。その師である細井 [平洲] は、すぐれた学者で高潔 [訳注30] の士でもあり、世に埋もれた身からこの責任の重い地位に就いた。この有徳の師が好んで鷹山に語った忠順な弟子の話は次のようなものである。「大藩紀州の藩主、徳川頼宣は、師の言いつけを聞かなかったために、腿 [よりのぶ] をきつくつねられたことがある。頼宣はそのときにできた痣を感慨深く見つめるのが常だった。偉大な藩主 [あざ] は、『これは、偉大な師の残してくださった警告である。これを見るたび、自分にも領民にも誠実であるかと問うて、内省している。だが、残念なことに、痣は年々色薄れ、それにつれて私の慎みも消えつつある』とよく口にしたと伝えられている」。若い鷹山はこの話を聞くたび涙した。大名の子弟が、ほとんど隔離されたような環境で育てられ、たいていは富と権力に恵まれた生活を続けられる理由も、下の者たちに対する自分の義務も、自覚しなくなっていた時代には、ほとんど見られない感性である。中国の賢人 [孟子] の「民を視る、

## II– The Man and His Work

Yōzan was a mere lad of seventeen when he came to the inheritance of the territory of Yonezawa in the now province of Uzen. Born of the Akizuki family, a rather inconsiderable daimiō[*8] of Kiūshū, he was adopted by the Uesugi, higher in rank and larger in territorial possession. But as we shall presently see, the adoption was a thankless privilege on his part, as he was thus involved in responsibilities, the like of which were not to be found in the whole land. The boy was recommended by his aunt to the elder lord of Yonezawa as "rather reticent and meditative, filial piety very characteristic of him." Unlike the common sons of the noble, he was singularly submissive to his tutor, Hosoi by name, who as a scholar and man of high principle, was raised to this responsible position from a state of total obscurity. The favorite story of a dutiful pupil often repeated to him by his worthy tutor was on this wise: "Tokugawa Yorinobu, the powerful lord of Kii, always looked with tender care upon a scar that was left upon his thigh, caused by a sharp pinch given by his teacher for some disobedience to the latter's will. 'This,' the great lord is reported to have often declared, 'is the warning my revered teacher has left on me, that on looking at it always, I may always examine myself, and be true to myself and to my people. But alas, the scar is fading with my age, and with it my vigilance too." The young Yōzan always wept when this story was repeated to him,—a sensitiveness of the rarest occurrence at the time when princes were reared in the closest seclusion, and were, as a rule, no more conscious of their duty toward their inferiors, than of the reason that kept them in power and opulence. That saying of a Chinese sage "*Be ye as tender*

傷つくがごとし」という言葉は、鷹山の心の奥底に刻みつけられたようで、彼はこの言葉を己のものとし、終生、民を治める指針とした。

　これほど鋭い感性の持ち主は、信仰心があつくないはずはない。藩主となる日のこと、鷹山は生涯あつく崇敬した春日神社<sup>訳注31</sup>に次のような誓詞を奉納した。

一、文武の修練は自ら定めたとおり怠りなく励むこと

二、民の父母となることを第一の務めとすること

三、次の言葉を日夜忘れないこと
　　贅沢なければ危険なし
　　施して浪費するなかれ

四、言行の不一致、賞罰の不公平、不実と無礼を犯さ
　　ぬよう慎むこと

　これを今後堅く守することを誓う。もし怠るときはただちに神罰を下し、家運を永年にわたり消失されんことを。

　　　以上
　　　上杉弾正　大弼<sup>だんじょうのだいひつ</sup>
　　　藤原治憲<sup>訳注32</sup>
　　　明和4（1767）年　8月1日

*to your people as to a wound in your body"* seemed to have impressed him to the very bottom of his heart, and the text became to him *his own*, and guided him in all his future dealings with his people.

The man so sensitive cannot but be religiously so as well. On the day of his installment in his office, he sent in the following oath to the temple of Kasuga, his guardian god through his life:

"I.   The exercises, literary and military, which I have prescribed to myself shall I pursue without negligence.

"II.  To be a father and a mother to my people shall be my first and chief endeavor.

"III. The words that follow shall I not forget day and night:
      No extravagance, no danger.
      Give in charity, but waste not.

"IV. Inconsistencies of words with actions, injustice in reward and punishment, unfaithfulness and indecency,—from these shall I diligently guard myself.

"The above shall I strictly observe in future, and in case of my negligence of the same, let divine punishment overtake me at once, and the family fortune be for ever consumed.

These,
Uesugi, of the Office of *Danjō*,*
Fujiwara Harunori.
The First day of the Eighth Month of the Fourth Year of Meiwa
    (1767)."

---

* His official title.

この人物は、他の人間ならとても引き受けないような仕事に直面することとなる。鷹山が養子に入った上杉家は、太閤の世になるまでは強大な勢力を誇る大藩だった。越後に広大で豊かな領地を持ち、日本の西海岸にも数カ所の領地があった。太閤によって会津地方に移されて、大幅に勢力をそがれたが、それでも100万石以上を領する雄藩であり、当主は全国の五大名の一人に数えられていた。しかし、関ケ原の戦い（1600年）で反徳川方（西軍）に味方したため、ふたたび領地を移される。今度は30万石に減封され、辺鄙な米沢の地を与えられた。その後も事態は悪化し、石高はさらに半分に減らされ、鷹山が藩主になったときは、上杉家は15万石の大名であった。それでも、100万石当時と変わらない数の家臣を抱え、その頃の慣例をすべて踏襲していたのである。したがって、新しい領地では藩の財政が支えられず、その負債は何百万両にも及び、領民は税とその厳しい取り立てに恐れをなして逃げ出し、領内全域を貧困が襲ったのも不思議ではない。米沢は羽前の南部に位置し、海がなく、全国でも土地がやせて、天然資源も乏しいほうだった。このような状態ではどうにもしようがなく、遠からず藩は崩壊し、その保護を受けている領民の破産も避けられないと思われていた。藩の総力をあげても、5両の金も工面できないことがたびたびあったと聞けば、この藩がいかに逼迫していたかがよくわかる。750平方マイルの領地に、10万人以上の人口を抱えた大名としては、信じがたい極貧状態だった。年若い鷹山のやるべき仕事は、まずこの状態に歯止めをかけ、なんとか我慢できるところまで回復させ、さらに、氏神の春日大明神の加護を得ら

The work this man was to face was one, which no soul less than his, would dare to undertake. His adopted clan of Uesugi was in time before Taikō one of the most powerful in the whole country, holding, as it did, the large and wealthy province of Echigo, together with parts of several other provinces on the western coast of Japan. The clan was removed by Taikō to the Aidzu[*9] district, and its power was greatly reduced thereby. Yet it was still a powerful clan, with a revenue of over 1,000,000 *koku* of rice and its lord was counted among the five great daimiōs of the country. Through its siding with the anti-Tokugawa party in the battle of Sekigahara (1600), the seat of the clan was again removed, this time to an out-of-the-way district of Yonezawa, with the reduced revenue of 300,000 *koku*. Then to make bad worse, the revenue was once more cut off one half, and when Yōzan came to be the chief, the Uesugi was a daimiō of 150,000 *koku*, with subjects once supported by 1,000,000 *koku*, and all the habits and practices established upon the latter basis. We need not wonder, therefore, when we hear that the new territory scarcely supported the clan, that its debts amounted to millions, that taxes and exactions scared off the population, that penury and destitution prevailed everywhere in the district. Yonezawa is in the southern part of the [former] province of Uzen, has no sea-coast, and its fertility and natural resources ranked very low in the country. The whole made the case a most hopeless one, and the dissolution of the clan, and the bankruptcy of the people under its protection, seemed to be inevitable at no distant future. We can well understand the extremity to which the whole clan was reduced, when we hear that often-times they were unable to raise five pieces of gold by their united effort,—a state of poverty hard to

れるならば、領地を、古の賢哲のいう理想の国にすることだった。

　藩主の地位に就いて2年後、鷹山ははじめて自分の領地である米沢に入った。国入りは晩秋のことで、ただでさえ悲しい状況に、自然がさらに悲哀の色を加えた。行列が、捨てられて住む人もなく荒れた村を通り過ぎるたびに、多感な年若き藩主は、目の前の光景に強い衝撃を受けた。やがて、鷹山が乗り物のなかで火鉢の炭を一生懸命吹いているのに、供の者が気づいた。家来の一人が「よい炭をお持ちしましょう」と言った。鷹山は「今はよい。すばらしい教訓を学んでいるところだ。後で話す」と答えた。その晩の宿で藩主は家来を集め、午後に学んだばかりの貴重な教訓について説明した。「わが民の惨状を目の当たりにして絶望していたとき、目の前の炭が消えかけていることに気づいた。大事にそれを取り上げ、そっと辛抱強く息を吹きかけていると、炭の火をよみがえらせることができて、実にうれしかった。『同じようにして、わが領地とわが民をよみがえらせることができないだろうか』と自問すると、希望が湧いてきたのだ」

believe about a daimiō, who owned 750 square miles of land, with a population of over 100,000. The boy Yōzan's business was first to put a stop to this state of things, then to restore it to something of tolerability, and if his guardian god of Kasuga would bless him more, to make of his territory an *ideal state* as laid out by philosophic sages of old.

Two years after his installment in the office, he made his first entrance to his own territory of Yonezawa. It was in late autumn when Nature lent sadness to the state of things already sad enough in themselves. As the procession passed by village after village, deserted, neglected, and depopulated, the sensitive heart of the young chief was deeply touched by the sights before him. It was then that his attendants observed him in his *norimono* diligently engaged in blowing at a charcoal fire in a little *hibachi* before him. "We can serve your Lordship with good fire," said one of them. "Not now," Yōzan replied; "I am now learning a great lesson. What it is I will tell you afterward." In a hotel where the procession stopped for the night, the chief called his attendants together, and explained to them a new and valuable lesson he had learnt that afternoon. He said: "As despair took hold of me, as I witnessed with my own eyes my people's miseries, my attention was called to a little charcoal fire before me, that was on the point of going out. I slowly took it up, and by blowing at it gently and patiently, I succeeded in resuscitating it—to my very satisfaction. 'May I not be able in the same way to resuscitate the land and the people that are under my care?' This I said to myself, and hope revived within me."

# III– 藩政改革

　**他**の国と同じように日本でも、人は変革を嫌う。若き鷹山は変革をもたらさなければならず、それ以外に救済の道はなかった。しかし、他人を変えるには、まず自分を変えることから始めなければならない。当然のことながら、当面の問題は財政だった。秩序や信用などを回復するには、可能なかぎり倹約するしかない。藩主自ら、生活費を1050両から209両に切り詰めることにした。50人いた奥女中を9人に減らし、着物は木綿に限り、食事は一汁一菜と決めた。家臣も同じように倹約を求められたが、それは鷹山の場合とは比較にならない程度の倹約だった。年間の手当を半分に減らし、それで浮いた分は、積もり積もった負債の返済に充てられた。重い債務から逃れるには、このような状態を16年間も続ける必要があった。しかし、これはまだ財政改革における消極的な面にすぎない。

　「民の幸福は治者の幸福である」。「統治を誤りながら民から富を期待するのは、胡瓜の蔓に茄子が実るのを期待するようなものだ」。そして適材適所なしに善政はしけない。「能力に応じた人の配置」という民主的な考えは、封建制度の世襲的な性質とは相容れないものだったが、鷹山はあらゆる手段を尽くして優秀な人材を登用しようとした。鷹山は能力のある人物には乏しい財源から惜しみなく手当を支給し、その者たちを3種類の異なる役目に振り分けて、民の上に配置した。まず上級の役職として、郷村頭取と次頭取、その下に郡奉行をおき、「民の父母」として、この小藩の行政全般に関わる一切を監督させた。この役職に対する鷹山の指

# III– The Administrative Reform

Men are natural enemies of changes, in Japan as elsewhere. Young Yōzan must effect changes, else salvation was impossible. But changes in others must begin with changes in one's own self. Naturally, finance was the first question to be settled. Only by the utmost frugality could it be restored to anything like order and credit. The chief himself would curtail his family expense of 1,050 pieces of gold to 209 pieces. He would keep only nine maids in his household instead of fifty as before; would wear nothing but cotton stuff, and would eat no more than soup and one dish at a meal. His subjects were to be likewise economical, *but not in the proportion he himself would be*. The annual allowances were reduced one-half; and the savings thus realized were to be used to liquidate the accumulated debt of the clan. This state of things must continue for *sixteen years* before the clan could be free from its pressing obligations! This is, however, only the negative aspect of the finance reform.

"The people's happiness is the ruler's wealth." "As well expect an egg-plant fruit from a cucumber-vine as to look for wealth from misgoverned people." And no good government is possible without right men in right places. And men he would have by all means, though the hereditary nature of the feudal government was against this democratic idea of "a man according to his abilities." Out of his impoverished treasury he paid very liberally to men of ability, and these he placed over his people in three distinct capacities. First, there were the governor and his sub-officers who were general supervisors, "fathers and mothers of the people," taking upon themselves all the duties of the general administrative affairs of the little state. To these one of Yōzan's

示は次のようなものである。

「子供には自分の知恵がない。だが、母は子の要求を
汲み取って世話をする。それは真心があるからである。
真心は慈愛を生み、慈愛は知恵を生む。真心を尽くし
さえすれば、できないことはない。役人は、民に対し
て母のように接しなければならない。民を慈しむ心さ
えあればよいのであって、自分の力不足を嘆くことは
ない」

その下の役職は、道徳や礼儀を人々に教える巡回説
教師のように、「親孝行のこと、寡婦や孤児への慈悲、
婚姻のこと、着物の作法のこと、食物と食事の作法、
葬式のこと、家の修理のことなど」を教える役目だっ
た。そのために領内を12の地区（教区）に分け、各地
区に一人の郷村教導出役（平信徒の司教）がおかれた。
この教導出役は年に2回集まって会議を開き、また、民
の間を回る仕事の進捗状況を随時、藩主に報告するこ
とになっていた。

3番目の役職は、非常に厳しい警察官のような役だっ
た。その仕事は、領民の悪事や犯罪を突き止め、罪状
に応じて厳しく罰することだった。情け容赦なく、村
や町の隅々までが念入りに調べられた。罪人を出すこ
とはその地区の恥となり、教導出役は、自分の地区か
ら警察の厄介になる者が出ると、自ら責任を取った。
この二つの役職に対して、鷹山は次のような指示を与
えた。

「教師である教導出役は、地蔵菩薩の慈悲を持ち、心
には不動明王の正義を忘れるな」

injunctions read as follows:

"The child has no knowledge of its own; but she who mothers it understands its needs and ministers thereto, because she does this from her sincere heart. Sincerity begets love, and love begets knowledge. Only be sincere, and nothing is unattainable. As is the mother to her child, so must the officer be to his people. *If but the heart that loves the people lies in you, you need not lament that lack of wisdom in you.*"

The second class of his officers were a kind of itinerant preachers who were to teach the people in morals and ceremonies, "of filial piety, of pity toward widows and orphans, of matters of marriage, of decency in clothing, of food and ways of eating, of funeral services, of house-repairs, etc." The whole territory was divided into twelve districts (dioceses) for this purpose, each with a presiding teacher (lay-bishop) over it. These bishops were to meet twice a year for mutual conference, and to make occasional reports to the chief of the progress of their work among the people.

The third class were policemen of the strictest kind. They were to detect the people's vices and crimes, and to punish them severely for their just dues. Mercy they were to show none, and every nook and corner of villages and towns was to be carefully investigated. It was a diocese's shame to produce offenders, and every preacher took upon himself responsibilities for the troubles his district gave to the police. Yōzan's injunction to the two classes of officers was as follows:

"Go with Zizō's[*10]* mercy, ye preachers, but forget not to carry Fudō's[†] justice within you.

---

* God of mercy.    † God of justice.

「警察である廻村横目は、閻魔大王の正義と義憤を示
し、心には地蔵菩薩の慈悲を保て」

　この三つの役職は見事にかみ合って機能した。鷹山
の一般行政の政策は、郷村頭取と郡奉行によって実施
された。しかし、鷹山は「教育のない民を治めるのは
手間がかかって効果があがらない」と言い、「国中に活
気を与え、あたたかい血を通わせる」教育が、教導出役
によって行われた。だが、教育をしても社会に規律が
なくては効果がない。そのため、警察制度をきわめて
厳しくして教育の効果をあげ、さらに慈悲をたれるこ
とによって、よりいっそう効果を高めようとしたのであ
る。このような統治制度を作り上げることのできた若
き藩主は、人間性を相当に見抜いていたにちがいない。

　この新しい制度は、どこからも邪魔が入らずに、5年
間実施された。秩序が現れてくると、見込みがないと
思っていた社会が回復するかもしれないという希望が
よみがえった。そこを、とてつもなく厳しい試練が襲
った。鷹山のような強い精神の持ち主でなければ、挫
折していただろう。保守派が反撃に出たのだ。私腹を
肥やすためでないとしても、昔からそうだというだけ
で旧態にしがみついている一派である。このような人
間は、いかなる改革にも異議を唱えるものだ。ある日、
7人の重臣が不満を訴えて若き藩主に詰め寄り、新体制
をすぐに廃止すると約束させようと強引に迫った。藩
主は黙っていた。自分の評価は民の判断に委ねようと
したのだ。もし、民が新しい行政方針に反対なら、潔
く地位を退き、もっと能力のある人物に委ねるつもり
だった。そこで、ただちに家臣全員を召集した。城内
には武装した家臣が何千人と集まり、待機した。その

"Show Emma*'s justice and righteous wrath, ye police; but fail not to store Zizō's mercy in your bosom."

The three functions together worked admirably. His general administrative policies went out through the governor and his subsidiaries. But Yōzan says, "To rule a people that is not taught is costly and ineffectual." And such teaching was furnished by his lay-bishops, to give "life and warm circulation to the whole." But teaching without discipline is also ineffectual. Hence the strictest police system to make the teaching more effectual, and the mercy shown, more conspicuous. The young lord must have had no little insight into human nature to have enabled him to frame such a system for governing mankind.

The new machinery was put in operation for five years without meeting any molestation from any quarter. Order began to show itself, and hopes revived of the possible resuscitation of the despaired-of society. Then came the trial, the severest of all, under which souls weaker than Yōzan's would have surely succumbed. Conservatives showed themselves,—those who love the old for its own sake, if not for their bellies' sake. Renovations of any kind are objectionable to such men. One day, seven of the highest dignitaries of the district approached the young chief with their grievances, and tried to wrest from him words for the immediate abrogation of the new system of government. The chief was silent. He would have his people judge him; and if *they* objected to the new administration, he would willingly give its place and his own to the better and the abler. So he called the general con-

---

* God of justice.

間、藩主は春日神社に参拝し、事が穏便に収まるように祈願した。それから、登用した家臣たちを集めて、自分の政治の方針が天意に背いていると思うかと尋ねた。執政と城代は「いいえ」と言い、廻村横目も一人残らず「いいえ」と答えた。三千宰配頭と三十人頭も「いいえ」と言った。「異口同音」の「いいえ」である。藩主は満足した。民の声は神の声である。鷹山の決意は固まった。7人の重臣を面前に呼び出し、処分を言い渡した。5人は所領の半分を没収され、「隠居閉門」となった。首謀者の2人は、サムライのしきたりにしたがって、名誉ある自決の方法である切腹、ハラキリを言い渡された。

　こうして保守派や不満を抱く勢力は一掃され、事態は大きく好転し始めた。改革を遂行するには、こういうことを乗り越えなければならないものだ。若き藩主は、信仰あつく、感性豊かではあったが、真の英雄だった。そして、民を富ませる治世が始まる。

## IV – 産業改革

産業改革を行う上で、鷹山は二つの方針を打ち出した。(1) 領内に荒れ地を残さないこと、(2) 民のなかに怠け者をなくすことである。もともと肥沃ではない土地だが、自分と領民の懸命の努力で、15万石の領地から30万石の収穫をあげることができると鷹山は考えた。そこで、真剣に農業経営に取り組んだ。藩主の座について数年後、鷹山は [古代中国の周の儀

ference of all his subjects at once. Armored and weaponed, they in thousands gather in the castle, and wait for the business. Meanwhile our lord resorts to the temple of the god Kasuga to pray for the peaceful issue of the trouble. Then he meets his beloved subjects, and asks them if in their opinions his administration is against Heaven's will. The governor and his associates say, No. The police, one and all, say No. Captains and sergeants say, No. "Different mouths with one voice," say, No. Our lord is satisfied. *Vox populi est vox dei.*[*11] His mind is made up. He calls the seven before him, and passes sentences upon them. Five of them had halves of their fiefs forfeited, and "shut up within their gates forever. Two of them, the head conspirators, were dealt with according to the manners of samurai,—were "given *harakiri*," bowel-cutting, a dignified method of self-destruction!

Conservatives and grumblers thus disposed of, good began to flow in in abundance. No reform is complete till this is done. The young chief is a veritable hero notwithstanding his religiosity and sensitiveness of heart. We may now expect a prosperous reign from him.

## IV – The Industrial Reforms

Yōzan's industrial policies were two: (1) *to leave no waste places in his territory*, (2) *and no idlers among his people*. Though not naturally fertile, he thought he could make his land give 300,000 *koku* instead of 150,000, by sheer industry on his and his people's part. Agriculture he encouraged therefore with his whole heart. So, a few years after he assumed the government, he went through the ceremony of "Earth-Worship" on a grand scale. The lord, the

式にならって〕大がかりな「藉田の礼」（天子みずから田<sup>せきでん</sup>におりて耕す儀式）を執り行った。藩主、郷村頭取、郡奉行、代官、教導出役、廻村横目の全員が礼装して春日神社に詣で、神に行事の目的と決意を報告する。それから一行は開墾されたばかりの土地へ向かい、そこでまず藩主が鍬を手に取り、厳粛に大地に3回鍬入れをする。次に郷村頭取が9回。それから郡奉行が27回、代官が81回と、最後は「土を耕す者」に至るまで大地に鍬を打ち込む。これは、今後大地を神聖なものとして扱い、ここから命の恵みを受け取るのだと宣言する、もっとも威厳ある儀式である。断じて迷信などではない！

　鷹山は、平時にはサムライにも農民の仕事をさせ、これにより荒廃していた耕地を何千エーカーもよみがえらせた。また、漆栽培の普及を命じた。武家は庭に15本の苗木を植えるように求められ、それ以外の家は5本、寺は境内に20本、植えるように定められた。割り当て以上の苗木を植えた場合は、1本につき20セントの報奨金が出た。木を枯らしてしまい、その代わりを植えなかった場合には、同額の罰金が課せられた。その結果、この価値ある苗木は、ごく短期間で100万本以上も領内に植えられた。これはやがて大きな実を結んで後世に伝えられたのである。耕作に向かない土地には、100万本ものコウゾ<sup>訳注33</sup>が植えられた。しかし、鷹山が目指していたのは、自分の藩を全国有数の絹の産地にすることだった。これに必要な資金を、藩の乏しい財政から出せるはずもない。そこで、鷹山は藩主の生活費209両のうち50両を倹約して援助にふりむけ、できる限り領民のあいだにこの事業を広めようとした。若き藩主は「わずかな金でも、長くつづければ巨額に達する」

governor, county-officers, village-officers, lay-bishops, the heads of the police, all dressed in sacerdotal robes, proceed first to the temple of Kasuga, to inform the god of their aim and purpose. The procession then marches to a piece of ground recently opened, and there with all solemnity the chief first takes up a hand-plough, and strikes three times into the ground. The governor comes next, and strikes nine times. Then county-officers twenty-seven times, village-officers eighty-one times, and so on to the very "tiller of the soil." The whole was a public announcement of the most august kind, that from that time on the earth was to be sacredly handled, and all blessings of life were to be expected from it. No bad worship after all!

His samurai he turned into farmers in time of peace, and recovered thousands of acres from desolation and wilderness in that way. He ordered lacquer-trees to be extensively planted. Every samurai family was required to plant 15 nurslings in its yard; every family other than samurai, 5; and every temple, 20 within its enclosure. For every one tree that was planted above the required number, the reward of twenty cents was given; and for every one that died and was not replaced by another, a fine of the same sum was required. Over one million nurslings of this valuable plant were thus planted in his territory within a very short period,—a matter of very great consequence to the posterity. A million more of *kōzo**  were planted in those places which allowed of no cultivation. But Yōzan's chief aim was to make his territory one of the greatest silk-producing districts in the land. For this a fund was required which his impoverished treasury was not able to supply. He therefore cut fifty more out of the two hundred and

---

* Paper-plants, *Broussonetia papyrifera*.

と言う。鷹山はこれを50年も続け、彼が初めに植えた数千本の桑の木は増えつづけ、やがて領内に植える余地がなくなるまで普及した。今日の米沢と、名産の見事な絹織物が、この昔の藩主の忍耐と仁愛を証明している。米沢織は今では最高級品の一つに数えられている。


　それでも、領内にはまだ荒れ地が残っていた。日本のような米の生産国では、水利の便がよくなければ豊かな収穫は期待できず、灌漑が不十分だと土地の大部分がやせたままになってしまう。長い用水路を引くことは、財政が底をついている鷹山の藩にはできない相談だった。しかし、鷹山は倹約はしても、けちではなかった。「施して浪費するなかれ」が彼のモットーである。資金不足を補うだけの忍耐力があった鷹山は、領民が幸福になるならば、できないなどと考えもしなかった。昔の日本で行われた最大級の土木工事のうちの2事業を計画して完成させたのは、この最も貧乏な大名だった。まず、高い堤防を延々と築き、全長28マイルにおよぶ堰を作って水を引くという、水力工学技術の粋を集めた工事が行われた。もう一つは、トンネルを通して川の流れを変えるという、堅い岩盤を1200フィートも掘り抜く工事だった。この事業は鷹山の治世の20年間を要し、藩への最大の貢献となった。鷹山の家臣に黒井［忠寄］という、おっとりした無口な男がいた。藩主に登用されるまでは、役立たずと思われていた。その男が、実はたぐいまれな数学［和算］の能力を持っ

nine pieces of gold which he had reserved for his family-expenses, and did with it as much as he could to forward this industry among his people. The young chief says, "Slender means is a large sum if long continued." So he continued for fifty long years, till the few thousands of mulberry stocks he had commenced with propagated themselves, and his whole territory had no more space left for them. The Yonezawa district of to-day and its splendid silk-produce testify to the patience and benevolence of its ancient chief. The Yonezawa brand now ranks highest in the market.

Still waste lands remained in his territory. In a rice-producing country like Japan, fertility means abundance of water-supply, and insufficient irrigation leaves large portions of land in comparative sterility. Conveyance of water through long distances seemed an impossibility with Yōzan's exhausted treasury. But frugality with him meant no parsimony. "Give in charity, and waste not," was his motto. When public welfare was assured, he could think of no impossibility, for he had patience to make up the lack in his means. So it was that the poorest of daimiōs projected and completed two of the most stupendous engineering works ever undertaken in Old Japan. One was the conduction of water for a distance of twenty-eight miles through viaducts and long and high embankments, all of which are master-pieces of hydraulic engineering. The other was the turning of the water-course of a large stream through a tunnel, 1,200 feet of which was through solid rocks. This latter work took twenty years of Yōzan's administration, and is by far the most important of his services to his territory. Among his subjects he had one Kuroi, a slow speechless man, passing for a good-for-nothing till the chief found out his usefulness. The man was a mathematician of the rarest ability.

ていた。黒井は粗末な器具で領地を細かく測量し、当
時の人々には狂気の沙汰としか思われないような工事
計画を立てた。黒井は第一期工事を完成させ、第二期
工事にとりかかったが、半ばで亡くなった。しかし、
彼の設計通り工事は続けられ、起工から20年の歳月を
経て、両側から掘り進められていたトンネルが貫通し、
開口部が上下にずれた誤差は4フィートだった。まだト
ランシットやセオドライトなどの測量器具が知られて
いない時代に、これほど正確な計算ができたのは驚き
である。荒れ地に花が咲き、鷹山の領地は豊かな実り
を生むようになった。それ以来今日まで、東北地方で
も米沢だけは水不足に見舞われたことはない。

　領民の幸福のために、藩主が見落としたものはなか
った。品種改良された馬を他国から買い入れ、池や小
川には鯉や鰻を飼い、他国から坑夫や織工を呼び、商
いの障壁となるものはすべて取り除き、領内にある資
源はすべてあらゆる方法を用いて開発するように努め
た。怠け者はいなくなり、みな働き者になったことも
手伝って、かつては全国で最も貧しい土地であったと
ころが、鷹山の晩年には模範的な生産性の高い土地に
変わり、現在もそれは変わらない。


# Ｖ― 社会改革と道徳改革

東洋思想の一つの美点は、経済を道徳と分けて考
えないことである。東洋の思想家にとって、富
は常に徳の結果であり、富と徳の関係は、木と実の関
係と同じである。木に肥やしをやれば、労せずして確

With his rude instruments he made careful surveys of the territory, and planned out the works, which to his contemporaries, appeared like real madness. He completed the first, and died while engaged in the second. The work was continued nevertheless following the plan laid out by him; and twenty years after its commencement, the tunnel was bored through from both ends, the lower section meeting the upper four feet *below* the latter,—a wonder of accuracy in calculation when the transit or the theodolite was an unknown instrument in the land. Deserts began to blossom, and fertility flowed in abundance into Yōzan's territory. Yonezawa alone of all northern provinces knows of no drought to this day.

That nothing might escape the solicitous attention of the chief for his people's welfare, he imported improved breeds of horses, stocked ponds and streams with carps and eels, invited miners and weavers from other provinces, removed all the commercial obstructions, and endeavored to develop in every way all the resources of which his territory was capable. These with his extermination of idlers from among his people, and their conversion into useful laborers, brought about changes such that the once poorest district in the land became a type of productivity near the close of his life, and has continued so ever since.

## V– The Social and Moral Reforms

One beautiful feature of Oriental knowledge is that it has never treated economy apart from morality. Wealth with their philosophers is always the *effect* of virtue, and the two bear the same relation to each other that the fruit bears to the tree.

実に実がなる。「民に愛を与えれば」、自ずと富がもたらされる。「ゆえに君子は木を思って実を得る。小人は実を思って実を得ない」。これは、鷹山が師の細井から授かった儒教の教えである。


　鷹山の産業改革のうちで最も素晴らしいのはこの点である。彼は家臣を徳の高い人間にすることを目指した。快楽主義的な幸福は、彼の理念に反していた。富を得るのは、それによって「礼節を知る人」になるためである。「衣食足りて礼節を知る」と、古の賢者も言っている。鷹山は当時の慣習にはまったくこだわらず、天から託された民を、「人の道」へ導こうとした。それは、大名も土を耕す者も、同じように従わなければならない道だった。

　藩主となって数年後、他の改革が順調に進み出すと、鷹山は長らく閉鎖されていた藩校を再興し、興譲館と名付けた。「謙譲の道を繁昌させる所」という意味で、鷹山が重んじていた徳を的確に表現している。藩校は、当時の財政事情には不釣り合いな規模と設備でできあがった。館長に、鷹山自身の師であり、当代屈指の碩学であった細井[平洲]を招き、そのうえ、貧しくても才能ある者は高等教育を受けられるように、学費を免除する学生も多かった。創立以来100年近くの間、米沢の藩校は全国の模範であった。この学問所は、現在も昔の名前のまま存続している。おそらく、この種の学校では国内最古であろう。

　しかし、仁政とは病人を治療する機関を備えてはじ

You manure the tree, and the result will surely be fruit without your effort. You "fertilize love to the people," and wealth will be a necessary outcome. "Therefore the great man thinketh of the tree, and he hath the fruit. The small man thinketh of the fruit, and he hath it not." Such was the Confucianism indoctrinated into Yōzan's mind by his worthy teacher Hosoi.

In this lies the grandeur of all of Yōzan's industrial reforms that his chief aim was to make *virtuous* people out of his subjects. The hedonistic view of happiness was repugnant to his idea. Wealth was to be had that all might be made "decorous people" thereby, for, said the ancient sage, "Decorum is known only when life's necessities are had." Remarkably free from the conventionalities of the time, he aimed to lead his heaven-entrusted people into "the ways of man," alike binding on the daimiō and the tiller of the soil.

Some years after he came to his office, when his other reforms were fairly set a-going, he revived the clan-school long in suspense, and named it *Kōjōkwan*,[*12] or the "Institute for the Promotion of Humility," very expressive of the dominant virtue he had in view. The magnitude and equipment of the school were out of all proportions to the then financial state of the clan, for besides having one of the greatest scholars of the day for its provost,—Hosoi Heishū, Yōzan's own tutor,—it provided many free scholarships to enable the worthy poor of his dominion to get the advantage of a high-class education. For nearly a century after its establishment, the Yonezawa school continued to be a type and example to the whole country. The institute still remains, retaining its old name, and is perhaps the oldest of the kind in the land.

But no administration of love is complete till it provides means

めて完成したと言える。その点でも、この名君に抜かりはなかった。医学校［好生堂］を開設し、教師に当時の日本の名医を2人招いた。薬草を栽培するための植物園も開かれ、そこで採取された薬草を使って、その場で薬学の講義と実習が行われた。西洋医学が恐れと疑いの目で見られていた時代に、鷹山は数人の家臣に、日本初の蘭学医として名高い杉田玄白の新しい医学を学ばせた。そして、それが和漢の医学にまさると確信すると、費用を惜しまず手に入るかぎりの医療器具を買い求め、医学校で十分な教育と実習が行えるようにした。このように、ペリーの艦隊が江戸湾に来航する50年前、北日本の山間地では西洋医学が一般に取り入れられていたのである。鷹山は中国から入った儒教の教育を受けたが、中国人になりはしなかった。

　鷹山の清い社会改革のうち、ここでは二つを紹介するにとどめる。

　遊女を廃止したのは、鷹山の目指す「仁政」に完全に一致していたからだ。それでは欲情のはけ口を断たれて、別のもっと凶悪なかたちで社会が乱されるという、ありきたりの反論に、鷹山は「もし欲情がそんなことで治まるのなら、いくら遊郭があっても足りないだろう」と答えた。鷹山は遊女を廃止したが、それによって社会に不都合が生じることはまったくなかった。

　最も重要な階級である農民には「伍什組合の令」を布告した。これには鷹山の考える理想国家が如実に表

for the healing of the sick, and in this, as might be expected, our good chief was not wanting. A medical school was started, for which two of the then most notable physicians of the country were invited to be instructors. A botanical garden was also opened for the cultivation of medicinal plants, and pharmacy was taught and practiced on the spot with the products thus obtained. At the time when the European medical art was looked upon with fear and suspicion, Yōzan caused several of his subjects to be trained in the new system by Dr. Sugita Genpaku, of great celebrity as the first Japanese physician after the Dutch method. Once convinced of its superiority over the Japanese and Chinese medicine, he spared no expense to get all the medical apparatuses he possibly could, and deposited them in his school to be freely used in instruction and practice. Thus fifty years before Perry's squadron appeared in the Bay of Yedo, one of the mountain-districts of north Japan had the Western medicine adopted by the general public. Yōzan's Chinese education had not made a Chinaman out of him.

Of his purely social reforms, we have space for but two of them.

His abolition of public prostitution was in entire accordance with his views of "administration of love." To the usual objection that thus might be cut off a channel for the vile passion to spend itself, and endanger social purity in other and more heinous ways, his plain answer was, that "if the passion is to be thus allayed, no amount of prostitution is enough for the purpose." He had it abolished, and could keep it abolished without any social inconvenience whatever.

His instruction to the farming class,—by far the most important in his dominion,—on "the Institution of the Associations of

されているので、ここにできるだけ原文に忠実に全文を紹介したい。

「農民の天職は、農（農作物を作る）、桑（蚕を育てる）にある。これに励み、父母と妻子を養い、藩の庇護に対して税を納め［れば一家は安全で栄え］る。しかし、自分だけでは容易でないので、互いに助け合う組合が必要である。すでに組合がないわけではないが、十分頼りになるものでもないと聞いている。そこで新たに、次のように伍什組合と近隣の五ヵ村組合を設ける。

一、五人組（脚注・戸主のみ数える。以下同じ）は、常に睦じく交わって苦楽を共にすること、同一の家族のようでなければならない。

二、十人組は、ときどき親しく出入して家事を聞くこと、親類のようでなければならない。

三、同一村の者は、互いに助け合い、互いに救い合い、その頼もしさは友人のようでなければならない。

四、五ヵ村組合の村は、隣村が苦難にあっているときは、真の隣人が親切に行なうように、進んで助けなければならない。

Five and Ten" (Go-Jū-kumiai) is so characteristic of his ideal of the perfect state that we give it here entire, keeping ourselves as close to the original as possible.

"The farmer's mission is in soil (農, tillage) and mulberries (桑, silk-raising). Diligent in these, he feeds his father and mother, wife and children, and gives his dues to the government to have its protection. But all this is possible by the mutual dependence of one upon another, for which purpose associations of some kind are necessary. Not that you had them not already, but as we hear of none that can be thoroughly depended upon, we herein institute anew the *Associations of Five and Ten* and the *Associations of Five Villages* as follows:

"I.  The members of the Association of Five* should be in constant intercourse one with another, share the joys and sorrows of each, as do the members of one and the same family.

"II.  The members of the Association of Ten should have frequent intercourse one with another, and bear to the family affairs of each, a tie equal to their blood relationship.

"III. They of one village should be like friends in helping and serving one another.

"IV. The villages that constitute the Association of Five Villages should help one another in time of troubles, as befit true neighbors in all such cases.

---

* Only heads of families were counted. The rest, the same.

五、このように組合で交るべきである。老いて子のない者、幼くて親のない者、貧しくて養子の取れない者、連れ合いに先立たれた者、身体が不自由で自活できない者、病気で身寄りのない者、死んでも埋葬してもらえない者、火事にあって雨露に曝<sup>さら</sup>されている者、変災で一家が困っている者がいれば、十人組が力を合わせ、身内のように世話をしなければならない。十人組の力では足らないときは、村で世話をしてその難儀を取り除き、生きて行かれるようにしなければならない。もしも、一村が災害に見舞われて存続の危機に陥ったならば、近隣の村は救援の手も差し伸べずに傍観していてよいはずがない。五ヵ村組合の四ヵ村は進んで救済にあたらなくてはならない。

六、善を勧め、悪を戒め、倹約を守らせ、贅沢を抑える。自分の天職を捨てて他の仕事に走る者、また歌舞伎、狂言、酒宴や他の遊興に耽ったり、博打<sup>ばくち</sup>や賭事をなす者があれば、まず五人組が教えさとし、次に十人組が意見し、それでも相手が従わないときは、ひそかに村役人に訴え、相応の処分を受けさせなければならない。

享和2（1802）年2月」

"V. Be ye thus kindly disposed one toward another, and fail not.[*13] If there is one among you who is old and has no child, or is young and has no parents, or is poor and cannot adopt sons, or is widowed, or is a cripple and cannot support himself, or is sick and has no means of help, or is dead and is left without burial, or has met fire and is exposed to rain and dew, or if by other calamities his family is in distress,—let any such who has no one else to depend upon be taken up by his Association of Five, and be cared for as its own. In case it lies not in the said Association's power to succor him, let his Association of Ten lend him its help. If his case is more than the latter can do for him, let his village see to the removal of his distress and make possible his existence. Should some calamity overtake one village so that its existence is endangered thereby, how can its neighboring villages stand aloof without extending help to it? The four of the Association of Five Villages should give it willing salvation.

"VI. To encourage the good, to teach the bad, to promote temperance, to check luxury, and so to enable each to abide in his mission,—these are the aims for which these associations are formed. If there is one who neglects his farm, or follows not his trade and runs to other employments, or indulges in dances,[*14] theaters, banquets and other laxities, such and such like should have peremptory admonition, first of his Association of Five, and then of Ten; and in case he is still refractory, he must be privily reported to the village authority and receive due treatment.

February, 2nd year of Kyōwa (1802)."

この布告には役人の形式主義がまったく見られない。しかも、鷹山の米沢藩以外に地球上のどこかで、このような布告が出されて、その通りに実施されたという話は聞いたことがない。アメリカにおける農業組合は、産業組合に他ならず、その主な目的は利得である。鷹山の農民組合にあたるものを挙げるならば、使徒たちが作った初代教会にまでさかのぼらなければならない。

　鷹山は、廻村横目や教導出役、いろいろな学校やさまざまな「教示」により、そして特に自らが範を示すことで、15万人からなる藩を、徐々にしかし着実に自分の理想のかたちに近づけていった。それがどこまで成功したかは、「聖人の治世」を見聞するために米沢藩を訪れた著名な学者、倉成竜渚（くらなりりゅうしょ）が記述した文章の、次のような抜粋からうかがえる。

　「米沢には『棒杭の商い』（ぼうぐい）（正札市）と呼ばれるものがある。人里離れた道の傍らに、草履（ぞうり）、草鞋（わらじ）、果物、その他の品々が値札をつけて棒杭にぶら下げてある。持ち主はそれを見張ってはいない。人々はそこへ行き、値札通りの金を置き、品物を持って帰る。こういった市場で盗難が起こるとは誰も思っていないのである。

　鷹山のもとでは、最も位の高い重臣が一番貧乏である。莅戸六郎兵衛（のぞき）［善政］（よしまさ）は筆頭家老で、だれよりも藩主の愛顧と信頼を得ている人物である。しかしながら、その暮らしぶりをみると、衣食は貧しい学生と変わらない。

　藩内には税関もなく、国境には自由な交易を妨げるものは何もないが、それでいて密輸が企てられたことはない」。

　これは、いつの世とも知れぬおとぎ話の世界の夢物

Not much of officialism in all these; yet we declare we never have seen the like of them promulgated and put into practice in any other portion of the globe except in Yōzan's dominion of Yonezawa. What is called the farmers' guild in America and elsewhere is nothing more than an industrial coöperation, with selfishness as its main motive. We should go to the Apostolic Church itself to find anything like our chief's Associations of farmers.

With his polices and lay-bishops, schools and various "instructions," and above all, with his own example, he molded his clan of 150,000 souls to his ideals slowly but effectively. How far he succeeded in so doing can be seen by the following few extracts from an account of his dominion given by a well-known scholar, Kuranari Ryūsho, who went there for the special purpose of observing "how the saint rules his people."

"In Yonezawa there is what they call the Label-Market. Away from the habitations of men, by the side of public roads, sandals, shoes, fruits and other articles are exposed for sale with their prices labeled upon them, and their owners all absent. Men go there, leave the prices as marked, fetch the goods, and pass on, and nobody imagines that any stealing will be done in these markets.

"In Lord Yōzan's government, the men highest in office are usually the poorest. Nozoki Rokurobei is his prime minister, and no body can be compared with him in the chief's favor and confidence. Yet, as I observed his ways of living, his food and raiment reminded me of those of a poor student.

"The dominion has no custom-houses and all such obstructions to free commerce on its borders, and yet no smuggling is ever attempted."

Let not our readers imagine that we are writing here an idyl

語などではない。ここに記したことはわずか100年足らず前に、この地球上の誰もが知っている土地で実際にあった出来事である。たとえ、このようなことを行わせた偉大な人物の時代の現実が、今は現実でなくなっているとしても、後世への影響は、それらが行われた土地と実行した住民の中に、確実に読みとることができる。

# VI– 人となり

当今では、人間をアダムのふつうの子孫以上のものだと思うのは時代遅れであり、特に「神の恩寵と啓示の外」にある異教徒となれば、なおさらだ。それに我々は、自国の英雄を神に祭り上げることで、たびたび非難を浴びている。しかし、誰と比べても鷹山ほど欠点や弱点をあげるのが難しい人物もいないだろう。それは鷹山自身がどの伝記作家よりも、自分の欠点や弱点を知っていたからだ。鷹山は文字通り、一人の人間であった。弱い人間であったからこそ、藩主の座につくとき、神に誓詞を献じたのだ。自身や藩の危機に面して、鷹山が神霊に祈願したのは（それを弱さと呼ぶなら）弱さゆえである。江戸屋敷にいたある日のこと、国で孝行者に褒美を与えるため、その名を記した名簿が鷹山のもとに届けられた。藩主が吟味し、承認を与えることになっていたからである。鷹山はそれにざっと目を通すと、師の講義が終わるまで物入れにしまっておくように命じた。しかし、講義が終わったときには、すっかり大事な用件を忘れてしまっていた。近臣の一人が「千乗の君」にあるまじき怠慢と、

about some mythic land of unknown ages. The things of which we write were practical realities; not yet one hundred years have passed since they were enacted in a well-known portion of this globe; and if they are no more realities such as they were in the days of their great enactor, their after-influences are distinctively readable in the place where they were tried, and among the people who practiced them.

## VI– The Man Himself

It is not fashionable in these days to make any mortals more than *common* sons of Adam, especially so if such happen to be heathens, "outside of the pale of grace and revelation"; and we are often criticized for making gods out of our heroes. But perhaps of all men, Yōzan has the least need of having his faults and weaknesses counted up; as he himself was more conscious of such than any of his biographers could possibly be. He was *a man* in the full sense of the term. Only a weak man sends in oaths to a temple on his entrance to a responsible office. It was his weakness (if we may so term it) that drove him to his guardian god when a crisis overtook him and his clan. One day, while in his residence at Yedo, a roll containing the names of those subjects of his who were to be rewarded for their filial piety was sent to him for examination and approval. He looked it over, and ordered it to be kept in a drawer till his tutor's lecture was over. It was over, but the important business slipped from his mind. One of his attendants severely reprimanded him for the negligence that was unforgivable in a "lord of a thousand." The chief's shame knew no bound. There he sat, for the whole night in repentance, weeping,

藩主を強く諫めた。藩主は深く恥じ入った。その場に座ったまま悔恨の涙を流しながら一夜をあかし、「恥ずかしさで朝食にも手をつけなかった」。その朝呼ばれた師が孔子の書物から一節を引いて、鷹山の自責の念を取り除いた。そして、ようやく「食べ物が喉を通った」のである。これほど鋭い感性の持ち主に対して、あまりに厳しい歴史批評を加えるのはやめようではないか。

しかし、鷹山の純粋さと高潔さは、家庭や家族関係に最もよく現れていた。倹約ぶりにはすでに触れた。米沢藩の財政への信用が十分に回復し、いくらでも豊かな暮らしができるようになってからも、鷹山は最期まで木綿の着物と質素な食事で通した。畳は修理がきかなくなるまで新しいものと取り替えず、破れた畳に自分で紙を貼っている姿がたびたび見かけられた。

鷹山の家庭観は実に立派なものだった。賢者の言う「自己を修める者にしてはじめて家を治め、家を整える者にしてはじめて国を統治することができる」[修身斉家治国]という言葉を文字通り実行した。とくに、鷹山のような社会的地位の人間が側室を持つ権利をだれも疑わず、大名ともなれば4、5人は側室を抱えていた時代に、鷹山は10歳年上の側室を一人持っていただけだった。それも特別の事情があったからだ。鷹山は当時の習慣に従い、成人前に親の決めた相手と結婚したが、その女性には先天的な知的障害があり、知力はせいぜい10歳ぐらいだった。しかし、鷹山は心からの愛情と尊敬をもって妻に接し、玩具や人形を作り、あらゆる手を尽くして慰め、20年の結婚生活の間、自分の運命に対する不満を微塵も見せなかった。二人はもっぱら

and "could not touch his breakfast because of his shame." The next morning the tutor was called in, absolution was passed over him by a quotation from the book of Confucius, and then "his food passed through his throat." Let not Historical Criticism be too harsh to a soul so sensitive as this.

But nowhere do we find the transparency and integrity of his character more than in his home and domestic relations. His frugality we have already touched upon. He kept up his cotton stuff and meager table till the very end of his life, when the credit of his treasury was fully restored, and he had abundance at his command. His old *tatami* he would not replace till further remedy became impossible; and he was often seen patching up torn mats by pasting papers over them.

His idea of home was a most exalted one. Herein he followed literally the words of the sage who said, "He alone ruleth his family who ruleth himself; and he alone can rule a nation whose family is in right order." At the time when nobody doubted the *right* of concubinage, especially in men of his social standing, and when few daimiōs had less than four or five concubines, Yōzan had only one *who was his senior by ten years*, and under the following exceptional circumstance. The lady to whom he was wedded in his minority by their parents, according to the then custom of the land, proved to be a born imbecile, and her intellect was never above that of a child of ten years of age. Her however he treated with genuine love and respect, made for her toys and dolls, and comforted her in all ways, and for twenty years of their wedded lives he never showed any dissatisfaction with his fate. His other

江戸で暮らし、側室の方は国元（米沢）に留め置かれ、障害のある妻にならぶ尊敬と地位は許されなかった。そういうわけで正妻は子供を残さなかった。[訳注36]

　鷹山は当然のことながら、わが子を深く思いやる父親で、子供の教育には熱心に取り組んだ。封建時代の藩主は世襲制なので、民の将来の幸福は、彼がどのような後継者を残すかにかかっていた。鷹山は後継者教育の責任の重さをよくわかっていた。息子たちが、「大きな使命を忘れて、自分のことしか考えない人間にならないように」、「貧しい人々への思いやり」を教えた。鷹山の子供の育て方をみるため、彼が孫娘たちに送った見事な手紙の1通を紹介しよう。夫と江戸で暮らすために実家を出る最年長の孫娘に宛てたものである。[訳注37]


　「人は三つの恩義を受けて成長する。父母と師と君である。それぞれの恩義の深さは計り知れないが、とりわけ深く貴いのは父母の恩である。…この世に生を受けたのは父母のおかげである。この身体が父母の一部であることを常に忘れてはならない。だから、心の底から父母を大切にしなさい。真心さえあれば、もし過ちを犯したとしても、届かないことはない。力不足だからこれはできないと思ってはいけない。真心がその不足を補ってくれる。…領地を治めるということは、大きすぎて想像がつかないかもしれない。しかし、領地を治める「もと」は、よく整った家にあると思いなさい。よく整った家というのは、妻と夫の関係が正しいことが基本である。水源が乱れている川から、どうしてまともな流れが期待できよう…年若い女である以

consort was left in Yonezawa while they lived mostly in Yedo, and was never allowed the dignity he attached to his imbecile wife. The latter of course left him no children.

Naturally he was a benignant father, and he made strenuous efforts for the education of his children. He clearly saw the importance involved in this part of his duty, as in the hereditary system of the Feudal Government, his people's future happiness depended wholly upon the kind of rulers he would leave after him. His boys he trained in "the knowledge of the poor," that "they might not forfeit their great mission and sacrifice it to their selfish purpose." That we may have a look into his ways of training his children, we give here one of many beautiful letters he wrote to his granddaughters. It was addressed to the eldest of them when she was leaving her paternal mansion to join her consort in the metropolis.

"Three influences make a man; his parents, his teacher, and his master. Each is unfathomable in beneficence, but the parents excel all others…. Our being in this universe we owe to our parents. That this body is a part of theirs should never be forgotten. In thy service to them, therefore, comport thyself with a heart that dissembles not; for if sincerity reside there (in heart), even though thou miss the mark, thou art not far from it. Think not a thing is out of thy power because of thy lack in wisdom. Sincerity makes up the lack thereof…. The ruling of a dominion may appear a stupendous task to thee. But know that the 'root' of a dominion is in its well-ordered families. And there can be no ordered families without the right relation of the wife to her husband. The source in disorder, how canst thou expect a well-ordered stream?…. In thy youthful womanhood, it is very

上、着る物などに関心が向くのは当然である。しかし、これまで教えられた質素の心を忘れてはいけない。養蚕などの女の仕事に励むとともに、和歌に親しんで心を磨きなさい。文化や教養にはしり、それだけを目的としてはならない。学問は、この身を修める道を知るためのものである。したがって、善を行い、悪を避けることを教える学問を選ばなくてはならない。歌を詠むと、ものの哀れを知る。月や花を歌に詠むことは品位を下げず、情操を高める。…あなたの夫は父として民を導き、あなたは母として民を慈しみなさい。そのとき民はあなたたちを親として敬う。これにまさる喜びがあろうか…

　繰り返しになるが、夫の両親には孝養を尽くしなさい。ご両親の心を安んじ、主であり夫である人に従って、あなたが限りなく栄え、私の娘が生まれた国にふさわしい賢婦人と仰がれることを願っています。


　　　武蔵野の江戸なる館に赴き給うはなむけに

　　　　　春を得て花すり衣重ぬとも
　　　　　　　　わが故郷の寒さ忘るな

　　　　（春が訪れ、花の衣装を身にまとう季節となっても、
　　　　　山里の父の家で過ごした冬を忘れるなよ）

　　　　　　　　　　　　　　治憲」


　この勤勉な節制家は、健康に恵まれて70年の人生をまっとうした。若き日の望みはほとんどかなった。藩は安定し、民の暮らしは楽になり、領内に豊かさが満

natural that thy mind should often be taken up with the matter of dress. But forsake not the frugal habits thou hast been taught. Devote thyself to silk-worm raising and other womanly industries; and at the same time feed thy mind with poems and books of poetry. Seek not culture and enlightenment for their own sake. The aim of all knowledge is to lead us into ways of virtue. Select such knowledge therefore as shall teach thee to do good and avoid evil. Poetry softens the heart. With it the moon and flowers abase us not, but our sentiments are lifted up thereby.... Thy husband is to teach the people as their father, and thou art to love them as their mother. Then they honor you both as their parents; and what joys can excel this?....

"To repeat the same things to thee, serve thy parents-in-law with all fidelity, and comfort them. With obedience to thy lord and husband in all quietness, may your prosperity know no end, and may my daughter be honored as a virtuous woman worthy of the land that gave her birth.

"*On My Beloved Daughter's Leaving for the Metropolis:*

> When Spring overtaketh thee,
> And raiment of flowers thou puttest on,
> Forget not Winter thou hast had,
> In thy father's mountain-home.
>
> Harunori."

The hard-working abstemious man enjoyed continuous health of three-score years and ten. He had his early hopes mostly realized;—saw his clan firmly established, his people well supplied,

ちた。藩をあげても5両の金さえ工面できなかったのが、一声で1万両も集められるようになっていた。このような人物の最期が安らかでないはずはない。文政5 (1822) 年3月19日、鷹山は最後の息をひきとった。「民はよき祖父母を失ったかのように泣いた。身分を問わず誰もが悲嘆にくれる様子は筆に尽くしがたい。葬儀の日、何万人もの人が沿道を埋め尽くして葬列を見送った。合掌し頭を垂れ、一斉に号泣する人々につられ、山川草木もこぞってこれに和した」と、伝えられている。

and his whole dominion abundantly replenished. The clan that had not been able to raise five pieces of gold by their united effort, could now raise ten thousands at a moment's notice. The end of such a man could not be anything but peace. On the 19th of March, the 5th year of Bunsei (1822), he breathed his last. "The people wept as if they had lost their good grandparents. The lamentations of all classes no pen could describe. On the day of his funeral, tens of thousands of mourners filled the way-side. Hands clasped, and heads all bowed, deep wailings went up from them all, and even mountains, rivers, and plants, joined in the universal sorrow."

1787–1856 （天明7年～安政3年）

# 二宮尊徳

## 農民聖者

---

# NINOMIYA SONTOK

## A Peasant Saint

# I- 19世紀初めの日本の農業

わが国のように海運や貿易に有利な条件がそろっていても、国民の生活が農業で支えられている国にとっては、本質的に「農業は国家存立の大本である」。土地の自然の産出力だけでは、限られた国土に密集している巨大な人口を養っていくことはできない。4800万人が15万平方マイルの国土に住み、そのうち耕作可能な土地はわずか2割なのだ。土地から最大の収穫を得るために、人はあらん限りの知恵を絞り、勤勉に働かなければならない。日本の農業は世界でも際だっていると我々は考える。一塊の土くれに至るまで大切に扱われ、土から顔を出した苗の一つ一つが、子供を育てる親の愛に似た心づかいで世話をされている。科学が不足している分はたゆまぬ勤労で補い、その結果、庭園のように整然と完璧に仕上がった1300万エーカーの耕地を有するまでになった。

このように高度な農耕は、国民が並外れて勤勉であってこそできるものだ。少しでも怠ければ、実に見苦しい荒廃を招く。かつて耕作されていた土地が、手入れもされず打ち捨てられているのを見るほど、心が痛むことはない。原生林の持つ活力や繁茂力もない荒地

# I– Japanese Agriculture in the Beginning of the Nineteenth Century

"Agriculture is the ground-basis of the national existence"; essentially so in a country like ours, where, despite all its maritime and commercial advantages, the main support of the people comes from its soil. Natural fertility alone cannot support so immense a population upon so limited an area,—48,000,000 upon 150,000 sq. miles, only 20 per cent of which are cultivable. The land must be made to yield its maximum, and human genius and industry must be exerted to the utmost for that end. We consider Japanese agriculture to be the most remarkable of the kind in the world. Every clod of earth receives thoughtful manipulation, and to every plantlet that starts from the ground is given a care and attention well nigh bordering upon parental affection. The science we lacked in we supplied with strenuous industry, and as a result we have 13,000,000 acres of cultivated surface, kept with all the nicety and perfection of market-gardens.

Such a high degree of cultivation is possible only by more than ordinary industry on the people's part. A little negligence is sure to call in desolation of the most unattractive character. We know of nothing so disheartening as a once cultivated field abandoned by human labor. Without the vigor and luxuriance of the

の荒廃は、暗黒の絶望だ。処女地の開墾に挑もうとする人は10人いても、見捨てられた耕地を元に戻そうとする人は一人もいないだろう。南北アメリカ大陸には世界中からつましい人々が集まるのに、バビロンにはフクロウとサソリしか住まないのだ。

　19世紀の初め、日本の農業は実に悲惨な状態だった。泰平の世が200年も長く続いたため、あらゆる階層の人々が贅沢と浪費をおぼえ、怠惰になった影響はすぐに耕地に表れた。全国各地で耕地からあがる収入は三分の二も減った。かつては実り豊かであった耕地はアザミや草薮でおおわれ、わずかに残った耕作できる土地で、農地全体に課せられた年貢を差し出さなければならなくなった。どの村もひどく荒れ果てた姿になった。まじめに働く気がなくなった人々は、身を持ち崩した。優しい大地から豊かな恵みを求めようとしなくなり、破滅につながる生活を続けるために、本来は必要でないものを得ようと、互いにごまかし合い、だまし合うようになった。諸悪の根元は道徳（の貧困）にあり、見さげはてた息子たちに報いる気をなくした自然は、あらゆる災いを土地に及ぼした。そのとき、自然の法と精神を同じくする一人の男が生まれた。


## Ⅱ– 少年時代

尊徳（徳を尊ぶ人）の名で親しまれている二宮金次郎は、天明7（1787）年に生まれた。父は相模の国の名もない村の、ごく貧しい農民だったが、隣人たちには仁愛と公共心があることで有名だった。16歳のとき、尊徳は二人の弟とともに孤児となった。親族

primitive forest, the desolation of the deserted field is that of black despair. For ten men who would dare to break up the virgin soil, not one will apply himself to recover the abandoned land. While the Americas invite the thrifty nations of the world, Babylon remains as a habitation of owls and scorpions.

In the beginning of the nineteenth century, Japanese agriculture was in a most lamentable state. The long-continued peace of two-hundred years brought in luxuries and dissipation among men of all classes, and indolence thus introduced had immediate effects upon the cultivated fields. In many places, the revenue from land decreased by two-thirds. Thistles and bushes invaded the once productive fields, and what little was left in cultivation had to bear all the feudal dues levied from the land. Village after village wore an aspect of utter desolation. Honest labor becoming too onerous, men betook themselves to dishonest ways. From the kind earth they ceased to look for her ever bounteous gifts, and by cheating and defrauding one another they sought to acquire what little they needed to sustain their ill-doomed existence. The whole cause of their evils was moral, and Nature refusing to reward her ignoble sons, brought about all the miseries that befell the land. Then was born a man whose spirit was in league with Nature's laws.

## II– Boyhood

Ninomiya Kinjirō, surnamed Sontok[*15] (Admirer of Virtue), was born in the seventh year of Tenmei (1787). His father was a farmer of very small means in an obscure village in the province of Sagami, notable, however, among his neighbors for his charity and public spirit. At the age of 16, Sontok, with his

が相談して、哀れな家族は引き離されることになり、長男の尊徳は父方の伯父のもとへ引き取られた。伯父の家で、若者はできるだけ伯父の厄介にならないように懸命に働いた。一人前の大人の仕事ができないのを嘆き、少年であるために日中にできなかった分は、夜中まで働いて埋め合わせた。そのうちに、字の読めない人間にはなりたくないという思いを抱いた。古人の学問に対して「目明き見えず」ではいたくないと思ったのである。そこで、孔子の『大学』を手に入れ、一日の仕事をすべて終えてから、深夜にこの古典をこつこつと勉強した。しかし、やがてそれが伯父に見つかり、伯父の得にはならず、まだ若い尊徳にも実際に役立つとは思えないことに、貴重な油を使ったと厳しく叱られた。尊徳は、伯父の怒りももっともだと思い、自分の力で灯油を手に入れられるようになるまでは、勉強をあきらめた。そして翌春、持ち主のいない川べりのわずかな土地を開墾してアブラナの種を蒔き、休みの日をすべて使って、自分自身の作物を育てた。そして、年の終わりには大きな袋一杯の菜種を収穫した。自分の労力で手にした成果であり、自然から直接授かった、誠実な労働の報酬である。尊徳はこの菜種を近くの油屋へ持って行き、数升の油と交換した。これで伯父の油を使わずに勉強を再開できると思うと、言いようもなくうれしかった。尊徳は誇らしい気持ちで夜の勉強を再開し、自分のこのような忍耐と勤勉に対して、伯父からほめ言葉があるのではないかと少しは期待もしていた。しかし、そうはならなかった。伯父は、養ってやっているのだから、この若者の時間は自分のものであり、読書のような無駄なことをさせる余裕は

two little brothers, was orphaned, and the conference of his relatives decided upon the dissolution of his poor family, and he, the eldest, was placed under the custody of one of his paternal uncles. Here the lad's whole endeavor was to be as little burdensome to his uncle as possible. He lamented that he could not do a man's part, and to make up what he in his youth could not accomplish in daytime, he would work till very late at midnight. Then came a thought to him that he would not grow up to be an illiterate man, a person with "open, seeing eyes, yet blind" to the wisdoms of the ancients. So he procured a copy of Confucius' *Great Learning*, and in the depth of night after the day's full work, he applied himself assiduously to his classical study. But soon his uncle found him at his study, sharply reprimanded him for the use of precious oil for work from which he (the uncle) could not derive any benefit, and could see no practical good to the youth himself. Sontok considered his uncle's resentment reasonable, and gave up his study *till he could have oil of his own to burn*. So the next spring, he broke up a little land that belonged to nobody, on the bank of a river, and there planted some rape-seed and gave all of his holidays to the raising of this crop of his own. At the end of one year, he had a large bagful of the seed, the product of his own hand, and received directly from Nature as a reward of his honest labor. He took the seed to a neighboring oil-factory, had it exchanged for a few gallons of the oil, and was glad beyond expression that he could now resume his study without drawing from his uncle's store. Triumphantly he returned to his night-lesson, not without some hope of words of applause from his uncle for patience and industry such as his. But no! the uncle said that the youth's time was also his, seeing that he supported him, and that he could not afford to

ないと言った。尊徳は、今度も伯父の言うことは当然だと思い、言いつけに従って、一日の厳しい農作業が終わった後、むしろ織りやわらじ作りに励んだ。以後は、伯父の家で使う干し草や薪を、毎日山へ取りに行く往復に勉強をした。

　休みの日は自分のものだったが、遊んで無駄にすることはなかった。尊徳は菜種を収穫した経験から、まじめに働くことの価値を学び、この経験をもっと大規模に試してみたいと思った。村に、最近の洪水で沼地になったところがあるのを知り、休みを有益に使う絶好の機会だと思った。沼から水を汲み出し、底をならし、きちんとした小さな田になるようにした。その田に、いつも農民が捨てている余った苗を拾ってきて植え、夏中怠らずに世話をした。秋には1俵近くも見事な米がとれた。地味な努力が報いられて、生まれてはじめて生活の糧を得た孤児の喜びようが目に浮かぶ。その秋に収穫した米は、波乱に富んだ人生を始めるための資金となった。彼はまさしく、独立した人間だったのだ。尊徳は、自然が正直にこつこつと働く者の味方であることを学び、後のすべての改革は、自然はその法に従う者には豊かに報いるという明解な原理に基づいて進められた。

　数年後、尊徳は伯父の家を出て、村の見捨てられていた土地を見つけては改良して作りためた、わずかばかりの米を抱えて、何年も住む人のなかった親の家に戻った。彼の忍耐と信念と勤勉をもってすれば、混沌と荒廃を秩序と多産に変えようとする試みを妨げるも

let any of his men engage in so unprofitable a work as book-reading. Sontok again thinks his uncle is reasonable, follows his behest, and goes to mat-weaving and sandal-making after the day's heavy work upon the farm is done. Since then, his studies were prosecuted on his way to and from hills whereunto he was daily sent to fetch hay and fuel for his uncle's household.

His holidays were his, and he was not one to throw them away for amusements. His experiment with the rape-seed taught him the value of earnest labor, and he wished to renew his experiment upon a larger scale. He found in his village a spot changed into a marsh-pond by a recent flood, wherein was a capital opportunity for him to employ his holidays for useful purposes. He drained the pond, levelled its bottom, and prepared it for a snug little rice-field. There he planted some seedlings that he picked out of the surplus usually cast away by farmers, and bestowed upon them a summer's watchful care. The autumn brought him a bagful (2 bushels) of golden grain, and we can imagine the joy of our orphan-boy who for the first time in his life had his life-stuff provided him as a reward for his humble effort. The crop he gathered that autumn was the fund upon which he started his eventful career. True, independent man was he! He learnt that Nature is faithful to honest sons of toil, and all his subsequent reforms were based upon this simple principle that *Nature rewardeth abundantly them that obey her laws.*

A few years afterward he left his uncle's house, and with what little grain he gathered with his own hand out of the mere refuse lands he discovered and improved in his village, he returned to his paternal cottage now deserted for many years. With his patience, faith, and industry, nothing stood in his way on his

のはなかった。山の斜面や川岸の空き地、道端、沼地
をことごとく活かして使う尊徳に、富と資産が増えて
いき、何年もたたないうちにかなりの資産家になって、
近所の誰からも倹約と勤勉の模範として尊敬されるよ
うになった。なにごとも自力で克服した尊徳は、同じ
ように自力で克服しようとする人たちの力になろうと
思っていた。

## III– 能力の試練

尊徳の名声は日増しに高まり、小田原藩主（大久
保忠真<small>ただざね</small>）の認めるところとなった。尊徳はその
領民であり、当時の小田原藩主は幕府の老中として全
国に並ぶ者のない影響力を持っていた。これほど有能
な領民を、村の生活に埋もれたままにしておくべきで
はなかったが、当時の社会は身分制度が厳しく、一農
民を影響力のある地位に抜擢するには、社会の慣例を
破る時に必ず起きる世間一般の抗議の声を黙らせるだ
けの、並はずれた能力があることを実証するほかはな
かった。そのために尊徳に課せられた仕事は、不屈の
忍耐力をもつ尊徳のような人間でなければ、心がくじ
けるような難事業だった。小田原藩の領地として下野<small>しもつけ</small>
<small>訳注41</small>の国に物井、横田、東沼の3村があり、何代にもわたっ
て放置されていたため、ひどく荒廃していた。かつて、
3村は450戸まで人が増え、公正な領主に1万俵の年貢を
差し出していた。しかし、今では厳しい自然が田畑を
荒廃させ、狐や狸が住みつき、人口は以前の三分の一
まで減少し、貧窮した農民から取り立てられる年貢は、
よくて2000俵どまりだった。貧困は道徳の退廃をもた

attempt to convert chaos and desolation into order and productivity. Declivities of hills, waste spots on river-banks, roadsides, marshes, all added wealth and substance to him, and before many years he was a man of no little means, respected by his entire neighborhood for his exemplary economy and industry. He conquered all things for himself, and he was ready to help others to make similar conquests for themselves.

## III– The Test of His Ability

His fame daily increasing, his worth was recognized by the Lord of Odawara, whose subject he was, and who as the then Prime-Minister of the Tycoon's Government, wielded an influence second to none in the Empire. So valuable a subject was not to be left buried in the obscurity of village life; but in the society of his time, when class-distinctions were so strong, the promotion of a peasant to any position of influence was possible only when he gave unmistakable evidence of extraordinary ability, enough to silence popular protest that was sure to be brought against any such infraction of regular social routine. The job that was selected for this purpose was of most disappointing nature to any but one of Sontok's indomitable patience. Among the feudal possessions of the Lord of Odawara were the three villages of Monoi, Yokota, and Tōshō in the province of Shimotzuke, which, through the neglect of several generations, had gone into fearful desolation. The three villages once counted 450 families, and tendered as their annual feudal dues 10,000 bags (20,000 bushels) of rice to their rightful Lord. But now that wild Nature invaded their fields, and badgers and foxes shared habitations with men, the population

らし、かつてつましく暮らしていた村々は、博徒の巣窟となっていた。村の再建が幾度となく試みられたが、村人自身が物を盗み、怠ける態度を改めないので、いくら金と権力を使っても効果がなかった。藩主にもっと自信があったならば、全住民を立ち退かせ、もっとよく働く新住民を移住させて、怠け者の領民が荒廃させた田畑を生き返らせようとしたかもしれない。


　しかし、このような何の目的にもかなわぬ村こそ、小田原藩主の胸に秘めた目的にかなうものだった。この3村を復興して、元の富と繁栄を取り戻すことができる人物なら、領内のすべての廃村（非常に多い）の復興を託せるだろう。また、これまで誰もが失敗してきたことに成功するほどの人物なら、正当な指導者として世間に通用するであろうし、特権階級の不満を恐れずにふさわしい権力を授けることができるはずである。尊徳はこのような仕事を、藩主から引き受けるように説得されたのである。一農民である尊徳は、低い身分であることと、そのような公共性の高い仕事をする能力はまったくないことを理由に、その栄誉を辞退した。貧しき土を耕す者である自分が、一生のうちにできることは、せいぜい自分の家の財産を回復することであり、それも自分の力によるのではなく、先祖から受け継いだ余得によるのだと考えていた。3年もの長い間、藩主はこの領民に頼み続けた。領民の方も、謙虚な態度を譲らず、茅葺き屋根のわが家で平穏に暮らしたいと懇願し続けた。しかし、立派な領主の懇請を断り切

numbered only one-third of what it had been, and 2,000 bags were the utmost that would be levied from the impoverished farmers. With poverty came moral degradation, and the once thrifty villages were now dens of gamblers. Their restoration was attempted several times; but neither money nor authority was of any avail when the villagers themselves were confirmed thieves and idlers. A more sanguine master might have determined upon the withdrawal of the entire population, and by the importation of new and more virtuous labor, might have begun to recover the fields left desolate by his indolent subjects.

But, these villages, if good for no purpose, just served the purpose which the Lord of Odawara had in view. A man who could restore these villages to their original wealth and prosperity might be entrusted with the restoration of all deserted villages (of which there were a great many) in the country; and he who succeeded where all before him had failed might be brought before the public as their rightful leader, and be clothed with proper authority without fear of discontent from the titled classes. This was the job then which Sontok was prevailed upon by his master to undertake. The peasant declined the honor upon the ground of his humble birth and his total inability for a work of so public a nature;—he a poor tiller of the soil, and the utmost he expected to accomplish in his life was the restoration of his own family-property, and that not by his ability, but by the inherited merits of his ancestors. For three long years the Lord insisted upon his demand from his subject, who as persistently maintained his modesty and request for peaceful domesticity under his own thatched roof. When, however, the importunities of his worthy superior were no longer to be resisted, Sontok asked for permission to carefully examine the

れなくなり、尊徳は自分が復興する村々の状況を詳しく調べる許可を願い出た。彼は、130マイルの道を歩いて各村まで出向き、数ヵ月村人とともに過ごし、一軒一軒訪ね、暮らしぶりを注意深く観察した。さらに、土壌の質や荒れ地の広がり具合、排水、灌漑の手だてなどを詳細に調査し、荒廃した村の復興の可能性を見定めるために必要な情報をすべて集めた。尊徳が小田原藩主に提出した報告書では、見通しは暗かった。ただ、まったく見込みがないわけでもなかった。「仁術さえ施せば、この貧しい人々に平和で豊かな暮らしを取り戻すことができます」と尊徳は報告書に書いた。「金銭を下付したり、税を免除したとしても、この困窮は救えないでしょう。実際、救済の秘訣は金銭援助をことごとく撤回するところにあります。このような援助は、強欲と怠惰を引き起こし、人々の不和の種となります。荒れ果てた土地を開くには荒れ果てた土地の力をもってし、貧乏を救うには貧乏の力をもってするべきです。どうか、この痩せた地からは無理のない年貢を取り立てるだけにして、それ以上を望まないでください。もし1反（1反は1エーカーの約4分の1）の田から2俵の米が取れるなら、1俵は村人の生活を支えるために用い、もう1俵は荒れ地をさらに開墾する費用として使わなくてはなりません。そのようにしたからこそ、この実り豊かな日本は神代に開拓されたのです。当時はみな荒れ地でした。いかなる資金援助もなく、自らの努力で、土地そのものが持つ力を頼みとして、今日のような田畑や肥えた農耕地帯、道路、町が生まれたのです。仁愛、勤勉、自助の徳を徹底して行えば、これらの村にも希望が生まれます。もしも、誠心誠意、忍

situation of the villages he was to revive. Thither he went upon his own feet, a distance of 130 miles, and for months remained among the people, visiting them from house to house, and carefully watching their ways of living; made a close study of the nature of the soil, the extent of wilderness, drainage, possible means of irrigation, etc., and gathered all the data for making his full estimate for the possible restoration of the deserted district. His report to the Lord of Odawara was most discouraging; but the case was not one to be wholly given up. "The art of love (仁術) alone can restore peace and abundance to those poor people," said he in his report. "Grants in money, or release from taxes, will in no way help them in their distress. Indeed, one secret of their salvation lies in withdrawing all monetary help from them. Such help only induces avarice and indolence, and is a fruitful source of dissensions among the people. *The wilderness must be opened by its own resources, and poverty must be made to rescue itself.* Let my Lord be satisfied with the revenue that can be reasonably expected from his famished district, and expect no more from it. Should one *tan*\* of such a field yield two bags of rice, one bag should go to the sustenance of the people, and the other to the fund for the opening-up of the rest of the wilderness. In this way alone was this our fruitful Nippon opened to cultivation in the days of the gods. All was wilderness then; and without any outside help, by their own efforts, with the land's own resources they made fields, gardens, roads, and cities, as we see them now. Love, diligence, self-help,—in the strict enforcement of these virtues lies the hope of these villages; and I should not wonder, if, ten years from this date, with patient

---

\* *Tan* is about one-fourth of an acre.

耐強く仕事に励むならば、今から10年後には、以前の繁栄を回復できるのではないかと思われます」

　実に大胆で、理にかなった、安上がりな計画である。そのような改革に賛成しない人間がいるだろうか。道徳の力を経済の改革の要素として重視する、そのような村の再建計画が提案されたことはほとんどなかった。信仰を経済に応用したのである。この人物にはピューリタン的なところがあった。いやむしろ、西洋からの輸入品である「最大多数の最大幸福の思想」に汚されていない正真正銘の日本人だった。そして尊徳には、自分の言葉を信じてくれる人々がいた。とりわけ、良き藩主が信じてくれた。たかだか100年あまりの間に、西洋「文明」は日本人をなんと変えてしまったことか！

　尊徳の計画は採用され、この農民道徳家は10年間、実質的に3村の行政の責任者になった。しかし尊徳は、先祖から伝えられた財産を回復する仕事を、中途半端のまま残してきたことが悲しかった。尊徳のような誠実一途な人間には、どんな事業でも精魂込めて取り組まないならば、それは罪であった。そして公共の事業に取り組むからには、私利は完全に無視しなくてはならないのである。「一家を廃して、万民の苦を除く」のだと尊徳は自らに言い聞かせた。長年の望みを犠牲にすることについて、妻の同意を得て、「祖先の墓前に詣り、これを告げ」決意を述べた。家を処分し、別世界に旅立つ者のように「背後の船を焼き払って」故郷の村を後にし、主君と村人に約束した仕事に着手した。

　尊徳の「土地と人心の荒廃との闘い」については、ここでは詳しく触れない。そこには術策も駆け引きも

application of ourselves in the work with all sincerity, we bring them back to their original prosperity."

Bold, reasonable, inexpensive plan! Who will not consent to such a plan? Seldom was such a scheme of restoration of villages ever proposed, making *moral forces* prominent factors in reforms of economic kind. It was the economic application of Faith. The man had a tincture of Puritanic blood in him; or rather he was a genuine Japanese undefiled yet by the Greatest-Happiness-Philosophy of the Occidental importation. He also found men who believed in his words, his good Lord the first of all. How did the Western "civilization" change us within a hundred years or so!

The plan was adopted, and our peasant-moralist was to be the virtual governor of these villages for ten years. But sad was he to leave the restorative work of his ancestral property only half-completed. To a man of his ardent sincerity anything but a whole-souled devotion to any enterprise is sin; and now that he undertakes a public work, his private interests are to be wholly disregarded. "He that would save the homes of thousands can do so only at the expense of his own home," he says to himself. He gets his wife's consent to the sacrifice of their cherished hope, tells all of his decisions "audibly at his ancestors' graves," finishes up his home, and like a man bound for another world, he leaves his native village, "burning all ships behind him," and enters upon the task he so boldly guaranteed to his Lord and countrymen.

With the details of his "battles with wilderness, and wildness of his people's heart," we will not concern ourselves at present.

なかった。あるのは「誠意を尽くせば、天地をも動かす」という信念だけだった。尊徳はあらゆるぜいたくを避け、木綿以外は身につけず、村人の家では食事をしなかった。1日の睡眠はわずか2時間で、畑には部下の誰よりも早く出て、最後まで残り、貧しい村人たちにふりかかる過酷な運命に、自らも耐えた。尊徳は、自分自身を評価するのと同じ基準で、つまり動機が誠実かどうかで部下を評価した。尊徳が考える最良の労働者とは、最もよく働く者ではなく、最も崇高な動機で働く者だった。尊徳のところへ一人の男が紹介されてきた。人の3倍は仕事をする働き者で好人物という触れ込みだった。そのような誉め言葉を、尊徳は長い間気にも留めなかった。しかし、その「好人物」に相応の表彰をするよう同僚から促されたので、その男を呼んで、他の役人に見せたのと同じやり方で、1日の仕事を自分の前でするように求めた。男にはできなかった。そして即座に、見回りの役人が見ている時だけ3人前の仕事をしてみせたと、邪な動機を白状した。尊徳は、自分の経験から一人分の仕事の限界を知っていたから、そのような報告にだまされることはなかった。その男は罰を受け、偽善を厳しく戒められて畑に送り帰された。

働き手のなかに、年老いて一人前の仕事ができない男がいた。この男はいつも切り株を取り除く仕事をしていた。骨の折れる、目立たない仕事である。それでも自分で選んだ境遇に明らかに満足している様子で、他の者が休んでいる間も働いていた。男は「木の根掘り」と呼ばれ、ほとんど顧みられることもなかった。

Of arts and policies he had none. His simple faith was this, that *"the sincerity of a single soul is strong enough to move both heaven and earth."* He denied to himself all sweet things, put on nothing but cotton stuffs, never ate at his people's houses, slept only two hours a day, was in the field before any of his men was, remained there till all left, and himself endured the hardest of lots that befell his poor villagers. He judged his men with the same standard with which he judged himself,—the sincerity of motives. With him the best laborer is not he who does most work, but one who works with the noblest motive. A man was recommended to him as the hardest worker, one who did three men's work, the most affable fellow, etc. To all such recommendations our peasant-governor was for a long time indifferent; but when pressed by his associates for the due reward of this "affable fellow," Sontok called the man to himself, and required of him to perform the day's labor in his presence in the same way that he was reported to do it before other officers. The man owned his inability to do so, and straightway confessed the sinister motive he had in forcing himself to three-men's labor before the eyes of the attending officials. The governor knew by his own experience the limit of a man's capacity, and he was not to be deceived by any such report like that. The man was punished, and sent back to the field with due admonition for his hypocrisy.

Another among his laborers was an aged man, hardly equal to one man's capacity. He was always found working at stumps,—a toilsome job, not the kind of work that can make much show. There he would work even when others were at rest, with an evident contentment in the lot he chose for himself. "Stump-digger" they called him, and very little notice was taken of him. But the

ところが、尊徳の目はこの男をとらえていた。ある賃金支払日のこと、いつものように尊徳によって、労働者一人一人の成績と働き分に応じた評価が言い渡されたが、最も高く評価され、褒美を与えられたのは、他でもない「木の根掘り」だった。誰もが驚いたが、一番驚いたのは、その男自身だった。男は通常の手当の他に15両（約75ドル）が与えられた。労働者の1日の稼ぎが、やっと20セントであった時代には、破格の額である。「だんな様」、年老いた男は声を上げた。「私はごらんのような年寄りで、一人前の日当をいただく値打ちはございません。仕事の量も他の人たちにはるかに及びません。勘違いをなさっているにちがいません。めっそうもない、このお金はいただけません」。尊徳は「いや、そうではない」と真顔で言った。「おまえは、他の誰もがしたがらない仕事をしたのだ。目立とうという思いはなく、本当に村のためだけを考えて働いていた。おまえが切り株を取り除いたおかげで邪魔物がなくなり、こちらの仕事がとてもやりやすくなった。おまえのような人間に報償を与えないで、これから先の仕事をどうやって片づけられよう。おまえの誠実な仕事ぶりに報いる天からの褒美である。ありがたく受け取り、老後の安楽な生活の足しにするがいい。おまえのような誠実な人間を知って、私はこの上なく嬉しい」

　男は子供のように泣き「涙で袖を濡らした」。村中の人々が感動した。神のような人が現れて、人々の前で隠れた徳行に報いたのだ。


　尊徳は反対にもあったが、「仁術」によって一掃した。小田原藩主が同僚として派遣した人物を、自分と自分

governor's eyes were upon him. On a certain pay-day, when, as was usual with our governor, judgment was passed upon each laborer according to his merit and share in the work, the man who was called up for the highest honor and reward was no other than the "stump-digger" himself, to the great astonishment of all, and to none more than to the man himself. He was to have fifteen pieces of gold (about $75) besides his regular wages,—an immense sum of money when a laborer earned only *twenty cents* a day. "I, my Lord," exclaimed the old man, "am not worthy of even one man's hire, seeing that I am advanced in age, and am far behind others in the work I have accomplished. Your lordship must be mistaken. For conscience's sake, the gold is not mine." —"Not so," gravely remarked the governor. "You worked where no body else liked to work. For men's observations you cared not, and you aimed only at real service to our villages. Stumps you removed cleared obstructions, and our work was greatly facilitated thereby. If I reward not such as you, by what other ways shall I carry on the work that is yet before me. The gift is from heaven to reward your honesty. Accept it with thankfulness, and use it to add comforts to your age. Nothing makes me rejoice more than the recognition of such an honesty as yours."

The man weeps like a child, "his sleeves wet almost to be wringed." Whole villages are impressed. One godlike has appeared among them, one who rewardeth openly the virtue that is done in secret.

Oppositions he had many, but these he removed by "arts of love." Once it took the patience and forbearance of three years to

のやり方に従わせるのに、忍耐と辛抱の3年を要した。村人のなかに手に負えない怠け者がいて、尊徳の計画にことごとく猛反対した。この男の家は倒れかかっており、自分が貧乏なのは、新しくやってきた役人たちのやり方が間違っている確かな証拠だと近所中に言いふらしていた。たまたま尊徳の家の者が、この男の便所を借りたことがあったが、長年放置されたままだったために傷みがひどく、軽く触れただけで倒れてしまった。男の怒りは留まるところを知らなかった。棍棒を手に家から出てきて、壊したことを詫びている者を一度、二度と殴りつけ、主人の家まで追いかけてきた。そして門前に立ち、まわりに集まった大勢の人々に向かって、自分が大損害を被り、尊徳ではこの地に平和と秩序をもたらすことはできないと言いたてた。尊徳は、その男を面前に呼び、この上なく穏やかに、家の者の過失を詫び、それからこう言った。

「おまえの家の便所がそれほど壊れやすくなっているのなら、さぞかし母屋の方もひどい状態であろう」

「貧乏だからね」男はぶっきらぼうに答えた。「家を直すことなどできはしない」

「それなら、修理する者をこちらから出そう。承知してくれるか」というのが、この道徳家の親切な答だった。

男は仰天して、いささか羞恥の念にも襲われて、こう答えた。

「それほどまでのご好意をお断りできましょうか。身にあまるお情けでございます」

reconcile to him and his ways of doing, a man whom the Lord of Odawara sent as his associate. One of his villagers was an incorrigible idler, and a vehement opposer to all of his plans. The man's house was in a tottering state, and his poverty he would recount to his neighbors as a sure sign of the weakness of the new administration. It happened that a certain member of the governor's household was under the man's manure-shed, which, by the negligence of many years, was in so rotten a state that a slight touch brought it down to the ground. The man's wrath knew no end. With a club he came out, gave a blow or two to the suppliant transgressor, and pursued after him till he reached his master's house. There in the front of the governor's gate the man stood, and recited to the hearing of a large crowd that gathered around him, the severe ills he suffered, and the governor's inability to give peace and order to the district. Sontok ordered the man to his presence, and in the mildest possible way, begged forgiveness for his servant's transgression, and continued:

"Seeing that your manure-shed was in so fragile a state, I am afraid your residence also is not in the best of conditions."

"You know I am a poor man," the man bluntly replied, "and I am unable to repair my house."

"So," was the gentle answer of the moralist. "How is it then if we send men to repair it for you? Will you give your consent to it?"

Taken with surprise, and already a sense of shame coming over him, the man replied.

"Could I object to so kind a proposal? That is a mercy too great for me."

その男はただちに家に戻り、古い家を取り壊して、家を新築するための地ならしをするように言われた。翌日、尊徳の家の者が新しい家を建てる資材をもって現れた。数週間のうちに、近所でも立派な部類に入る家が完成した。便所も触ったぐらいでは壊れることがないように修理された。こうして、村一番の困り者が降参した。それ以来、この男は誰よりも尊徳に忠実であり続けた。男は後年、その時に学んだ真の恥について語るとき、いつも涙を浮かべていた。

ある時、村人の間に不満が広がり、どんな「仁術」をもってしても収拾がつかない状態になった。尊徳は、すべての責任は自分にあると考えた。「天は私の誠意が足りないのを、このようなかたちで罰しているのだ」と胸の内で思った。そして、ある日突然、人々の前から姿を消し、村人はみな、その行方を案じた。数日後、尊徳は遠方にある寺に行ったことがわかった。そこには、祈り、瞑想するために行ったのだが、それ以上に村人を導くためにもっと誠意を身につけようと、21日間の断食をしていたのだ。尊徳に早く村へ帰ってもらおうと、迎えの使者が出された。尊徳がいなくては村の秩序が保てず、もう尊徳なしではやっていけないことがわかったからだ。尊徳は断食を終えると、軽い食事で体力をつけ、「村人が非を悔いていると聞いて喜び、3週間の断食が明けた翌日、25マイルの道を歩いて村まで帰った」。この人物は鉄のように頑健な体だったにちがいない。

数年におよぶ不断の努力と倹約、そしてとりわけ「仁術」によって、荒れ地はほぼなくなり、生産力が満

He was at once sent back to his home, to pull down the old house, and to prepare the ground for the erection of the new. The next day, the governor's men appeared with all preparations for the new structure, and within a few weeks there was finished one of the nicest-looking houses in the whole neighborhood. The manure-shed also was repaired, so that it could stand any man's touch. The worst of the villagers was thus brought down. Ever afterward none remained more faithful to the governor than this man. Tears always gushed out when he told afterward of the *real* humiliation he experienced then.

Once discontent became general among the villagers, and no "art of love" could subdue it. Our governor thought he himself was to be blamed for all such. "Heaven punishes thus my lack in sincerity," he said to himself. One day he disappeared suddenly from among his people, and they all became uneasy about his whereabout. Some days after it was found that he had resorted to a distant Buddhist temple, there to pray and to meditate, but chiefly *to fast* for one-and-twenty days, that he might be furnished with more sincerity in leading his people. Men were sent thither to entreat him for his speedy return, as his absence meant anarchy among his people, who now had learnt that they could not get along without him. The term of his fasting over, he strengthened himself with a slight meal, and "the day after his three weeks' abstinence from food he walked twenty-five miles to his villages, rejoicing in his heart to hear of the repentance of his people." The man must have had an iron constitution with him.

With several years' unabated diligence, economy, and above all, "arts of love," the wilderness had fairly departed, and

足できる程度まで回復し始めた。尊徳は他の地域から入植者を募り、「不案内な者にはわが子に対するよりも親切にしなければならない」と言って、元からいる住民よりも配慮をして遇した。尊徳にとって、地域の完全な復興とは、元の肥沃な土壌に戻ることだけではなく「凶作に備えて10年分の食料備蓄」があることまでを意味していた。それで、「9年分の食料備蓄のない国は危ない。3年分の備蓄のない国はもはや国とはいえない」という中国の賢人の言葉に文字通り従った。ということは、この農民聖者の目から見れば、現在大国を自負しているいずれの国も、「まったく国とはいえない」ことになる。ところが、食料備蓄が整う前に飢饉がやってきた。1833年という年は、東北地方全域が大変に困窮した年だった。尊徳は、夏に茄子を口にした時に、その年の凶作を予言した。秋茄子のような味がするのは、「太陽がすでにその年の光を使いつくした」確かなしるしだと言ったのである。尊徳はただちに、その年の米不足を補うために、一家に1反の割合でヒエを蒔くように村人に命じた。命令は実行され、次の年になって近隣地域は、ことごとく凶作だったが、尊徳が治めていた3村では、食料不足で苦しむ家は一軒も出なかった。「誠実に生きていれば、前もって知ることができる」。尊徳は予言者でもあったのだ。

約束の10年が終わると、全国で最も貧しかった土地が、どこよりも平穏で、十分な蓄えのある土地になり、地力の点でも最も生産性が高い地域になった。豊かだった昔のように、年貢として米1万俵を納められるようになっただけでなく、主要穀物で満杯の倉をいくつも所有し、凶作が数年続いても耐えられるほどの備蓄が

something like tolerable productivity began to return. The governor invited immigrants from other provinces, and them he treated with more consideration than he did the native-born inhabitants, "because," said he, "strangers need more kindness from us than our own children." To him the complete restoration of any district does not mean the mere return of fertility to the soil, but "provisions enough for ten years of scarcity." Therein he followed literally the words of a Chinese sage who said, "A country without nine years' provisions is in danger; and that without three years' is no country at all." According to the views of our peasant-saint, then, the proudest of nations of now-a-days is "no nation at all."—But famine set in before these provisions were made. The year 1833 was one of great distress to all the north-eastern provinces. Sontok foretold the year's poor harvest when eating an eggplant fruit in summer. He said that it tasted very much like that of autumn, an evident sign that "the sun had already spent forth its rays for the year." He at once gave orders to his people to sow millet at the rate of a *tan* to a family, so as to supply the deficiency of the rice-crop of the year. This was done; and the year following, when scarcity reigned throughout the neighboring provinces, not a single family in the three villages under Sontok's supervision suffered from lack. "The ways of sincerity [we] can know beforehand." Our governor was a prophet as well.

At the end of the promised ten years, the once poorest land in the empire became the most orderly, the best provided, and as far as its natural fertility went, the most productive district in the whole country. Not only were the villages made to yield a revenue of 10,000 bags of rice as in their former days of prosperity, but they had now several granaries well-filled with substantial

できた。さらにうれしい知らせを付け加えると、尊徳自身にも数千両の蓄えができ、彼は後年人助けのためにその金を惜しみなく使うこととなった。尊徳の名声は広く知れ渡り、国中の大名が領内の貧村復興の助言を得ようと使いをよこした。誠実だけで、これほど大きな成果があがったことはかつてなかった。これほど素朴で、これほど低い身分の人間でも、天に従いさえすれば、これほど大きな業績を成し遂げることができるのだ。尊徳が公人として最初に取り組んだ仕事で大きな功績をあげたことは、当時の怠惰な社会に道徳面で強烈な印象を与えた。

## IV− 個人的援助

尊徳がこの国の公共の利益のために行った仕事について話す前に、困っている人々の求めに応じて彼が与えた援助について触れておきたい。尊徳自身全くの独学であったため、勤勉で誠実であれば、独立自尊の精神が育たないはずはないと考えていた。「天地は休まずに動いていて、私たちをとりまく万物の成長は、止むことがありません。人がこの永遠の成長の法に従って、働かないことがなくなれば、貧困は求めても襲ってこないでしょう」と、尊徳は貧困にあえぐ農民の一団に言った。彼らは封建領主の悪政を嘆き、先祖伝来の土地から出て行こうとまで思いつめ、尊徳の指導と助言を求めて訪ねてきたのだ。尊徳はさらに言葉を継いで、「皆さんに鍬を一丁ずつさしあげましょう。私のやり方を採用して、それを守るなら、皆さんは必ずや荒れた田畑を楽園に変えることができ、借金もす

grain to provide for many years of scarcity; and we are glad to add that the governor himself had several thousand pieces of gold left for himself which he was to freely use for philanthropic purposes in after years. His fame now spread far and wide, and nobles from all parts of the country sent in messengers to ask his instructions for the restoration of desolated villages in their provinces. Never before had sincerity alone given so prominent a result. So simple, so cheap, a man with Heaven alone can accomplish so much. The moral impression of Sontok's first public achievement was tremendous upon the indolent community of his time.

## IV – Individual Helps

Before speaking of his other public services to his country, let me narrate here something of the friendly help he was called upon to offer to his suffering fellowmen. Himself a wholly self-made man, he knew of no case which industry and sincerity of heart could not bring up to independence and self-respect. "The universe moves on and on, and a stop there is not in the growth of all things around us. If but a man conforms himself to this law of everlasting growth, and with it ceases not to work, poverty, though he seeks it, is impossible." So he said to a group of poverty-stricken farmers, who, complaining of the misgovernment of their feudal lord, were on the point of leaving their ancestral homes, and came to Sontok for his guidance and instructions. "A hand-plough shall I give each of you," he continued, "and if you adopt my way, and abide by it, I assure you, with it you can make a paradise out of your desolated field, pay back all your debts, and can

べて返済して、再び豊かさに恵まれ、他国に富を求めなくともよくなります」と言った。農民たちは、その言葉に従って「鍬一丁ずつ」をこの農民聖者の手から受け取り、助言通りに懸命に働いた。数年後には、失ったものをすべて取り戻しただけでなく、それ以上を手にしていた。

　村人への影響力を完全に失った名主が、尊徳の知恵を借りにきた。この聖者の答えは実に簡単ではあったが、なるほどと思わせる答だった。「それは、自分可愛さが強すぎるからです。利己心はけだもののようなものだ。利己的な人間はけだものの仲間だ。村人を左右する力を持ちたいのなら、村人に献身的に尽くし、自分の持っているもの一切を与えるしかないでしょう」

　「それには、どうすればよろしいのでしょうか」名主が尋ねた。

　「自分の土地や家屋敷、衣類など、すべての持ち物を売り、それで得た金をすべて村の財産にし、身を捨てて村人のために尽くすのです」尊徳は答えた。

　これほど極端な方法には、普通の人はなかなか応じることはできないものだ。名主は、決意するのに数日の猶予を願い出た。

　そして名主が、自分の払う犠牲があまりにも大きすぎると言うと、尊徳はこう答えた。「ご家族が飢えるのを恐れているのですか。あなたがあなたの役目を果たすのに、あなたの相談役である私が私の役目を果たさないとでも思っているのですか」

　名主は帰り、教え通りに実行した。その影響力と人望はすぐに回復した。しばらくは暮らしに困る分は、名主が師と仰ぐ尊徳が自分の蓄えから補っていたが、

rejoice once more in plenty, without seeking fortune outside of your own land." The men did so, accepted "a hand-plough each" from the saint's hand, went earnestly to work as he advised, and in a few years got back all they had lost and more.

A village-mayor who had entirely lost his influence with his people came to Sontok for his wisdom. The saint's answer was the simplest that could be imagined, "Because love of self is strong in you," he said. "Selfishness is of beasts; and a selfish man is of beast-kind. You can have influence over your people only by giving yourself and your all to them."

"How can I do so?" the mayor inquired.

"Sell your land, your house, your raiment, your all," was Sontok's reply, "and whatever money you get thereby contribute to the village fund, and give yourself wholly to the service of the people."

No natural man can easily commit himself to so severe a procedure like this. The manor asked for several days' delay before he could give his decision.

When told that the sacrifice was altogether too much for him, Sontok said: "I suppose you are afraid of the starvation of your family. Think you that if *you* do *your* part, I, your adviser, know not how to do *my* part?"

The man returned, and did as was instructed. His influence and popularity returned at once. His lack for a time his revered instructor supplied out of his own store; but soon the whole

やがて全村あげて名主を支援するようになり、まもなく名主は以前にもまして裕福になった。

　藤沢の米商人は、凶作の年に穀物を高値で売って相当な財産を築いたのだが、家が相次いで災いに襲われ、破産寸前になった。その親戚の一人が尊徳の親しい知人であったので、失った財産を回復する手だてを教えてほしいと、この聖者に相談がもちかけられた。尊徳は、自分の利益しか頭にない人の相談には、いつも気が乗らなかったが、度重なる懇願にあって、ついに依頼に応じた。そして、その米商人の道徳を診断してみたところ、すぐに不幸の原因は一つであることがわかった。「解決法は、残っている全財産を人に施し、裸一貫で出直すことだ」と尊徳は言った。尊徳の目からすると、悪銭は財産とはいえなかった。自然の正しい法則に従い、自然から直接得たものだけが自分のものなのだ。その男の財産がなくなったのは、もともとその男のものではないからなのだ。残りの財産にしても「汚れている」から、そのような財産はないほうがよいのだ。

　強欲をこれほど急激に直すには、長い間苦しみもがくことになる。しかし、この道徳の医師の名声は非常に高く、その処方箋の有効性を誰も疑わなかった。米商人は尊徳の助言に従い、その友人や親戚をことごとく驚かせた、いや仰天させた（といった方がよいだろう）。米商人は、残っていた700両（3500ドル）の全財産をすべて町の人に分け与え、自分は船頭になった。子供の頃に覚えた仕事のうち、ただ一つ「裸一貫」でできる回漕業を始めたのである。その男の決断が、本人にも町の人全体にも与えた道徳的影響のほどは、容

village came to the mayor's support, and within a short period, he was a wealthier man than before.

A rice-merchant in the township of Fujisawa, who had made a considerable fortune by selling his grain at high prices in a year of scarcity, came very near to bankruptcy by successive misfortunes that befell his family. A relative of his was an intimate acquaintance of Sontok, and the saint's wisdom was asked to devise some means for the restoration of the lost property. Always very reluctant to confer with the people who had personal interests in view, he yielded to their request only after long importunity. His moral diagnosis of the man revealed to him at once the sole cause of the trouble. "The way is to give in charity all you have left now," Sontok said, "and to begin anew with your bare hand." To his eye, ill-gotten fortune was no fortune at all. A thing is ours only as we have it directly from Nature by conforming ourselves to her righteous laws. The man lost his property because it had not been originally his, and that which he had left was also "unclean," and hence nothing could be done with *it* also.

Avarice cannot be made to yield itself to such a radical reform without long and painful struggles. But the reputation of the moral-physician was too great to doubt the efficacy of his prescription, and his advice was followed to the amazement, and (may we say) consternation of all his friends and relatives. The man distributed all he had left, amounting to 700 pieces of gold ($3,500) among his townsmen, and he himself went to rowing, the only "bare-hand" trade he was acquainted with from his boyhood. We can easily imagine the moral effect of such a decision on the man's part both upon the man himself, and upon the townsmen at large.

易に想像できる。男の欲深さが買った恨みは、すぐに忘れ去られた。男の不幸を喜んでいた人々も、今や助けてくれるようになり、権（かい）を握っていたのは、ほんの短い間にすぎなかった。この男に幸運が微笑みはじめ、今度は町の人々全員の善意も伴われ、それからの人生は、それまで以上に成功したと聞いている。ただ、残念なことに、歳をとるにつれて男はまた貪欲になっていき、晩年は貧乏をしたということだ。孔子の本[左伝]にこう書かれてはいないだろうか。「禍福門なし、ただ人の招く所なり」

　尊徳に会うのは容易なことではなかった。初めての人間は、その身分にかかわりなく、「多忙につき」という東洋的な口実の決まり文句を聞かされて、必ず門前払いにあった。追い返されても何度も繰り返し訪ねて来る人だけが、話を聞いてもらうことができた。来訪者の忍耐が切れて来なくなると、尊徳はいつも「私が助ける時期には、まだ至っていないようだ」と言った。ある時、檀家を救済するための助言を求めて、一人の僧侶が徒歩で遠方より訪れた。面会はそっけなく拒絶されたが、忍耐強い僧侶は、門前の地面に着衣を拡げ敷き、そこに3日3晩座り込んだ。苦行に耐え、不屈の精神であたれば、この師も会ってみようという気になると信じていたのだ。しかし尊徳は「犬のような」、「乞食坊主」が門の外に座っていると聞いて激しく怒り、僧侶にすぐに立ち去って「人々の魂のために、祈るなり断食するなりせよ」と命じた。このような扱いが何度も繰り返されてから、ようやく僧侶は信頼を得て受け入れられ、以後は尊徳からいつでも自由に、金銭も知恵も親交も与えられるようになった。尊徳から親交

All the bitterness against him caused by his avarice was removed at once, and those who rejoiced in his misfortunes now came to his help, and he was upon his oars only for a very short time. Fortune began to smile upon him, this time *with* the good-will of all his townsmen, and we are told that his latter end was more prosperous than his beginning. Only we are sorry to hear that with age avarice returned to him once more, and his last days were spent in penury. Does not a book of Confucius say, "Misery and happiness come not by themselves; *only men invite them*"?

Our teacher was not an easy man to approach. Strangers of whatever ranks were always repulsed at his gate with the customary oriental excuse "I am pressed with duty." Only the most importunate could get a hearing from him. Should the inquirer's patience fail, the teacher would say "My time of helping him is not come yet." Once we are told that a Buddhist priest, who came a long distance walking to get instruction for the relief of his parishioners, was bluntly refused audience; but he a patient man spread his garment upon the ground in front of the teacher's house, and there for three days and nights he sat, believing that by penance and pertinacity, the teacher might be induced to give him a hearing. But Sontok was extremely wroth to hear that "dog-like" a "beggar-priest" sat near his gate, and he ordered him to begone at once and "pray and fast for people's souls." Such a treatment was repeated several times before he received the priest in confidence, and this was he, who in after years, was to be a free recipient of his gold, wisdom, and friendship. His friendship was always very costly to get, but when once procured, nothing was so precious and lasting. He could do nothing with false

を得るのは、いつも大変な努力が必要であったが、いったん得たなら、これほどありがたく、また長続きするものはなかった。不実な人間は相手にされなかった。そのような人間は、宇宙とその法則に反しており、尊徳の力でも、いや誰の力をもってしても、不幸や堕落から救い出すことはできないのだ。そのような人たちに対して、尊徳はまず彼らを「天地の理」に従わせ、それから人間の援助を、どうしても必要なことなら何でも与えた。「キュウリを植えたのならキュウリとは別なものが収穫できると思うな。人は自分が植えたものを収穫するのだ」。「誠実にして、はじめて禍を福に変えることができるのだ。術策は役に立たない」。「一人の人間は、宇宙にあっては限りなく小さな存在であるが、その誠意は天地をも動かすことができる」。「なすべきことは、結果に関係なく、なさなくてはならない」。このような多くの教訓を与えて、尊徳は指導と救済を求めてやってきた苦しんでいる人々を救った。こうして尊徳は自然と人との間に立ち、正しい道徳を忘れて、自然の惜しみない恵みを受ける権利を失っていた人々を、自然へと引き戻した。このような福音に比べて、近年わが民族の国土に氾濫している西洋の学問とは、何であろうか！

## V‒公共事業一般

尊徳の信念によって、荒廃した下野の国の3村が復興されると、その名声は疑いようもなく確かなものになり、尊徳は全国各地の大名に絶えず煩わされるようになった。尊徳は例のそっけない応対の仕方で

insincere men. The universe and its laws were against such men, and nothing in his power or any man's power could rescue them from misery and degradation. Them he would first reconcile with the "Reason of Heaven and Earth," and then administer to them whatever human helps that might be absolutely necessary. "Think not you can get anything else than cucumber-fruit when you plant cucumber. The thing a man planteth, the same he must reap also." "Sincerity alone can turn misery into happiness; arts and policies avail nothing." "An individual soul is an infinitesimally small thing in the universe, but its sincerity can move heaven and earth." "Duty is duty irrespective its result." Such and many like them are the precepts with which he helped out many a struggling soul that came to him for guidance and deliverance. Thus he stood between Nature and man, restoring to the former them, who, through their moral obliquity, had forfeited the right she so freely bestowed upon them. What are all the wisdoms of the West that have recently flooded our soil, in comparison with an evangel such as this, of our own kin and blood!

## V – Public Services at Large

His faith once worked out in the restoration of the three deserted villages in the province of Shimotzuke, and his fame thus indubitably established, he became an object of constant interruption by nobles from all parts of the country. He fenced

来訪者を受け流したが、彼の「信念の試験」に合格する人も少なからずいて、その人々には尊徳が相談にのり、実際に力も貸した。尊徳の一生の間に、広い領地を持つおよそ10人の大名が、荒廃した自領の改良の仕事を尊徳に依頼した。同じように尊徳の力を借りた村の数は、数え切れないほどだった。晩年には幕府にも登用されるほど、国家に重要な貢献をするようになった尊徳だが、彼の使命は本来地味なものであったから、特権階級の公的、社会的な慣例尊重の制約を受けずに、自分と同じ階級の貧しい労働者とともにいる時が最も生き生きとしていた。それにしても不思議なことに、卑賎の生まれで、まったく教育を受けていない農民の尊徳が、「上流階級の人たち」とつき合うときには、「真の貴人」のようにふるまうことができたのである。

　当然ながら、尊徳の領主である小田原藩主は、尊徳から特に多くの恩恵を受けた。小田原城下の広大な領地は尊徳の監督下におかれ、領内の多くの荒廃地は、尊徳のたゆまぬ勤勉と、変わらぬ「仁術」によって復活した。1836年の大飢饉は、尊徳が同じ藩の人々のために最もすぐれた働きをした一例となった。数千の人々が餓死寸前にあった時、尊徳は領主（その時は江戸にいた）から迅速に救済にあたるように命じられた。尊徳は、当時は江戸から丸2日の道のりであった小田原に急行すると、飢えた民をすぐさま救うために城の穀物倉を開ける鍵を渡すよう、役人に求めた。すると「殿の直筆の許可状がなくては」というなんとも横柄な答が返ってきた。尊徳はそれに応じて、「よろしい。だが、今から直筆の許可状が到着するまでの間にも、飢えた領民が餓死する数はさらに増えることになりまし

himself against such intrusions by his usual blunt ways of receiving his visitors, but such as endured his "test of faith" were not few, and these had all the benefit of his wise councils and practical help. During his life-time, some half-a-score nobles representing a wide extent of land had his services in improvement of their impoverished dominions, and the number of villages likewise benefited was innumerable. Near the end of his life his service to the nation became so invaluable that he was employed by the Central Government; but the homely nature of his mission made him appear at his best when he was among his own class of poor laborers, unhampered by the official and social conventionalities of the titled classes. The wonder is, however, that he a peasant of the meanest birth and the simplest culture could have managed himself like a "real noble" when associating with "men in high places."

Naturally his own Lord of Odawara was to get most from him. The large dominion attached to the castle-town of the same name was placed under his supervision, and much of the desolated and waste places in it was recovered by his tireless industry and never-failing "arts of love." The great famine of 1836 witnessed one of his most signal services to his fellowmen. When thousands of people were on the point of death from starvation, he was commissioned by his Lord (then residing in Yedo) to undertake their speedy relief. Sontok hastened to Odawara, then a journey of two full days, and asked the men in authority there to hand him the key to open the castle-granary for the immediate relief of the starving people. "Not till we have the Lord's written permission," was their rather contemptuous answer. "All right, then," Sontok responded. "But, gentlemen, seeing that during the interval between this and the arrival of the written permission of the Lord

ょう。そのことを思うならば、領民を心をこめて守る
べき役目の我々は、領民が食を断たれているように食
を断ち、この城内で使者が戻るまで断食をするのが当
然の義務だと思います。そうすれば、領民の苦しみが
どのようなものか、多少なりともわかるでしょう」。役
人たちは、4日間も断食するなど考えるのも嫌だった。
鍵は即座に尊徳に渡され、ただちに領民の救済が実施
された。いつの時代のいかなる国にあっても、領民を
守る立場にある者はだれもが、飢饉が迫った時には、
この道徳家の提案を肝に銘じてほしいものだ。そして、
役所は形式を重んじて無益な手続きにこだわるから、
苦しんでいる民の救済に取りかかれないのだ。

　尊徳が「年饑て民を救うの道を得ず。この時にあた
り何の術を以て飢渇の民を救い、これを安んぜんや」
という名高い講話を行ったのは、このときのことだっ
た。主な聴講者は、領主から藩政の責任者に任じられ
ていた国家老だった。この講話には、講師のひととな
りがよく現れているので、その一部をここに紹介しよ
う。

　「国が飢饉に見舞われ、穀物倉は空になり、民は食べ
るものがない。この責任はだれにあるかといえば、そ
れは治者以外にありません。治者は天民を託されてい
るのであって、民を悪から遠ざけて善へと導き、末永
く無事に暮らせるように教えることが、その使命では
ないのでしょうか。その使命をまっとうすると期待さ
れているからこそ、高禄を得て、自分の家族を養い、
家は安泰なのです。ところが今や、領民が飢えに苦し
んでいるのに、平然と見すごしています。これほど嘆
かわしいことが天下にあるでしょうか。この時にあた

many more of our starving people shall die of hunger, I believe it behooves us as their faithful guardians that we should abstain from food as they are now doing, and should stay here in this office-room fasting till the return of your messenger. Thus we may learn somewhat of the nature of our people's suffering." Four days' fasting was too horrible to think of to these officers. The key was instantly delivered to Sontok, and the relief was effected at once. Would that *all* guardians of people of whatever clime at whatever time may be mindful of our moralist's proposal when hunger waits at the people's door, and officialism must go through useless formalities before it can bring relief to the sufferers!

It was upon this occasion that he delivered his famous discourse upon "the Ways of Famine-Relief in default of Means for that End." His chief audience was the governor of the dominion appointed by his Lord as the chief executive of the provincial government. We give here some fragments of the discourse, as it is very characteristic of the man who gave it.

"That the land famishes, the granaries are empty, and the people have nothing to eat,—whose blame is this but that of the ruler himself! Is he not intrusted with Heaven's children (天民), and is it not his mission to lead them into good and away from evil, and so enable them to live and abide in peace? For this service which is expected from him he is paid abundantly, and he brings up his family, and they are safe. But now that his people are reduced to hunger, he thinks not himself responsible for it:—Gentleman, I know of nothing under heaven so lamentable as this. At this time, should he succeed in devising some means of

り、よく救済策を講じることができればよし、もしでき
ない場合には、治者は天に対して自分の罪を謝し、自ら
進んで飲食を断ち、死ぬべきです。ついで家臣の、藩
を治める家老が治者の後を追い、次に村を治める郡奉
行や代官がその後を追って、飲食を断ち、死ぬべきで
す。彼らもまた職務を怠り、領民に死と苦しみをもた
らしたからです。そのような犠牲が、飢えた人々に与
える道徳的影響は、すぐに明らかになるでしょう。犠
牲を知った人々はこう言い交わすでしょう。『御家老様
と御奉行様は、本当は何の責任もないのに、我々の困
窮の責任を取られた。我々が飢えているのは、豊作の
時に贅沢や浪費をして、将来の備えを怠ったせいだ。
我々には、立派なお役人の痛ましい死に対する責任が
あり、飢え死にするのも当然のことだ』。こうして飢饉
に対する恐れは消え、それと共に餓死に対する恐れも
消えるでしょう。すると民の心は安らぎます。恐怖が
消え去りさえすれば、じきに食料は十分に行き渡るよ
うになります。富める者は貧しい者に持っている物を
分け与えるでしょう。そうでない場合は、山に登って、
木の葉や根を食べて飢えをしのぐでしょう。たった1年
の飢饉では、国内の米や雑穀をすべて食べ尽くす心配
はなく、丘や山には山菜もあります。国が飢えるのは、
民の心が恐怖に支配され、食物を探し求める気力を奪
い、死に至らせるからなのです。空砲が臆病な鳥を撃ち
落とすことがあるように、何年も凶作に苦しんでいる
民は、飢餓と聞いただけで驚いて死ぬのです。ですか
ら、民を治める者がまず進んで餓死するのなら、飢え
の恐怖は民の心から消え去り、心が満たされて救われ
るでしょう。郡奉行や代官が犠牲になるのを待つまで

relief, well; but if not, the ruler should confess his sin before Heaven, and himself go to voluntary fasting and *die*! Then his sub-officers,—county-officers after him, and then village-officers,—they also should abstain from food and *die*, for they too have neglected their duty and brought death and suffering upon the people. The moral effect of such sacrifices upon the famished people will be evident at once. They will now say among themselves: 'The governor and his sub-officers held themselves responsible for the distress that is upon us, when they have really nothing to blame themselves with. Starvation is upon us because of our own improvidence, luxury, and extravagance in times of abundance. We are accountable for the lamentable end of our honored officers, and that we should now die of hunger is entirely proper.' Thus the fear of famine shall depart, and with it the fear of death also. Their mind is now at peace. Fear once gone, abundance of food-supply is within their reach. The rich may share his possession with the poor; or they may climb mountains, and feed upon leaves and roots. A single year's famine cannot exhaust all the rice and millet of land, and hills and mountains have their supply of green things. The nation famishes because Fear reigns dominant in the people's mind, and depriving them of energy to seek food, causes them to die. *As guns fired without shots often bring down timid birds, so men in years of scarcity are astounded with sound of hunger, and die.* Therefore let the leaders of the people die first of voluntary starvation, and the fear of hunger shall be dissipated from the people's heart, and they all shall be filled and saved. I do not believe you need wait for the sacrifice of your county and village-officers before you realize the result you aim at. I believe the sacrifice of the governor alone is sufficient for this purpose. This,

もなく、望み通りの結果が得られると思います。家老の死のみで十分でしょう。みなさん、これが、何の手だても残されていない時に、飢えた民を救う方法です」

講話は終わった。家老は恥じて恐れ入り、長い沈黙の後にこう言った。「あなたの話に反論することはできない」

この痛烈な皮肉は、真剣に語られた話ではあるが、もちろん実行させるつもりはなかった。尊徳の仕事の特徴は、迅速、勤勉、苦しむ者への深い同情心、自然や自然の情け深い法則への信頼だったが、この時の救済には明快さも発揮された。困窮している農民に、分割で5年以内に収穫物で返すという条件で、穀物と金銭が貸し与えられた。そして、このような援助をした側の誠実だけでなく、援助を受けた純朴な農民にも敬意を表して付け加えるならば、この取り決めは忠実に自発的に守られ、救われた40,390人の窮民のうち、決められた期日に返済できなかった者は一人もいなかった。

自然とともにある者は急がない。目先のことだけのために計画を立てることもない。いわば自然の流れのなかに身を置き、その流れを助けたり強めたりして、それによって自分が助けられ、前進させられるのである。宇宙に後押しされているのだから、仕事の大きさにたじろぐこともない。「万物には自然の道がある」、尊徳は常々言っていた。「自然の道を探し出し、それに従わなくてはならない。それによって、山はならされ、海は干拓されて、大地は我々の役に立つようになるのだ」。ある時、尊徳は幕府から利根川下流の大きな沼の干拓を可能にする計画を立てて報告するよう命ぜられた。そのような事業が完成すれば、三重の意味で計り

gentlemen, is one way of saving your hungry people when you have nothing left to give them for their relief."

The discourse ended. The governor in shame and dismay, said after a long silence, "I should say it is impossible to gainsay your argument."

The sarcasm, though seriously spoken, was not of course intended to be carried into practice. The relief was effected with the same simplicity as that which characterized all his other labors,—promptness, diligence, intense sympathy with the sufferer, and trust in Nature and her beneficient laws. Grain and money were loaned to the suffering farmers, to be paid back in instalment within five years by crops; and be it mentioned in honor of the simple-hearted peasants thus succored, as well as of the *good faith* in which the succor was offered, that the promise was faithfully and willingly kept, not one of the 40,390 sufferers so relieved proving himself insolvent at the end of the stipulated term!

He that is in league with Nature hastes not; neither does he plan works for the present alone. He places himself in Nature's current, as it were, and helps and enhances it, and is himself helped and forwarded thereby. With the universe at his back, the magnitude of the work astounds him not. "There are natural courses for *all* things," Sontok used to say, "and we are to seek out Nature's ways and to conform ourselves thereto. Thus can mountains be levelled and seas be drained, and the earth itself be made to serve our purpose." Once he was appointed by his government to report upon some possible plans of draining the great marshes on the lower course of the river Toné. If accomplished, such an enterprise would serve triple purposes of inestimable public

知れない公共の利益があった。毒気を放つと思われていた浅い沼地が埋め立てられて何千エーカーもの沃地が生まれ、洪水の時には放水して、毎年この地方が受ける被害の大半を未然に防ぐことができ、利根川と江戸湾を結ぶ短い水路が新しく開かれるはずだった。水路の正確な長さは、沼地と湾の間が10マイル、沼地の2地点の間が5マイルで、全長15マイルにわたって沼地の丘や砂地が切り開かれることになる。この計画はそれまでも一度ならず試みられながら、あきらめて放棄されていた。この仕事は、日本のレセップスともいうべき有能な人物によって完成されるのを待っていたのだ。

この巨大事業に関して尊徳が提出した報告書はかなりつかみどころのない内容だった。だが、同じような規模の土木工事がいくつも失敗した点に関しては急所をついていた。「可能かもしれないし、不可能かもしれない」と報告書は述べていた。「無理のない唯一の可能な方法を採用して、その方法に従えば可能でしょう。しかし、人間の本性は概してそのような方法に従うことは嫌いますから、その場合は不可能でしょう。水路を通す地域の民は、道徳的に堕落しているようなので、この仕事に着手する前に不可欠な準備として、まずその点を仁術によって正さなければなりません。そのような民に金を使えば、悪い効果を生じるのは必至で、当然のこと実際の作業ははかどらないでしょう。この事業の本質を再検討してみますと、金や権威からはほとんど何も期待できないでしょう。強い報恩の念で人々が一致結束してこそ、初めて可能になる事業なのです。それゆえ、幕府は民に「仁術」を施し、寡婦を援助し、孤児を保護し、道徳を忘れた住民を有徳の民

benefit: it would recover thousands of acres of fertile land from the shallow and miasmatic marsh; would drain off surplus water in time of flood, and obviate much of damage yearly done in those quarters; and would afford a new and short passage between the river and the bay of Yedo. The distance to be cut is ten miles between the marsh and the bay, and five miles between the two main sections of the former,—in all, fifteen miles of excavation through mud-hills and sand. The attempt has been made more than once, only to be given up in despair; and the work is still there waiting for some master mind,—a Japanese Lesseps—to carry it into completion.

Sontok's report upon this gigantic enterprise was rather enigmatic; but it hit the point upon which many an engineering work of like magnitude made ship-wreck. "Possible, yet impossible," said the report: "Possible, if the natural and only possible course be adopted and followed; but impossible, because human nature in general is loath to follow such a course. I see the demoralization of the district through which the canal is to be dug, and *that* must be righted first by 'the arts of love' as the essential preliminary to the work to be undertaken. Money spent among such people cannot but have vicious effects upon them, to say nothing of the amount of actual work accomplished thereby. But the nature of the undertaking under review is such that little can be expected from either money or authority. Only a united people impelled by a strong sense of gratitude can do it. Let the government therefore apply 'the arts of love' upon them, comfort their widows, shelter their orphans, and make a virtuous people out of the present demoralized population. Once you have called forth their sincerity, the boring of mountains and breaking of rocks will

に変えることです。いったん民の誠実な心が呼び起こされれば、山をうがつことも岩を砕くことも思いのままになるでしょう。回り道のように見えても、これが最短にして最も効果的な方法です。植物の根があってこそ、花が咲き、実がなります。まず道徳があり、それから作業があるのです。作業を道徳の前にもってくることはできません」

　今日では、これをあまりにも夢のような計画として、幕府が受け入れなかったのはもっともだと思う人がほとんどだろう。しかし「パナマ疑獄事件」を見守っていた人なら、あの巨大事業の失敗の主な原因が、財政面ではなくて道徳面にあることがわかるはずだ。コロンとパナマを盗人の巣窟に変えた黄金は、どぶに捨てられたようなものであり、実際にどのような成果があがったかといえば、二つの大洋は、シャベル一杯の土が地峡からはじめて取り除かれた時と変わらず、離れたままだ（脚注・我々の予想に反して、運河はアメリカの黄金によって完成された。拝金主義は強し、である）。偉大なフランス人技師が、多少なりともこの日本人農夫の先見の明をもって、道徳を考えていたらどうであったろう。6億ドルの資金をすべて事業に使わないで、その一部を「仁術」による人への投資にまわしていたなら、必ずやレセップスの白髪頭には二つの運河の成功を称える王冠が載せられ、一つの運河の不名誉な失敗で、もう一つの運河の輝かしい成功を帳消しにすることはなかっただろう。金は多くのことを可能にするが、徳はそれ以上のことを可能にする。運河建設の計画を立てる上で道徳的要因を重視する人は、つまりは誰よりも実際的な人なのだ。

be according to your wish. The way may look tortuous, but it is the shortest and most effective one. Does not the root of a plant contain all its flowerage and fruitage? Morality first, then work; —you cannot place the latter before the former."

Most of the present-day readers may sympathize with his government that rejected so visionary a plan as this; but who has watched the "Panama scandals" and fails to see that the main cause of the failure of that gigantic enterprise was moral and not financial? The gold that turned Colon and Panama into veritable dens of thieves lies buried there like so much rubbish, and to all practical purposes, the two oceans are as yet as far apart from each other as when the first shovel of dirt was removed from the isthmus*. Would that the great French engineer had possessed something of the moral foresight of the Japanese peasant; and instead of disbursing his six hundred millions wholly upon the work itself, had a part of it invested in human souls through "arts of love";—then who doubts that Lesseps would have had *two* canals to crown his gray hairs, instead of the disgraceful failure of one covering up the glorious success of the other? Money can do much, but virtue more; and he who takes into account *moral elements* in forming his plan for canal construction is NOT after all the most unpractical of men.

---

* Now accomplished by American gold, *against* our prophecy. Great is Mammonism!

尊徳が一生のうちに手がけた仕事は、地理的にはそう広い範囲に及んではいないが、厳格な身分差別のあった時代に、彼ほど社会的地位の低い人間にしては相当なものだった。なかでも最大の業績は、今日の磐城地方にあたる相馬領の復興である。相馬は230村からなり、もともと貧しくはなかったが、今や国内でも特に豊かで栄えた土地になっている。尊徳は、どのような規模の仕事でも、実に単純な取り組み方をした。まず、たいていはその地方で一番貧しい村を代表に選んで、その一村に全力を注ぎ、ただ一生懸命励むことによって、その村を尊徳の方法に従わせる。これが、仕事のなかで一番難しいところだった。最初にその一村を立ち直らせて、そこを基点に地域全体を変えていくのだ。尊徳は、一種の伝道精神を農民に教え、尊徳から助けられたように隣村の人々を助けるように求めた。驚くべき実例を目の当たりにしたり、新しい息吹を吹き込まれた人々の惜しみない援助を受けたりして、地域全体が同じ方法を取り入れるようになり、人々の心は伝播の単純な法則に従って変化していった。「一村を救済できる方法は一国を救済できる。その原理は同じである」、尊徳は尋ねる人に決まってそう言った。「この当面の仕事に全力を尽くそう。そうすれば、これが前例となって、時が来れば全国を救う役に立つ」、日光地方の荒廃した村々を復興する計画を立てている時に、尊徳は弟子たちにこう言った。この人物は、自分が宇宙の永遠の法則を会得していることを自覚しており、彼にとっては取り組めないほど難しい仕事はなく、全身全霊で取り組む必要がないほど簡単な仕事もなかった。

The geographical extent of Sontok's actual accomplishment in his life-time was not large, though considerable for a man of his social position at a time of rigid class distinctions. By far the most considerable of all his achievements was the restoration of the Sōma region in the present province of Iwaki,—itself a no mean district of two hundred and thirty villages, now one of the wealthiest and most prosperous in the country. The way he set himself to work in any work of magnitude was perfectly simple. He would first concentrate his whole energy upon one typical village,—usually the poorest in the district,—and by sheer dint of industry would convert it into his ways. This is usually the hardest part of the whole business. The one village first rescued, he had as a base to start from for the conversion of the whole district. He always infused a kind of missionary spirit among his peasant-converts, who were required to help their neighboring villages as they themselves were helped by their teacher. With a striking example furnished before their very eyes, and with help freely afforded by the men under the new inspiration, the whole district was brought to adopt the same method, and conversion was effected by a simple law of propagation. "The method that can rescue a village can rescue the whole country; the principle is just the same," he used to say to his inquirers. "Let us apply ourselves devotedly to this one piece of work; for the example may serve to save the whole nation in times to come," he observed to his disciples while preparing plans for the restoration of a few desolated villages in the Nikkō district. The man was conscious of his possession of the everlasting laws of the universe, and no work was too difficult for him to attempt, nor too easy to require his whole-souled devotion to it.

言うまでもなく、尊徳は死ぬ間際まで勤勉であった。遠い将来を見越して計画を立てて働いたので、その仕事と影響は、今もなお我々の間に生きている。尊徳の手で復興された数多くの村の晴れやかな姿は、尊徳の知恵と計画の先見性を証明している。また、尊徳の名前と教えで結ばれた農民の団体が日本各地に見られ、気落ちした農民に尊徳が教えた精神をそのまま今日に伝えている。

Naturally he was a hard-working man till the very close of his life. As he planned and worked for the distant future as well, so his works and influences still live with us. Many a smiling village of his own reconstruction witnesses to his wisdom and the permanence of his plans; while scattered through different parts of the empire are to be found societies of farmers bound by the name and teaching of this man, to perpetuate the spirit he made known to the disheartened sons of toils.

1608-48（慶長13年～慶安元年）

# 中江藤樹

## 村の先生

---

# NAKAE TŌJU

## A Village Teacher

## I — 昔の日本の教育

「**私**たち西洋人が助けに来る前は、日本ではどのような教育が行なわれていたのですか？　あなたたち日本人は異教徒の中でもとりわけ賢いように見えます。心と頭の両面でそれなりの教育を受けてきたからこそ、今日の姿があるに違いありません」

日本を離れ、初めて西洋の文明人のなかに入ったとき、このような問いかけを受けたり、それに近い口ぶりでよく話しかけられたりする。それに対する私たちの答えは、次のようなものだった。

「ええ、私たちは教育を受けました。それもかなりのものを。十戒のうち少なくとも八つの戒めを、母親の膝の上にいるころに父親の口から学んだと、私たちは自負しています。力は正義ではないこと、天地は利己主義のうえに成り立ってはいないこと、盗みはどんな場合でもよくないこと、生命や財産は結局のところ志すべきものではないこと、そのほか多くのことを知りました。また学校があり教師もいましたが、それは偉大な西洋を手本に、今日わが国で模倣されているものとはまったく違うものです。第一に、私たちは学校を知的な修行を積むための訓練場とは決して考えませんでした。学校に行かされたのは、修行を積めば生計を

# I– Teaching in Old Japan

"What kind of schooling had you in Japan before we Westerners came to save you? You Japanese seem to be the cleverest set of people among heathens, and you must have had some training, moral and intellectual, to make you what you have been and are."

Such are the questions, and oftentimes their tone, put to us by some civilized Westerners, when some of us appeared in their midst, fresh from our country. To which our answer has been somewhat as follows:

"Yes, we had schooling, and considerable of it. We believe, at least, eight out of the Ten Commandments we learnt from the lips of our fathers while in our mothers' laps. We knew that might is *not* right, that the universe does *not* stand upon selfishness, that stealing is *not* right in whatever form it appears, that life and property are *not* after all the things we should aim at, and many other things. We had schools too and teachers, quite different from what we see in your great West and now imitated in our land. First of all, we never have thought of schools as shops for intellectual apprenticeship. We were sent there not so much for earning livelihood when we had finished with them, as for becoming *true men*, *kunshi*, as we called them, akin to "gentlemen" in English.

立てられるからではなく、真の人間になるためでした。私たちはそういう人間を君子と呼びました。これは英語のジェントルマンに近いものです。さらに、一度にたくさんの異なる科目を教えられることはありませんでした。今も昔も頭脳には二葉しかなく、たくさんはないのです。それに、昔の教師は、わずかな年月にあらゆる知識をつめこんではいけないと考えていました。（これは、賢明なことだと思います。）それが、昔の教育制度の、ひとつのすぐれた特徴でした。私たちは「歴史」「詩」「礼儀作法」を少なからず教わりましたが、おもに教えられたのは「道徳」で、それも実生活に即したものでした。理論的な、あるいは神智学的、神学的な道徳は、私たちの学校では決して強要されませんでした。たしかにわが国の仏教学者は、山の洞窟にこもり、伝説上の亀の甲に毛が何本あるかとか、そのほか重箱の隅をつつくようなことを論じあっていましたが、下のほうの平地に住み、人間の実際的なことがらに対処しなければならない私たちは、そのような問題に心をわずらわせずにすんだのでした。ひとことで言えば、私たちは学校で神学は教わりませんでした。神学を学びたければ寺へ行けばよく、学校にはほかの国でよく見られるような教派上の争いはありませんでした。これもまた、昔の教育制度のすぐれた特徴でした。

　さらにまた、私たちにはクラス分けがありませんでした。魂を持つ人間を、オーストラリアの農場の羊のようにクラスに分けることは、昔の学校では考えられませんでした。人間は分類できないものであり、一個人として、顔と顔、魂と魂で向き合っていかなければならないと教師たちは信じていた、そう私には思われ

Then too, we were not taught on a dozen different subjects at the same time. We had only two lobes of the brain then as now, and not a dozen; and our old teachers thought (we think, wisely) that we must not be crammed with knowledges of all kinds in a few years. This was one good feature of our old system of education. We were taught considerable in History, in Poetry, in Manners; but chiefly in Morals, and that of practical kind. Morality of the speculative, or theosophical, or even of theological kind, was never forced upon us in our schools. Our Buddhist scholars indeed, in their mountain recesses, did dispute the number of hairs upon the carapace of the fabulous turtle, and other subjects of hair-splitting nature; but we who lived in the plains below, and had to deal with the practical affairs of men, were spared from conscientious scruples about these and similar questions. In a word, we were never taught theology in our schools. We had temples (churches) to resort to for that purpose, and our schools were free from the sectarian wranglings often witnessed in other lands. This was another good feature of our old system of education.

"Then also we were not taught in classes. The grouping of soul-bearing human beings into classes, as sheep upon Australian farms, was not known in our old schools. Our teachers believed, I think instinctively, that man is unclassifiable, that he must be dealt with personally, i.e., face to face and soul to soul. So they schooled us one by one, each according to his idiosyncracies—physical,

ます。ですから、教師は私たち一人一人を、体の状態やものの考え方や感じ方をみて、それぞれの個性に応じて教育しました。彼らは私たち一人一人の名前をちゃんと覚えていました。ロバと馬が決して同じ引き具につながれることがなかったので、ロバが愚かなあまり叩きのめされる恐れもなければ、優れた馬を鍛えすぎて死なせてしまう恐れもありませんでした。現代に見られるような適者生存の原理にもとづく教育制度は、寛大で人を愛する君子（ジェントルマン）になるには適していないように思われました。したがって、この点では、昔の教師は教育理論に関して、ソクラテスや<sup>訳注46</sup>プラトンと同じ考えでした。<sup>訳注47</sup>

　ですから、当然、教師と生徒の関係は可能な限り親密でした。私たちは教師を、あの近寄りがたい呼び名の、教授とは呼ばずに、先に生まれたという意味の「先生」と呼びました。これは、この世に生まれた時点で先──必ずしもそうではありませんでしたが──というだけでなく、真理を先に会得したという点で、先に生まれたことになるからです。そういうものとして彼らは、私たちが両親や藩主に対して示すものにも似た、この上もないほどの尊敬を受けていました。実際、「先生」と両親と「君」（主君）は、尊敬すべき対象の三位一体でした。日本の若者にとって最も頭を悩ますのは、この三者が同時に溺れようとしているとき、一人しか助けることができないとしたら、誰を助けるかという問題でした。したがって、「弟子」が「先生」のために命を投げ出すことは最高の美徳とされました。一方、現代の教育制度のもとで、生徒が教授のために死んだという話は聞いたことがありません。

mental, and spiritual. *They knew every one of us by name.* And as asses were never harnessed with horses, there was but little danger of the former being beaten down into stupidity, or the latter driven into valedictorians' graves. The system of education based upon the survival-of-the-fittest principle, as the modern one seems to be, was considered to be *un*fittest for making generous, man-loving *kunshi* (gentlemen). In this respect, therefore, our old-time teachers agreed with Socrates and Plato in their theory of education.

"So naturally the relation between teachers and students was the closest possible. We never called our teachers by that unapproachable name, professors. We called them *sensei*, "men born before," so named because of their prior birth, not only in respect of the time of their appearance in this world, which was not always the case, but also of their coming to the understanding of the truth. As such they claimed from us the highest veneration, akin to that which we were asked to show toward our parents and feudal lords. Indeed, *sensei*, parents, and *kimi* (lord) constituted the trinity of our worshipful regard; the most vexing question for the Japanese youth was which he would save if the three of them were on the point of drowning at the same time, and he had the ability to save but one. It was considered, therefore, a virtue of the highest kind for *deshi* (disciples) to lay down their lives for the sake of their *sensei* (master); while we never have heard of students dying for their professor in our modern *régime*[*16] of education.

このような「先生」と「弟子」の関係が頭にあった
ため、キリスト教の聖書に見られる師と弟子の親密な
関係をすぐに理解できた者もいました。弟子は師にま
さることなく、しもべは主人にまさることなく、よき
羊飼いは羊のために命を捨てる、などと聖書にあるの
をみて、私たちはほとんど直観的に、はるか昔からわ
かっていたことだと思いました。そして、師とは教授
にすぎず、弟子とは生徒にすぎないと考えているキリ
スト教徒が、私たちに教えようとしている聖書の教え
をどれだけ理解できているのだろうと、つい考えてし
まうのでした。

　もちろん、古いものがあらゆる点で新しいものより
優れていると主張しているわけではありません。ただ、
強く言いたいのは、古いものが必ずしも悪いとは限ら
ず、新しいものが必ずしも良いとも完全とも限らない
ということです。新しいものは改良されていくでしょ
うし、古いものは再活用されなければいけません。い
まのところは、古いものを捨て去り、新しいものを全
面的に受け入れるというのは、納得できません」

　このように私たちは語り、いまでもこの考えは変わ
らないが、あまり賞賛されなかった。つまり西洋人は、
思っていたほど私たちが柔順でもなく、言いなりにも
ならないと考えたのだ。このような私たちの「頑固さ」、
「非受容性」、「排外主義」をさらに伝えるものとして、
ここに理想的な学校教師（先生）の一人として私たち
が尊敬する、ある人物の生涯を記したい。それによっ
て、日本の若者たちの教育に深い関心を持つ西洋の良
き友人たちに、二、三の手がかりを提供することにな
れば幸いである。

"It was this idea of relationship between 'sensei' and 'deshi' which made some of us able to comprehend at once the intimate relation between the master and his disciples that we found in the Christian Bible. When we found written therein that the disciple is not above his master, nor the servant above his lord; or that the good shepherd gives his life for the sheep, and other similar sayings, we took them almost instinctively as things known to us long before; we often wondered how those Christians whose idea of master is only professor, and of disciple, only student, could have comprehended these teachings of the Scripture which they came to teach us.

"We do not maintain, of course, that the old was superior to the new in every respect. But we do maintain that the old was not all bad, and the new is not all good and perfect. The new is yet to be much improved, and the old is yet to be resuscitated. As yet we cannot advise ourselves to give up the old and owe our allegiance to the new altogether."

So we expressed ourselves, as we still continue to express ourselves, and we were not received with much applause. They thought, that is, these Westerners did, that we were not so docile, and pliable, as they imagined we were. That we may further maintain our "stubbornness," "non-receptivity," and "anti-foreignism," we give in this essay the life of a man whose name we revere as one of our ideal school teachers (sensei). Thereby we mean no more than to give a clue or two to those, our good friends of the West, who have the education of the Japanese youths at heart.

# Ⅱ- 少年時代と自覚

と きは西暦1608年、関ケ原の戦いからわずか8年後、<sup>訳注50</sup>
大阪城の落城に先立つこと7年という時代。男た
ちは戦場に赴き、女たちは銃後で涙を流すのが仕事と
され、実世界に生きる男が文学や哲学に走るなどもっ
てのほかと思われていた時代、日本にいまだかつてい
ないほど気高く、もっとも進んだ思想家が近江の地で<sup>訳注51</sup>
生まれた。琵琶湖の西岸、比良の峰が後背に迫り、鏡
のような湖面に影を投げかけている地である。父の住
む近江を遠く離れた四国で、藤樹はもっぱら祖父母の
手で育てられた。そして早い時期から、歳にも武芸一
筋の侍の息子にも似合わぬ感受性を発揮していた。孔
子の『大学』の一節に触れ、生涯の生き方を決定する
ことになる志を立てたのは11歳のときだった。『大学』
には次のように書かれていた。「天子から庶民にいたる
まで、人の第一の目的は身を修めることにある」。藤樹
はこれを読んで叫んだ。「このような本があるとは、あ
あ、ありがたいことだ。聖人になろうとして、できな
いはずがあろうか！」。藤樹は泣いた。このときの感動
を彼は生涯忘れなかった。「聖人になれ」とは、なんと
いう大志だろう！

だが、この少年は、祈ったり内省的になったりする
だけの、ただの神経質な弱虫ではなかった。あるとき、
祖父の家が暴徒に襲われたことがあったが、藤樹は刀
を手にして、真っ先に暴徒のなかへ突進し、首尾よく
追い払った。そして「いつもどおり平然としていた」。
このとき、まだ13歳だった。

## II– Early Years and Awakening to Consciousness

It was in the year 1608 of the Christian era, only eight years after the battle of Sekigahara, and seven years before the fall of Ōsaka, when as yet men's chief business was to fight, and women's to weep, and letters and philosophies were thought unworthy to be pursued by practical men of the world, that one of the saintliest and most advanced thinkers that Japan has ever produced was born in the province of Ōmi, on the west bank of Lake Biwa, near which the Hira rears up its rounded head, and casts its shadow upon the glassy lake below. Brought up mostly by his grandparents, on the island of Shikoku, away from his paternal residence at Ōmi, he showed early sensitivity unusual in one of his age, and in the son of a samurai trained mostly in the arts of war. It was in the eleventh year of his age that a text from Confucius' *Great Learning* roused in him an ambition which was to shape the whole of his future career. Therein he read: *From the Emperor down to the commonnest people, man's chief aim is in the right ordering of his life.* "Here is this book, oh Heaven be thanked," he then exclaimed; "and can I not by attempting be a saint myself!" He wept, and the impression remained with him throughout his life. "Be a saint,"—what an ambition this!

But the boy was not a mere over-sensitive weakling, bent wholly upon prayer and introspection. Once a mob attacked his grandfather's house, and he was among the first that rushed into their midst, a sword in his hand, and repelled them successfully, and "then was calm as before." He was but thirteen years of age then.

同じころ、藤樹は、漢詩と習字を習うために、天梁という学識のある僧侶のもとへ行かされた。この早熟な少年は、先生にたくさんの質問をしたが、そのなかでも次の質問はたいへん藤樹らしかった。「仏陀は生まれると、一方の手で天を、もう片方で地を指し、『天上天下唯我独尊』と言った、と先生はおっしゃいました。仏陀は天下でももっとも傲慢な人間ではないでしょうか。先生はそんな人間をどうして理想的な人物としていられるのでしょう」。少年は、その後決して仏教を好きになれなかった。藤樹の理想はどこまでも謙虚であることだったが、仏陀はそのような人間ではなかったのだ。

　17歳のとき、書物の乏しい時代のなかで、孔子の『四書』<sup>訳注52</sup>を一揃い手に入れることができた。このことは藤樹の学習意欲をさらに掻き立て、いまは自分のものとなった貴重な知識の宝庫に、ひまさえあれば夢中になっていた。けれども、侍の本分は戦いとされていた時代に、読書は僧侶や隠遁者のみに似つかわしいとして蔑視されていたので、若い藤樹も人目を避けて勉強を続けるより仕方がなかった。昼はすべて武芸に費やし、読書に打ち込むのは夜だけだった。だが、いつまでも隠し事をすることはできなかった。ある日、仲間の一人が藤樹のことを「孔子殿」と呼んだ。藤樹が毎晩読書に没頭し、しかも当時の粗野で喧嘩好きの若者たちとは違って優しい性格であるため、それをあからさまにからかったのだ。「無知なやつめ！」、おとなしい少年の口から怒りの言葉が飛び出した。「孔子様が亡くなられて2000年になる。そんなふうに呼んで聖人の名を汚す気か。それとも私の学問好きを嘲るつもりか。

About the same year, he was sent to one Tenryo, a Buddhist priest of great learning, to be trained in the arts of poetry and handwriting. Of the many questions that the precocious youth put to his teacher, the following was very characteristic of him: "You tell me," Tōju said, "that when Buddha was born, he pointed one hand heaven-ward and the other earthward, and said, 'I alone of all beings in heaven above and under the heaven, am worthy of honor';—is he not the proudest of men under heaven; and how is it possible that my revered master owns him as his ideal?" The boy never liked Buddhism afterward. His ideal was perfect humility, and Buddha was not such a man.

When he was seventeen, he was able to obtain the complete set of Confucius' *Four Books*, showing the scarcity of books at that time. This whetted his appetite for learning more than ever, and he was found devoting all his stray hours to acquiring of knowledge from the precious store now in his possession. At the time, however, when the samurai's chief business was to fight, and book-reading was despised as a work fit only for priests and recluses, the young Tōju was compelled to carry on his study in all privacy. His daytime was spent wholly in the use of arms, and he gave himself to his books only in the nighttime. But his secrecy was not to remain undiscovered. One day, one of his comrades addressed him as "Confucius," in evident derision of his nightly devotion to his books, as well as of his benignant temper wholly exceptional among the rude combative youths of the time. "You, ignoramus, you!" the gentle youth was now heard in indignation. "Holy Confucius is dead now for two thousand years. Meanest thou by that epithet to blaspheme the saint's name, or to deride me for my

哀れなやつだ！　戦いだけが侍の仕事ではない。平時の仕事もある。無学な侍は物や奴隷と同じだ。貴様は奴隷でいることに満足しているのか」。藤樹の一喝は効き目があった。その男は自分の無知を認め、その後は何も言わなかった。

　藤樹は22歳になった。善良な祖父母に世を去られ、父親も失ったばかりだった。父親とは生涯のうちわずかな期間をともに過ごしただけだった。不幸な出来事は藤樹をいっそう感じやすく、涙もろく、心優しい人間にした。いまや唯一の気がかりは近江に残した母親のことだった。学問と高潔な人柄で日増しに藤樹の名声は高まり、名誉と高禄が前途に約束されていた。けれども、藤樹にとってたった一人の母親は、全世界よりも重い存在だった。この頃から、藤樹はなによりも母親のことを気にかけるようになった。


## Ⅲ– 母親崇拝

藤樹はまず、母親を自分のもとに呼び寄せ、伊予[訳注53]の国で藩主に仕えようとした[訳注54]。それが駄目とわかると、藩主のもとを去って母親のそばを離れずにいようと心を決めた。この決断は、心の葛藤に悩んだあげくのことだった。藤樹は家老に一通の手紙を記し、そのなかで、特別な事情から藩主よりも母親につくすほうを選んだことを述べた。「二つのつとめのどちらをとるべきか、私は慎重に考えました。主君は、私のような家来なら手当てを出すことで、誰でも召し抱えることができます。しかし、私の老母はこんな私以外には誰も頼る者がいないのです」。「三位一体」に対する

love of knowledge? Poor fellow! War alone is not the samurai's profession, but the arts of peace as well. An unlettered samurai is a chattel, a slave. Art thou satisfied with thy being a slave?" Tōju's thundering had its effect. The fellow owned his ignorance, and was silent ever afterward.

He was now twenty-two. His good grandparents were now gone, and he had recently lost his father, with whom he had been only for a short time in his life. Adversities made him more sensitive, tearful, and compassionate. His sole concern was now his mother whom he left at Ōmi. He was now daily growing in fame for his learning and purity of character, and honors and emoluments were waiting for him in abundance. But to him a single woman, his mother, was weightier than all the world. She was to claim his whole attention from this time on.

## III– Mother-Worship

His first attempt was to call his mother to his side, and to serve his lord in the province of Iyo. In which failing he made up his mind to leave his lord, and to cling to his mother. This conclusion he reached only after severe struggles in his mind. He prepared a letter addressed to his lord's chancellor, wherein he stated the motives that induced him in his peculiar circumstance to prefer the service of his mother to that of his lord. "I carefully weighed the two duties in my mind," was one of the sayings. "My lord can invite with salaries any number of servants such as I, but my old mother has none to depend upon except my poor self." His "trinitarian" scruples thus disposed of,

良心の呵責はこうして解決し、相当な量の禄米、家屋敷、家財という全財産を後に残して、藤樹は母親のもとへと向かった。

いまや母親のそばで藤樹の心は安らかだったが、母親を慰めるものはなにもなかった。家に帰り着いたとき、手元には百文（現在の一銭貨幣、価値は一円ほど）しかなかった。その金で酒を少し買い、学者先生は行商人となって近くの村々を歩き回って酒を売り、わずかな利益を得た。すべて母親のためだった。また「侍の魂」である刀を処分して、銀十枚を手にした。この金を村人に貸し、そこから生じるわずかな利子で小家族のつましい生活をまかなった。こういう仕事を少しも恥ずかしいとは思わなかった。藤樹の至上の幸福は母親の笑顔にあり、それにまさる貴重なものはなかった。

2年間、藤樹はこのような貧しく人目につかない暮らしをしていた。その著作からわかるように、この2年間は生涯でもっとも幸福な時期だった。母親のそばを離れれば、夜よく眠れず、「夢に母を思い、寝返りをうった」。後ほどわかるように、藤樹の道徳観の中心にあるのは子としての義務（これを孝という）であり、この中心的な義務がなければ、すべてがないに等しく、心が落ち着かなかった。藤樹の一生の目的がなんであったか、私たちは知っている。聖人、すなわち完全な人となることは、藤樹にとっては学者、思想家であることよりも重要なことだった。けれども世の中は藤樹を学者、思想家としても必要とした。とうとう藤樹は自分の学問を人々に伝えるように説き伏せられた。

he made his way to his mother's home, leaving behind him all his possessions now amounting to a considerable sum in grain, houses, and furniture.

He was now by his mother's side, to his entire satisfaction; but means to comfort her was wholly wanting. When he reached her home, he had only a hundred *mon* (one *sen* in our present currency, perhaps a *yen* in value) left. With it he bought a little *saké*; a scholar and sensei now turned himself into a pedler, and went round the neighboring villages to sell the liquor with little interest on it—all for his mother's sake. Also he disposed of his sword, "the samurai's *soul*," and got ten pieces of silver for it. This he lent out to the villagers; and a small interest coming therefrom was another source of supply to the humble existence of the little family. The master felt not the slightest shame in all these menial labors. His heaven was in his mother's smiles, and nothing was too costly to have one of them.

For two years he lived in this state of menial obscurity. From what we gather from his writings, these were among the happiest years of his life. Away from his mother, he could not very well sleep at night, "remembering her in my dreams, as I rolled from side to side upon my bed." As we shall see afterward, his whole system of morality was centered in filial duty (孝, we shall call it *filiality*), and lacking in this pivotal duty, he lacked in all, and hence his uneasiness. His aim of life, we know what it was; and to be a saint, a perfect man, was grander in his eyes than to be a scholar and philosopher. But the world needed him in the latter capacity as well, and he was finally prevailed upon to give his knowledge to the public.

# Ⅳ - 近江の聖人

**28**歳のとき、藤樹は行商の仕事をやめ、自分の村に学校を開いた。当時は簡単に学校を開くことができたのだ。自宅が寄宿舎であり、礼拝所であり、教室だった。正面には孔子像が掲げられ、敬意を表して香が焚かれ、生徒たちを従えた先生が儀式を執り行った。科学や数学の授業はなかった。中国の古典、歴史、詩作、習字がそのころの授業のすべてだった。ささやかな、目立たない仕事、これが学校教育である。その影響はほんの少しずつしか現われない。天使のうらやむ、そして世の目立ちたがり屋の忌み嫌う仕事だった。

　草深い田舎に住み着き、藤樹は人生の最後の日まで穏やかで楽しい日々を送った。後述するように、まったくの偶然から世間の注目を浴びるようになったのである。有名になることをなによりも藤樹は嫌っていた。藤樹にとって、心こそ王国であり、己のすべてが、そしてすべてを超えたものが、わが内なる世界にあった。藤樹は村の出来事につねに関心を持ち、訴えられた村人のためにとりなし、あるときは自分を乗せた籠かきに「人の道」を説いたという。このような話はほかにもいくつか、近所の素朴な村人たちのあいだに伝わっていた。いずれも藤樹の人生観がよくうかがわれた。藤樹は「積善」について次のように述べている。

　「人は誰でも悪名を嫌い、名声を好む。小善が積らなければ名はあらわれないが、小人は小善のことを考えない。だが、君子は日々自分に訪れる小善を疎かにし

# IV – The Saint of Ōmi

He was twenty-eight years old, when leaving his pedler's business, he opened a school in his village. Nothing was simpler then than to start a school. His own house served as a dormitory, a chapel and a lecture hall at the same time. Confucius' image was hung up in the right place, and incense was burnt in his honor with due ceremonies by the master attended by his pupils. Sciences and mathematics found no place in his curriculum. The Chinese classics, some history, poetry-making and handwriting constituted the whole of the topics then taught. A modest, unseen business, this of school-teaching. Its influence was felt only very slowly—the work envied by angels, and despised by the show-loving men of the world.

Established there in that out-of-the-way section of the country, his life was a smooth continuity of peaceful enjoyment to its very close. Only accidentally his name was brought to the public notice, as we shall see soon afterward. Notoriety he hated above all things. His mind to him a kingdom was, and he had his all, and more than all, within himself. We hear of his taking constant interest in the affairs of his village; of his interceding for a villager prosecuted before the provincial court; of his teaching in "the ways of man" the very coolies who carried him in *a kago*; and of a few such incidents preserved by his simple neighbors. And such were in entire accordance with his views of life. Here is what he said "on the accumulation of virtue":

"All men hate bad names, and love good names. And as small deeds, unless accumulated, make not names, the small man takes no thought of them. But the *kunshi* despises not small deeds that

ない。大善も出会えば行なうが、自分からは求めない
だけである。大善は少なく小善は多い。大善は名声を
もたらすが、小善は徳をもたらす。世の人は、名を好
むために大善を求める。しかしながら、名のためにな
されるならば、大善さえ小さくなる。君子とは多くの
小善から徳を生み出す者だ。まさしく、徳にまさる善
はない。徳はあらゆる大善の源である」

　藤樹の教育には非常に特異な点が一つあった。生徒
の徳と人格の形成を重んじ、文芸や知的な面の向上を
ほとんど問題にしなかったのだ。ここに藤樹の考える、
真の学者とは何かを物語る一文がある。いわく、

　「『学者』という名は徳に与えられるのであって、芸に
与えられるのではない。文芸は芸であり、生まれなが
らにその才を授かった人間なら、苦もなく文人になれ
る。だが、たとえ文に秀でていても、徳を欠けば学者
ではない。文を知るただの人だ。一方、文は読めなく
ても徳のある人は、ただの人ではない。文才はないが
学者である」

　何年ものあいだ、この教師は、ごく限られた近所の
人々にしか知られずに「ものいわぬ控えめな生活」を
送っていた。やがて神の摂理で、無名の存在から、世
に知られる人物へとなった。一人の青年が先生として
仰ぐ聖人を求めて岡山を旅立った。この変わった旅の
目的は「東方の三博士」[訳注55]が「ユダヤ人の王」を探した
旅と同じだった。青年は都のある東へと急いだ。都に
行けば、当然、王侯貴族ばかりでなく聖人に出会える
だろう、と考えたのだ。青年は近江に来て、田舎の宿
に泊まった。薄い間仕切りだけを隔てて、隣には二人
の旅人がいた。どうやら知り合ったばかりらしい。二

come to him day by day. Great deeds he also does if they come in his way; only he seeks them not. Great deeds are few, and small deeds are many. The former make names; but the latter *virtue*. The world seeks great deeds, because name is what it loves. If done for the name's sake, however, even great deeds become small. A *kunshi* is he who makes virtue out of many small deeds. Indeed, no deed is greater than virtue. Virtue is the source of all great deeds."

One thing was very peculiar in his teaching. He made very much of virtue and character, and very little of letters and intellectual attainment in his pupils. Here is his idea of what a true scholar is:

"'Scholar' is a name for virtue, not for arts. Literature is an art, and a man with an inborn genius for it has no difficulty in becoming a man of letters. But though proficient in letters, he is not a scholar, if he lacks in virtue. He is an ordinary person knowing letters. An illiterate man with virtue is not an ordinary person. He is a scholar without letters."

For years, the teacher led a "mute, inglorious life," unknown save to the narrow circle in his vicinity, when Providence sought him out in his obscurity, and made him known to the world. A young man started from Okayama to seek out a saint in the land, whom he might own as his *sensei*. He had no better aim in this singular search than had the magi of old in their search after the King of the Jews. On he sped toward the east, toward the capital of the country, where, he naturally thought, can be found saints, as well as kings and other notables. He came to Ōmi and there stopped at a country hotel for a night. In a room next to his, separated only by a thin partition, were two travellers, evidently of but recent

人の会話に青年はひきつけられた。彼らのうちの一人
は侍で、次のような体験を語っていた。

「主君の命で都に上り、数百両の金を託されて帰る途
中だった。いつもなら肌身離さず持っている財布を、
この村に入った日は、習慣に反して、その日の午後に
雇った馬の鞍に結び付けておいた。宿に着き、鞍につ
けた大事なものを忘れたまま、馬方といっしょにその
馬を返してしまった。少したってはじめて、忘れ物を
したことに気づき、真っ青になった。どれほど困った
ことか。馬方の名前はわからず、捜しだすのは不可能
だった。たとえ捜しだせたとしても、その男がすでに
金を使い果たしていたら、どうしようもない。不注意
だったではすまされない。主君に対して釈明する方法
は一つしかない。（当時、人命にはそれほど値打はなか
った。）私は、家老と家族あてにそれぞれ手紙をしたた
め、最期を迎える決意を固めた。

　こうして、言いようのない苦悩に打ちひしがれてい
ると、真夜中近くになって、宿の戸を激しく叩く者が
あった。やがて、人夫の身なりをした男が私に会いた
がっていると知らされた。会ってみると、たいへん驚
いたことに、男は、その日の午後、私を乗せた馬方に
ほかならなかった。『お侍さん』、男はすぐに私に声を
かけた。『鞍に大事なものを忘れましたね。家に帰って
から見つけ、お渡ししようと思って戻ってきました。
さあ、お忘れ物ですよ』、そう言うと、馬方は私の前に
財布を置いた。私はあまりの嬉しさに呆然となってし
まった。しかし我に返って告げた。『あなたは私の命の

acquaintance with each other. The conversation they were engaged in attracted the youth's attention. One of them, a samurai, was telling his experience on this wise:

"I had gone up to the capital on my lord's errand, and was on my way home entrusted with several hundred pieces of his gold. I usually carried them close to my body, but on the day I reached this village, contrary to my usual custom, I fastened the purse to the saddle of the horse which I had hired for the latter part of the day. I reached my hotel, and forgetful of the treasure on the saddle, I sent the horse away with its *bettō*, and came to the knowledge of my fearful loss only some time afterward. You can imagine the extremity to which I was driven. I knew not the name of the *bettō*, and to seek him out was an impossibility. Or even if I could, what availed me if he had disposed of the gold already. My absence of mind was inexcusable. There was but one way left of explaining myself to my lord." (Human life was not very costly then.) "I prepared letters, one to the chancellor, and others to my relatives, and resolutely made up my mind for the last hour."

"While in this state of inexpressible anguish, now late in midnight, I heard somebody knocking hard at the hotel door; and I was soon informed that a man in a cooly's raiment wanted to see me. I met him, and to my great amazement, he was no other than the *bettō* who had carried me upon his horse that same afternoon. 'Sir Samurai:' he addressed me at once, 'I believe you left an important thing upon the saddle. I found it after I reached my home, and I came back for the purpose of handing it to you. Here it is.' So saying, he placed the purse before me. I knew not where I was; ecstasy transported me. But recollecting myself, I said, 'Man, I owe my life to you. Take a fourth of this as the price of

恩人だ。助けてくれたお礼に、この四分の一の金を持っていってください。再び命を授けてくれたのだから』。けれども馬方は聞き入れなかった。『私には、そのようなものを受け取る資格はありません。財布はあなたのものです。当然あなたが持っているべきです』。そう言って、馬方は自分の前に置かれた金に手を触れようとしなかった。私は馬方に十五両を、次いで五両、二両、ついには一両を受け取らせようとしたが、駄目だった。『では、私は貧乏人ですので』、馬方はとうとう言った。『わらじ代として四文（1セントの百分の四）いただけませんか。このことで家から四里（10マイル）の道をやってきたもので』。なんとか渡すことができたのは二百文（2セント）だけだった。喜んで立ち去ろうとする馬方を引きとめて、訊ねた。『どうしてそんなに無欲で正直で誠実なのか、教えてください。こんな時代に、この世でこれほどの正直者に出会うとは思いもよらなかった』。貧しい男は答えた。『私の住む小川村に中江藤樹という人が住んでいます。この方が私たち村人に、こういうことを教えてくださっているのです。先生は、利を得ることは人生の目的ではない、正直で高潔で人の道に従うことが大切だとおっしゃいます。村人はみな先生の話を聞き、日々教えに従っているのです』」

　青年はこの話を聞き、はたと膝を打って叫んだ。「その人こそ私が探し求めていた聖人だ。明日の朝には訪ねて、使用人か弟子にしてもらおう」。翌日、青年はすぐに小川村へ向かい、聖人を探し当てた。来意を告げ、へりくだって弟子にしてくれるように懇願した。藤樹先生は驚いた。自分は村の一教師であって、遠くからわざわざ来てもらうような者ではない。藤樹はていね

my existence. You are to me another father.' But the cooly was immovable. 'I am not entitled to any such thing. The purse is yours, and it is entirely just that you should have it.' So saying he would not touch the gold placed before him. I forced upon him fifteen pieces, then five pieces, two pieces, and finally one piece, without success. 'As I am a poor man,' he said at last, 'pray give me 4 *mon* (4-hundredths of a cent) for a pair of straw sandals, as I came all the way from my home four *riis* (10 miles) away for this special purpose.' The utmost I could force upon him was only two hundred *mon* (2 cents), and he was on the point of going gladly away. Stopping him I said, 'Pray tell me what made you so unselfish, so honest, so true. Never in this age have I thought of finding such an honesty upon this earth.' 'There lives in my village of Ogawa,' the poor man answered, 'a man by the name of Nakae Tōju, who teaches us villagers of these things. He says gain is not the aim of life, but honesty, righteousness, and the ways of man. We villagers all hear him, and walk by his teachings.'"

The young man heard the story. He clapped his knee, and exclaimed, "Here is the saint I seek after. I will go to him tomorrow morning, and be made his servant and disciple." The day after he proceeded at once to Ogawa Village, inquired after the saint, and found him. He confessed his purpose of coming there, and humbly implored the teacher to accept him into his discipleship. Master Tōju is surprised. He is a village teacher, and he is no

いに若い侍の頼みを断った。侍はあきらめない。いったん師と決めた人のもとから、どうしても立ち去ろうとしなかった。だが、教師の意思も固かった。この客はすっかり誤解しているに違いない、自分が先生であるのは村の子どもたちに対してだけだ。今や粘り強さと謙遜の張り合いで、二人とも決して一歩もひこうとしなかった。

　何を言っても、どんなに頼んでも、師の気持ちを動かせないとわかると、侍はただただ粘り強くお願いすることで聖人の謙遜に打ち勝とうと決心した。そこで、師の家の玄関先に上着を広げると、姿勢を正し、刀を傍らに、両手を膝の上に置いて座った。陽にさらされ、露に濡れ、道行く人々に噂されても、座り続けた。夏だったので、その辺りでは蚊にも悩まされた。だが、一途な気持ちが揺るがないように、どんなことがあっても青年は背筋を伸ばしたまま、姿勢を崩さなかった。三日三晩が過ぎ、無言の願いは家のなかにいる師にも伝わったが、許しの言葉は出てこなかった。藤樹にとって非常に大きな存在である母親が仲裁に入ったのは、この時だった。これほど心から願っているのに、息子は受け入れず追い払おうというのだろうか、と母親は思った。この青年を弟子にしてもよいのではないだろうか。そうした方が断るよりも立派なことではないだろうか。師も考え直し始めた。母親が正しいと思うなら正しいにちがいない。師はとうとう折れ、侍は彼の弟子になった。この侍こそ熊沢蕃山<sup>訳注56</sup>だった。蕃山は、のちに大藩岡山の財政および行政にたずさわり、その取りしきった地にいまでも残るほど数々の改革を導入した。この男のほかに弟子がいなかったとしても、藤

man to be inquired after by a gentleman from a distant province. He as humbly declines the young samurai's request. The latter is importunate. He would not move away from his sworn master. But the teacher also is determined. The stranger must be entirely mistaken, for he (Tōju) is not a sensei for any but the village children. Now it was a rivalry between importunity and modesty, and both determined to hold its ground to the end.

As neither words nor entreaties could avail to win the master's favor, the samurai made up his mind to overcome the saint's modesty by sheer importunity. So by the entrance-gate of the master's house, he spread his upper garment, and there in a posture befitting a gentleman, with swords on his side, and hands upon his knees, he sat, exposed to the sun, dews and the comments of the passersby. It was summertime, and mosquitoes are troublesome in those regions. But nothing could break his upright posture as well as his heart bent upon its single aim. For three days and nights, his silent request went up to the master within, without drawing from him a word of consent. It was at this time that Tōju's mother, his almighty mother, interfered on the youth's behalf. Should such sincerity of request be turned away without acceptance on her son's part, thinks the mother. Might he not just as well take the young man in to his discipleship, and be more honorable for so doing than not? The master begins to reconsider the situation. What his mother thinks right must be right. He yields at last, and the samurai becomes his *deshi*. The same was Kumazawa Banzan,[34] the future financier and administrator of the powerful clan of Okayama, an introducer of many permanent reforms still visible in the land he superintended. Had Tōju no other disciple than this man, he would yet be remembered as one

樹は国家の偉大な恩人の一人として記憶されただろう。今やこの教師の手に委ねられた仕事の重要性を十分に理解するためには、この生徒について別の話を書かなければならない。こうして神の摂理は、夜の影を好む宝石を白日の光のもとへといざなった。

　さらにもうひとつ話をあげて、この静かな男の外面の生活にはまったく意味のないことすべてを締めくくることにする。それは、岡山藩主[訳注57]の訪問である。家臣となった蕃山が、師の人格の偉大さを伝えたのだ。そのような人の訪問は、厳格な身分差別のあった時代にはまったく異例のことだった。藤樹はまだ無名で、一方、訪れた大名は全国有数の大藩の藩主だったことを思うと、この訪問は、された方ばかりでなく、した方も同じように、きわめてまれな賞賛すべき謙譲の行為だった。しかしながら、大藩の大名の期待に反して、師も村人も、そんな立派な客を迎える準備はなにもしていなかった。大勢の従者を引き連れて住まいに着くと、師は村の子どもたちに『孝経』を説いていた。岡山藩主が特別に面会に来たことが知らされると、師は、講義が終わるまで玄関のところで待っていてもらいたいと伝えた。大名はこのように変わった扱いを受けたことがなかったが、家来全員とともに、その場で待っていた。外ではべつに何も起こっていないかのように、家の中では講義が続けられていた。やがてこの立派な客は、ふつうの人々と変わらない態度で迎えられた。藩主の師かつ相談役として仕官してほしいと言われると、師は、自分の使命はこの村にあり、母との暮らしにあると言って辞退した。藩主がこの異例の訪問で得た最大の成果は、名前を門人に加えてもらう許可を得

of the nation's greatest benefactors. We need a separate essay for the pupil to fully appreciate the magnitude of the work now entrusted to the teacher's hand. How does Providence bring to light, the gems that love the shadows of night!

One more episode finishes up all that is worth noting of the outward life of this silent man; and that was a visit paid him by the Lord of Okayama, to whom Banzan, now his subject, communicated the grandeur of his master's character. Such a visit was entirely exceptional at that time of rigid class distinctions; and when we remember that Tōju was yet an unknown man, and the daimiō, one of the greatest in the land, the visit was a condescension of the rarest kind, honorable, alike to him who paid it, as well as to him who called it forth. Contrary to the expectation of the great daimiō, however, he found the master and his village wholly unprepared to receive so great a guest. With his large retinues, he proceeded to the master's residence, and found him there explaining the *Book of Filiality* to several of the village children. When it was announced that the Lord of Okayama was in for the special purpose of seeing him, he sent back word that he would like the guest to wait for him at the house entrance till the lecture was over. Never before had the daimiō received such strange treatment. But there he waited, his whole retinues with him, while the teaching went on within, as if nothing special was going on outside. The great guest was received with no more ceremony than that due to common humanity. When asked to enter the Lord's service as his master and councillor, the teacher declined by saying that his mission was in his village, and with his mother. The utmost the Lord succeeded in this extraordinary

たことと、師が自分のかわりに長男を岡山に行かせると約束したことだった。教えを求めてやってきた貧しい青年にはあれほど謙虚だった師が、栄華を極めて訪ねた君主には堂々とふるまったのだ。確かに師は、全国から人々が相談に訪れる「近江聖人」という名にふさわしい人物だった。藤樹は全国から尊敬を集めるようになり、ほかにも多くの大名が藩内の問題について特別に教えを乞いに、その門を叩いた。

　こうしたことを除けば、藤樹はきわめて淡々とした生活を送った。それを伝える話は終わりにするが、ここで西洋人読者は師と妻との関係を知りたいと思うだろう。彼らは、ほかの関係よりも妻との関係で人を判断すると思われる。藤樹は儒者であり厳格な一夫一婦主義者だった。中国の賢者の定めに従い、30歳で結婚した。けれども、伴侶となった女性は容貌があまり美しくなかったので、母親は家族の被る悪評を心配し、当時よく見られたように再婚を勧めた。だが、母親の願いはたいていどんなことでも聞いていた優しい息子も、このときは従わなかった。「たとえお母さんの言葉でも、天意に反していれば、聞くわけにはいきません」と言ったのだ。こうして、女性は生涯を藤樹とともに過ごし、二人の子どもを産んだ。「夫の名誉のためには、自分の名誉はすべて犠牲にする」典型的な日本の妻だった。藤樹に理想的な女性像を示唆したのは、妻の心の美しさだった。この女性像は藤樹の著した『女訓』という小冊子に、次のように書かれている。「男の女に対する関係は、天の地に対する関係と同じである。天は力（virtus）であり、万物の源である。地は受け入れる。地は天の生むものを受け、これを育む。ここに夫

visit was a consent to have his name enrolled among the master's disciples, and a promise to have his eldest son sent to Okayama in his stead. He who was so humble to a poor young man coming for his instruction was so dignified to a prince coming in all his glory. He certainly was worthy of the name which the nation at large came to confer upon him, *the Saint of Ōmi*. He became an object of universal admiration, and many daimiōs came to him for the special purpose of having his counsels upon the affairs of their dominions.

Before closing this part of his otherwise very uneventful life, our Western readers would like to know of the master's relation to his wife, as they seem to judge a man more by this relation than by any other. He was a Confucian and a monogamist of the highest order. In accordance with the injunction of the Chinese sage, he was married at thirty. It so happened, however, that the lady who became his consort was not very remarkable for her physical beauty; and the mother, solicitous of the disrepute his family might suffer, urged upon him remarriage, as such was not uncommon under similar circumstances. But the mildest of sons who would hear to almost anything that his mother wished to have done, was disobedient in *this* case; for he said, "Even the mother's word is not in force if contrary to Heaven's laws." So the lady stayed with him all her life, gave birth to two children, and was one of those typical Japanese wives "who shun all honors that their husbands may be honored thereby." It was this *spiritual beauty* of hers that suggested to him an ideal womanhood as depicted in his brochure entitled "Instructions to Women." Therein we read: "The relation of man to woman is that of Heaven to Earth. Heaven is strength (*virtus*),[*17] and all things have their origin in it. Earth is receptive. It accepts what Heaven makes, and nurtures. Herein is

と妻の和もある。前者は生み、後者は成す。云々」。キリスト教はこのような女性観に反対するものではない、と私は信じている。

## V – 内面の人

藤樹の外見の貧しさと簡素さは、内面の豊かさ、多様さとはまったく不釣合いなものだった。藤樹の内側には自分を絶対君主とする大いなる王国があった。内面が満たされているから自然と外面が穏やかになっていった。実際、藤樹は天使のような人であると言われるように、「九分の霊と一分の肉からなる」と言ってもいいだろう。もっと進んだ「救済論」や「終末論」を持っている私たちは、この人物の半分でも幸福だろうか。

最近、藤樹の著述が、二人の後世の弟子によって入念に編集され、十冊からなる大型の和本として刊行された。これらは、日本に体系的な思想が存在したかどうかいささか疑わしい時代に、かつて実在した人物の足跡を私たちの前にありありと示している。収められているのは、藤樹の小伝、村人の回想、中国古典の注釈、講義、詳論、問答、書簡、随想、座談、日本（歌）中国（詩）両方の詩歌だ。私たちはこの人物の内面へ読者を案内するだけである。

藤樹の学問上の歩みには、二つの段階がある。はじめは、同時代の人と同じく、保守的な朱子学のなかで育てられた。朱子学では、なによりも自分自身を常に

the harmony between a man and his wife. The former originates, and the latter completes, etc." I believe Christianity itself has no objection against such consideration toward womankind.

## V – The Inward Man

His outward poverty and simplicity were out of all proportion to his inward wealth and variety. He had a large kingdom within of which he was a perfect sovereign. His outward tranquility was nothing but the natural result of his inward satisfaction. Indeed we may say of him, as was said of another angelic man, that "he was nine parts spirit, and only one part flesh." I wonder whether we with all our improved Soteriology and Eschatology are half as happy as this man was.

Only very recently his works were carefully edited and collected by two of his distant disciples, and we have now before us ten good-sized Japanese volumes of his writings, the whole opening up a vista before us of the soul that once was a reality among us, at the time when we might almost doubt the existence of systematic thinking in Japan. The books comprise a short sketch of his life, the reminiscence of his villagers about him, his commentaries upon the Chinese classics, lectures, essays, dialogues, letters, stray-thoughts, table-talks, and poems both Japanese (*uta*) and Chinese (*shi*). We can do no more than to introduce our readers to what was in the man.

There were two distinct stages in his intellectual career. The first was when he, with his countrymen of the time, was brought up in the conservative Chū philosophy, which above all other

深く見つめるように要求する。この感じやすい若者が、自分自身の内部の欠点と弱点を絶えず反省するうちに、よけいに感じやすくなってしまったということは、容易に想像できる。過度な自己探求の結果は、若いころの生活や著述にはっきりと表れている。藤樹の『大学啓蒙』は21歳のこの状態のときに書かれた。もしも、進歩的な中国人の王陽明の著作に出会ったことで新しい希望が生まれていなかったとしたら、気の滅入るような朱子学の抑圧のもと、生まれつき控えめな藤樹は、よく似た者がそうだったように、不健全な世捨て人となっていただろう。すでに大西郷の話をしたときに、この優れた思想家について語る機会があった。日本の歴史のなかの既成事実だと思うのだが、陽明学という中国文化があったからこそ、私たちは内気で臆病で保守的な、後ろ向きの国民にならなかったのだと言えるだろう。聖人孔子その人は非常に進んだ考え方の人間だった、と今日の孔子論者はみな認めている。その孔子を勝手に解釈して、世の中に見えている姿に作り変えてしまったのは、後ろ向きに考える同国人だった。だが、王陽明は、孔子の内にあった進歩性を発展させ、そのように間違った解釈をしがちな人々に希望を吹きこんだ。この王陽明の力によって、わが国の藤樹は、聖人孔子を新しい目で見ることができた。近江聖人は、いまや実践的な人間となった。その陽明主義を詠みこんだ、いくつかの歌がある。

「暗くとも　たゞ一向にすゝみ行け
　心の月のはれやせんもし」

things, enforced ceaseless examination into one's own self. We can imagine the sensitive youth made doubly sensitive by his constant introspection into the lack and weakness within himself, and all the effects of undue self-examination are plainly visible in his early life and writings. His *Notes and Commentaries upon Great Learning*, composed in his twenty-first year, was written under this mood. We fear his natural modesty under the pressure of disheartening philosophy would have turned him into a morbid recluse, as it did many souls like him, had not a new hope been reached out to him in the writings of that progressive Chinese, Wang Yang Ming. We have had already some occasion to refer to this remarkable philosopher when we spoke of our great Saigō. I think I am stating a well established fact in Japanese History when I state my own observation that the Chinese culture in the form of Yang-Ming-ism has never produced timid, fearful, conservative and retrogressive people out of us. I believe all thoughtful critics of Confucius now agree that the sage himself was a very progressive man. It was his retrogressive countrymen who construed him in their own light, and made him appear so to the world. But Yang Ming developed the progressiveness that was in Confucius, and inspired hopes in such as were inclined to understand him in that light. The same helped our own Tōju to see the sage in the new light. The Saint of Ōmi was now a practical man. Here are some of his Yang-Ming-isms:


"Press right on, though thy ways be dark;
    Skies may clear ere thy course is done."

「志つよく
　引立（ひきたて）むかふべし

石に立つ矢の
　ためし聞くにも」

「上もなく　また外もなき道のために
　身をすつるこそ身を思ふなれ」

これらの歌から、静かな村の先生を思い浮かべる人がいるだろうか。

藤樹には中国の古典の注釈書がある、とすでに記した。実際にそれらは藤樹の全著作のなかでももっとも重要なものである。しかし、読者は藤樹を当時のふつうの意味での「注釈家」とは考えないでほしい。藤樹はとても独創的な人間だった。ただ、もともと控えめだったために、自分の考えを述べるのに、この種の文献を利用したのだ。藤樹がまったく自由な態度で古典に接したことは、門人に繰り返し語った言葉からも明らかだった。「いにしえの聖人の論文には、現在の社会状態には当てはまらない部分が多い」、藤樹はこう言うと、改訂版を作って教えた。藤樹が今日生きていたとしたら、異端裁判のかっこうの対象になっていただろう。

藤樹が人間の作り出した「法（ノモス）」と永遠のうちに存在する「真理（道、ロゴス）」とをはっきりと区別していたことは、つぎの有名な言葉に示されている。「道と法とは別である。一方を他方とみなすことが多いが、それは誤っている。法は時により、中国の聖人によっても変わる。わが国に移されればなおさらであ

"Tightly pull, man, thy heart's string,
    Prepare for a resolute march;

A case is known of an arrow,
    Piercing through a flinty rock."

"He loves his life who his life forsakes
    For Ways that no like or higher know."

Who can make a quiet village teacher out of these?

We have said he wrote commentaries upon the Chinese Classics. Indeed, these form by far the most important part of all his writings. But let not our readers imagine that Tōju was a *commentator* in the ordinary sense of that term. He was a most original man, and his natural modesty alone made him resort to this kind of literature for expressing himself. That he expressed perfect freedom in handling the ancient writings was evident from the words he often repeated to his pupils. "These *Discourses* of the holy men of old contain many things in them that are not applicable to the present state of society." So saying, he made an expurgated edition of the same for use in his school. Had he lived today, he would have made a fine subject for a heresy trial!

That he clearly made distinctions between man-made Laws (法, nomos) and eternally-existing Truth (道, logos) is shown by the following remarkable saying of his:

"The truth is distinct from the law. Many taking one for the other are greatly mistaken. The law changes with time, even with saints in their land,—much more when transplanted to our land.

る。だが、道は永遠から生じたものである。徳の名に
先だって、道は広く行きわたっていた。人間の存在よ
り前に、宇宙には道があった。人間が消滅し、天地が
無に帰した後でも、道はあり続けるだろう。しかし法
は時代の必要にかなうように作られたものである。時
と所が変わり、聖人の法でさえ、世に押しつけられる
ものとなれば、道のもとを損う」

　これは、聖書が今日の極端な霊感論者にとって絶対
であるように、いわゆる「経書」が誤りないものと考
えられていたときに語られた。このような精神で書か
れた注釈書は当然、大胆で印象的で新しいものだった。

　なにものも恐れず独立不羈の藤樹だったが、その倫
理体系でなにより注目すべきなのは、謙譲の徳を最高
位に置いたことである。藤樹にとって謙譲の徳とは、
すべての徳の源となる根元的な徳であり、謙譲の徳が
ない人間ならば、すべてを欠いているのと同じだった。
「学者はまず慢心を捨て、謙譲の徳を求めないならば、
どんなに学問や才能があろうとも、庶民から分離した
腐肉の地位に終わってしまう」「慢心は損失を招き、謙
譲は天の法である。謙譲は虚である。心が虚であるな
ら、善悪の判断は自然に生じる」。藤樹は、虚という言
葉の意味を説明して、次のように述べている。「昔から
真理を求める者はこの語につまずく。精神的である故
に虚であり、虚である故に精神的である。このことを
よく心得なければならない」

　この徳の高さに達するための藤樹の方法は、非常に
簡単だった。つぎのように述べている。「徳を抱くこと
を望むなら、日々善をしなければならない。一善をす
ると一悪が去る。毎日善をすれば、毎日悪は去る。昼

But the truth is from eternity. Before the name of virtue was, the truth was and prevailed. Before man was, space had it; and after he shall have disappeared, and Heaven and Earth have returned to nothingness, it will abide. But the law was made to meet the need of time. When time and place change, even saints' laws, if forced upon the world, are injurious to the cause of the truth."

And this was spoken when the so-called Classical Books (経書) were considered as inerrant as the Bible to the extreme inspirationists in our day. Commentaries written in such a spirit as this cannot but be bold, striking and new.

Yet with all his fearlessness and independence, nothing was more remarkable in his ethical system than the foremost position he gave to the virtue of humility. To him it was the primal virtue out of which all other virtues came, and without which a man lacked in all things. "Unless the scholar first purges himself of his spirit and seeks the virtue of humility, with all his learning and abundance of genius, he is not yet entitled to a position above the slough of low commonalty." "Fullness invites loss; humility is Heaven's law. Humility is emptiness. When the mind is empty, the judgment of good and bad comes by itself." Explaining the meaning of the word *emptiness*, he has this to say: "From of old, he that seeks the truth stumbles at this word. Because spiritual, hence empty; because empty, therefore spiritual. Consider this well."

As for attaining this height of virtue, his method was very simple. Said he: "If to cherish virtue is our aim, we are to do good day by day. One good done, and one evil goes. Good daily done, evil daily goes. Like as the day lengthens, the night shortens, we

が長くなれば夜が短くなるように、たゆまず善に励めば、すべての悪は消え去る」。この心の虚に藤樹は最高の満足を覚え、まだ利己心をまぬがれていない人々をあわれみ、次のように語っている。

「獄外獄あり、
　　　世界を納む。
　名・利・傲・意、
　　　その四壁。
　哀しいかな、世間多少の人
　　　這裡に拘攣し、長えに戚々たり」

（哀れなことに、たくさんの人たちが
その中につながれて、いつまでも憂い悲しんでいる）


「願い事」や欲望は、どんなものでも嫌った。藤樹が仏教をまったく信仰しようとしなかったのは、仏教にはこの要素が色濃かったからである。善事も、報奨を目的とするのならば、たとえそれが来世の報奨であっても、藤樹の肯けるものではなかった。正義は、それ以外の動機を必要とするものではない。来世にもたらされる報奨と生活を望む気持ちは藤樹にはなく、万が一そうした気持ちがあったとしても、藤樹の正義を愛する心と「天道」を実践する喜びを、なんら妨げるものではなかった。仏教の信仰から離れ、儒教にかわった息子のことを悲しんでいる一人の母親に、つぎのような手紙を書き送っている。「後生を大切にお考えになられることはよくわかります。しかし、後生が大切なら、今生はもっと大切だということにお気づきになってください。今生に迷うなら、後生にも迷い続けるこ

persevere in good, and evil all disappears." And finding his supreme satisfaction in this emptiness in his soul, he has these words of pity to say of those who are not yet exonerated of selfishness in them:

"A prison there is besides prisons,
    Large enough to take in the world;
Its four walls, love of honor,
    Of gain, and pride, and desire—
Alas! So many among men,
    Chained therein, mourn evermore."

"Wish," desire, he despised in all its forms. It was the predominance of this element in Buddhism that alienated him entirely from that faith. That good is done with a reward as its aim, even though the reward lies in the future existence, was objectionable to him. Righteousness with him needed no other incentive than itself. The hope of future reward and existence, even if he had it, influenced him not in the slightest degree in his love of righteousness and enjoyment in the practice of the Heavenly Ways. Writing to a mother who mourned over her son's leaving the Buddhist faith to turn a Confucian, he has this to say: "That you make so much of the future I can well understand. But I wish you to note that if the future is so important, the present is still more so, for if a man get astray in this life, it is all too probable that he will be forever lost in the life to come.... In a life so uncertain as this, where tomorrow is wholly unknown to us, nothing can exceed in

とになるでしょう。……このように不確かな、明日を
も知れぬ人生にありましては、わが胸のうちの仏をい
つも拝する態度がもっとも大切です。云々」。藤樹が無
神論者でなかったことは、わが国の神々に深い敬意を
払っていたことからもよくわかる。ただ藤樹の信仰は、
すべてに正しくありたいという願いを除いて、あらゆ
る種類の「願い事」からめずらしいほど無縁だった。

　それでいて藤樹は、人生を十二分に楽しんだようだ。
すべての著作を通して、意気消沈した様子は一点も見
つからない。私たち自身の神や宇宙の思想から見ると、
陽明学派の藤樹がどうしてこれほど幸福だったのか、
とても想像がつかない。

　つぎの「冬の日に」という歌を詠んだ心情には、永
遠の喜びが溢れていたにちがいない。

　　「世の中の桜をたえておもはねば
　　　　春の心は長閑(のどか)なりけり」

　つぎも同じ調子の歌である。

　　「思ひきや　つらく憂(う)かりし世の中を
　　　　学びて安く楽しまんとは」

　しかし、藤樹は長くは人生を楽しめなかった。妻に2
年前に先立たれた後、40歳になった1648年の秋、その<sup>訳注58</sup>

importance our constant worship of the Buddha within our breasts, etc." That he was not an atheist is abundantly shown by the profound respect he paid to the gods of the nation. Only his faith was singularly free from "wishes" of all kind, except that of being righteous altogether.


And yet he seems to have enjoyed his life thoroughly. In all his writings we fail to catch a single note of despondence. Indeed, we with our own views of God and universe, can hardly imagine how this man with his Yang-Ming-istic form of Confucianism could have been so happy.

Everlasting joyful must have been the heart that could sing "On a Winter Day":

"Whence flowers ceased to be
        Objects of my heart's desire,
How everlasting is the Spring,
        That reigns in my bosom."

The following is in a similar strain:

"Little knew I that this life,
        With sorrows hard pressed,
Could by Learning's benign help,
        Be spent in endless peace."

But he did not enjoy his life long. His wife predeceased him two years, and in the autumn of 1648, in his fortieth year, he died

人生にふさわしい最期を迎えた。藤樹は最期が訪れたことに気づくと、門人を呼び集め、ふだんのように正座して告げた。「私は世を去る。どうかわが道が、この国から消え去ってしまわないようにしてもらいたい」。そして、亡くなった。近所の人々は喪に服した。師に敬意を表して、諸大名からは代理の者たちが送られてきた。葬儀は国をあげての行事となり、徳と正義を愛する人々はみな、国にとって大きな損失である藤樹の死を悼んだ。何年も後に、藤樹の住んでいた家は村人たちによって修理され、今日まで保存されている。藤樹の名を持つ神社も建てられ、年二回、藤樹を記念する祭りが行なわれている。藤樹の墓を訪れれば、村人たちが質素な礼服を身につけて、案内してくれるだろう。300年前に生きていた人が、なぜかくも尊敬を受けているのかと問えば、村人はこう答えるだろう。

「この村でも近くの村でも、父は子に愛情を注ぎ、子は親孝行で、兄弟は仲睦まじくしています。家庭では怒りの声は聞かれず、みな穏やかな顔をしています。これもすべて藤樹先生の教えと遺徳のおかげです。私たちは誰もが、先生を畏敬し、その名を呼ぶときは、深い感謝をもって思い出すのです」

翻って今の時代、私たちは、笛や太鼓や新聞広告を使って騒ぎ立てれば、他人に「影響」を及ぼせるに違いないと思っているが、真の影響とはなんであるか、を藤樹に学ぶべきかもしれない。バラが自分の香りに気づかぬように、自分の影響力に気づかなかった藤樹。そんな藤樹のように静かに生きることがかなわなければ、たとえ一生を通じて書き、説き、叫び、手を振りかざしても、あとに残るのは「畳一畳ほどの墓場」だ

a death worthy of his life. When he found that his end had arrived, he called his disciples together, assumed his usual upright posture, and said, "I go away; see that my ways be not lost to the land"; and passed away. The whole neighborhood went into mourning. Deputies were sent by princes to render honor to the master. His funeral was a national affair, and all that loved virtue and righteousness mourned the death so costly to the land. Years afterward, the house he had lived in was repaired by his villagers, and is preserved to this day. They made a god of his name, and observe two annual festivals in his memory. You go to visit his grave, and a villager will guide you, not without a simple ceremonial robe cast over his shoulders. You ask him why his respect thus paid to a man who lived three hundred years ago, and he will answer you in this way:

"Here in this village and neighborhood, the father is kind to the son, the son filial to the father, and brothers are affectionate to one another. In our homes no angry voices are to be heard, and all wear the countenance of peace. All these we owe to the teaching and after-influence of the Master Tōju, and we, one and all, revere his name with grateful remembrance."

And we of this age, with so much of our drum-beatings, trumpet-blowings, and newspaper advertisements, that we might have "influence" over others, may well learn of this man what the real secret of influence is. If we cannot live quietly as Tōju did, who was no more conscious of his influence than the rose of its odor, we may write and preach and howl and gesticulate all our lives, and yet nothing will remain of each one of us except "a mound of sod one *tatami* wide." "There are saints scattered all over this land,"

けであろう。藤樹はかつてこう言った。「この国のいたるところに聖人はいる。谷の奥にも山あいにも。ただ、その人たちは姿を見せないので、誰にも気づかれない。それが真の聖人であり、世に名の鳴り渡った人々は、どれほどのものでもないのである」。幸か不幸か、藤樹の名は「世に鳴り渡った」（先刻承知のように、本人の願いとはまったく反して）。このことから、崇高な目的をもって生きるならば、静かな人生を送っても力を及ぼすことを藤樹から学ぶことができるかもしれない。このような聖人たちこそ、「谷の奥」の学校で、昔の日本をあらゆる卑しさから守った人々だった。徳と影響力に関してはわずかに教えているという程度の現在の教育制度では、私たちのあいだにはびこっている卑しさをうまく抑えることができるかどうかわからない。どこかで叫ぶ声が聞こえる。「頭に血がみなのぼってしまった。手足の血がすっかりなくなり、じきに脳溢血で死ぬ」。もしも多くの藤樹が、この国に現れなければ。

Tōju once said, "in nooks of valleys and sheltered by mountains; and we cannot recognize them because they do not show themselves. These are real saints, and those whose names sound in the world need not be counted as anything." Happily or unhappily his name did "sound in the world" (much contrary to his wish, we know), that *we* might all learn of him the power of a silent life if lived with a noble aim in view. These saints were they who in their schools "in nooks of valleys" did preserve Old Japan from meannesses of all kinds; and we know not whether our present system with virtues and geniuses all dabbed and professored, could as effectively keep down the meannesses so rife in our midst. "The blood has all gone up to the head," they cry; "the limbs are empty, and we shall soon die of apoplexy," *if not many Tōjus appear in the land*.

1222–82 （貞応元年〜弘安5年）

# 日蓮上人

## 仏僧

# SAINT NICHIREN
## A Buddhist Priest

# I– 日本の仏教

**宗**教は人間にとって、最大の関心事である。信仰のない人間は考えられないと言っていいだろう。人間とは妙なもので、自分の能力をはるかに越える願いを持ち、世界が与える、あるいは与えうる以上の望みを抱くので、行動はともかく、少なくとも思考においては、どうにかして矛盾のないようにしなければならない。確かに、あの人は「無宗教だ」という話はよく耳にする。それはただ単にその人たちが、特定の教義を奉じておらず、自分を導くものとしての教団を認めず、神として木や金属でできた像や、心に描いた偶像を崇拝していないというだけのことだ。しかし、そういう人たちでも信仰は持っている。彼らの内にある不可解なものは、たとえば拝金主義やウィスキーの献納といった、自分で選んだ心の鎮め方や眠らせ方で手なづけられている。人の信仰は、その人なりの人生の解釈であり、人生をなんらかのかたちで解釈することは、この争いの世で幸福に生きるためには、どうしても必要なのだ。

さらに、死というきわめて重要な問題がある。貧しい者には希望であり、富める者には恐怖となっている死こそ、何にもまして重大な問題だ。死のあるところ

# I– Buddhism in Japan

Religion is man's chiefest concern. Properly understood, a man without a religion is unthinkable. In this strange existence where our wishes are so much more than our faculties, and our hopes exceed all that the world does or can give, something must be done to remove these incongruities, in our thought at least, if not in our actions as well. Indeed we often hear some say that they are "men of no religion." By that they simply mean that they do not sign their names to any distinct set of dogmas, own no order of priests as their guides, and pay no homage to any wooden or metallic or psychic image as their god. But a religion they nevertheless have. The Inscrutable within them is tamed in some way, be it by Mammon-Worship or Whiskey-Oblations or some other soporific or sedative method of his own choosing. A man's religion is his own explanation of life; and *some* explanation of it is an absolute necessity for his well-being in this world of strifes.

Then that all-important question of death, the hope of the poor and the dread of the rich—*that* is the question of all questions. *Where death is, religion must be*;—a sure sign of our weakness it

には宗教が必要になる。それは人間の弱さを示す確かなしるしかもしれないが、それだけでなく、人間の誕生の尊さと人間の内にある不滅のものの確かなしるしでもあるのだ。死によって死なない。これは、アダムの子孫が切望し、信仰心の強いことで知られるヘブライ人やインド人と同じように、日本人も切望していることだ。我々は「キリストの復活」について何も知らずに2500年を過ごしてきたが、よい宗教のあったおかげで、なんとか死を迎える方法を身につけ、人によっては実に立派な死に方をしてきた。この美しい国土を現世の住処(すみか)として、うれしい春は桜の花で飾られ、静かな秋は紅葉で彩られ、平和な家庭生活を人生の定めとしてきた日本人にとっては、生きることが重荷となることはほとんどなく、従って死はいっそう悲しいものとなった。「千代に八千代に」生きたいと願えば、死を考える苦痛は倍増し、その苦痛を和(やわ)らげられるものは、もっとよいところへ、つまり神道なら天にある神々の住まいへ、仏教であれば極楽浄土の蓮の園へ導かれるのだという信仰だけだった。我々が死を恐れたのは、臆病だからではなく、この美しい国に愛着があったからである。運命や義務のために、自分が生まれた愛する国から召される時に、身をゆだねる宗教が必要だったのだ。

　日本人は独自の宗教を持っているが、それは中央アジアを起源として、日本に伝わった可能性が高い。この宗教が元々どういう性格のものであったのかはよくわからない。最近になって、モーセの宗教と似ているという指摘があり、また、イスラエルの失われた10支族の記録を日本人の中に見つけようとする試みもあっ

may be, but withal also of our noble birth, and of deathlessness within us. *Not to die by dying*,—that is what all the sons of Adam yearn after, and Japanese no less than Hebrews or Hindoos of famed religiosity. And for twenty-five centuries before we heard of any thing about Resurrection, we have managed to die in some fashion, some of us in very creditable fashion, thanks for all the good religions we have had. With this beautiful land as our earthly home, with cherry blossoms to adorn our joyous spring, and maples to paint our serene autumn, and peaceful domesticity as our lot in life, existence has been a burden to us only very seldom, and death has been grievous unto us so much the more. With our desire to live "a thousand and eight thousand years," the thought of death was a double pain, to be alleviated only by a faith that could introduce us into a still better land, be it a saint's home in Shintō heaven, or a lotus garden in Buddhist paradise. We feared death not so much from our cowardice as from our attachment to this beautiful land of ours. Religions we needed to resign ourselves when fate or duty called us from the beloved land of our birth.

The Japanese has a religion of his own, which in all probability he brought with him from his home in Central Asia. What the exact nature of that religion originally was is not easy to tell. Its similarity to the Mosaic Faith has been recently pointed out, and another attempt was made to find in us the Lost Ten Tribes of the Jewish record. But whatever it had been, the time came when it

た。しかし、原型がどのようなものであったにしろ、日本独自の宗教は、インドを起源とする、はるかに複雑で、おそらくずっと洗練されていた宗教にとって代わられ、力を失う時が訪れた。日本人の間に初めて広まったヒンズーの教えの印象の強さは、容易に想像がつく。華麗な儀式や高遠な神秘主義、奔放自在で迷路のように複雑な思索は、純真な人々を驚嘆させたにちがいない。無学な者の目を喜ばせ、博学な者の知性を刺激し、国を治める者の目的にかなう宗教だったのだ。外来の宗教を大々的に受け入れることについては、愛国心から反対もあったが、ヒンズーの教えは国中に急速に広まった。少なくとも一時は、古来の信仰はまったく陰に追いやられ、新しい信仰が何世紀にもわたって隆盛をきわめた。

仏教が日本に伝来したのは、第29代欽明天皇の治世の13年のことで、西暦でいえば552年、仏教年代学者にいわせれば「仏滅後1501年」にあたる。早くも587年には、聖徳太子によって難波（大阪）に天王寺という大寺院が建立された。聖徳太子は、日本が生んだ最も聡明な皇子であり、「日本仏教の父」である。次の世紀（7世紀）には、全国で仏教への改宗が相次ぎ、歴代の天皇も自ら率先して仏門に帰依した。その頃中国では、唐の名僧、玄奘<sup>げんじょう 訳注59</sup>の指導のもとに仏教の大復興が起こっていた。インドを目指した玄奘の冒険旅行は、バルテルミ・サンティレールが実に生き生きと描いている。そして、仏教の教義をその発祥の地まで求めに行った玄奘の教えを乞おうと、日本から多くの学者が海を渡った。奈良時代（708〜769）の歴代の天皇は、仏教を強力に擁護した。壮大な伽藍は、当時と変わらぬ名前

was superseded and eclipsed by a very much more complex, and, may we say, refined faith of Indian origin. We can easily imagine the effect of the Hindoo faith as it first made its way among Japanese. Its gorgeous ceremonies, high mysticisms, and speculations bold and labyrinthine, must have struck the simple-hearted people with wonder. It satisfied the eyes of the ignorant, whetted the intellect of the learned, and served the purpose of the ruler. Notwithstanding some patriotic opposition against the wholesale importation of an exotic faith, the Hindoo religion spread in Japan with gigantic strides. For a time at least, the ancient faith was placed wholly in the background and the new reigned supreme for centuries in succession.

The date of the introduction of Buddhism into Japan is the thirteenth year of the reign of Kinmei, the twenty-ninth emperor, which we make to be 552 of the Christian era, or "1501 (SIC.) year after Buddha's entrance into Nirvana," as Buddhist chronologists like to have it. The great temple of Tennōji was built as early as 587 A.D. at Naniwa (Ōsaka) by Shōtoku Taishi, the wisest prince the country has had, and "the father of Japanese Buddhism." The next century (seventh) saw active proselyting going on throughout the empire, the emperors themselves taking the initiatives in the work. About this time there was a great revival of Buddhism in China under the leadership of Hiuen Chwang [Xuan Zhuang], that famous priest of the Tang dynasty, whose adventurous journey into India was so vividly described by Barthélemy St. Hilaire; and scholars were sent from Japan across the water to study under the man who had sought the faith in the land of its birth. The

をもつこの古都を今も飾り、新しい宗教が、伝来後すぐに勢力を広げたことを物語っている。


　しかし仏教熱が頂点に達したのは9世紀の初頭、最澄と空海なる2人の僧侶が、それぞれの宗派をきわめて、中国留学から帰国してからであった。奈良から京都に遷都した桓武天皇は、最澄と空海に寺院建立にふさわしい土地を与え、あわせて寄付金と特権も与えた。最澄は、新しい都の鬼門にあたる北東の方角にある比叡山に延暦寺を建てた。空海は紀伊の国の高野山に金剛峯寺（こんごうぶじ）を建てたが、都の南端にも寺領を授かった。現在の京都駅の真南に塔のそびえる有名な東寺は、空海が建立したものだ。788年の比叡山と816年の高野山の開山をもって、日本仏教は国土にしっかりと根をおろしたといえるだろう。これをしのぐ宗教は他にはなく、二人の開祖が、仏教の基盤は寺院を創建した山のように不動であると考えたのも不思議ではない。


　こうして、9世紀の初頭には、いわゆる「仏教八宗」がこの国に確立した（脚注・八宗に馴染みのない人のために、ここに紹介すると、八宗とは三論、法相（ほっそう）、華厳、律、成実、倶舎（くしゃ）、天台、真言である）。空海が没してから400年の間は、日本には新しい宗派が興ることも伝来することもなかった。「八宗」がそれぞれ勢力と影響力を拡大していくなか、最澄の宗派（天台宗）が最も大きくなった。そして、やはりここでも、教団が権力を握ると、それに

emperors of the Nara dynasty (708–769) were all strong supporters of Buddhism, and the mighty temples that still adorn the
ancient capital of the same name witness to the power attained by
the new religion so soon after its introduction into the land.

But the new enthusiasm reached its acme, when by the beginning of the ninth century, two Buddhist scholars, Saichō and Kūkai,
returned from their study in China, each with a sect of his choosing. The emperor Kanmu, who removed the capital from Nara to
Kyōto, gave each a conspicuous site for temple-building, and
endowments and privileges affixed thereto. Saichō built [the
Enryakuji Temple on Mt. Hie, also known as] Eizan lying to the
northeast of the new capital, the direction from which all evils
were thought to come. Kūkai posted himself at Mt. Kōya in the
province of Kii, but had a temple-site given him in the south end
of the capital, the famed Tōji with its peering pagoda right south
of the railway station being his own establishment. With Eizan
founded in 788, and Kōya in 816 A.D., we may say that Japanese
Buddhism had rooted itself firmly in the native soil. No competi-
tion with it by any other faith was possible, and no wonder that
its founders thought that its foundations were immovably laid as
the mountains on which they builded.

Thus in the beginning of the ninth century we find the so-
called "eight sects of Buddhism"* firmly established in the land.
For four centuries after the death of Kūkai we hear nothing about
the introduction or formation of any new sect in Japan. The
"eight" grew on in power and influence, Saichō's (Tendai)

---

* For those who may not yet be familiar with them, we might just as well mention
them here. They are (1) Sanron, (2) Hossō, (3) Kegon, (4) Ritsu, (5) Jōjitsu, (6)
Kusha, (7) Tendai, and (8) Shingon.

伴ってあらゆる腐敗が生じた。やがて、僧侶が天皇をしのぐ勢力になったので、ある天皇は僧侶に対する苛立ちを表した有名な言葉を残している。訳注60「わが意に従おうとせぬものが二つある。賀茂川の水と山法師だ」。天皇も貴族も、先を争うように自分の祈りをこめた寺院を建立し、寄進をして、華やかに飾った。そのため、大都市京都とその近郊は、山門、塔、六角堂、鐘楼などの壮大な宗教建築が今も残り、かつて日本で栄えた信仰の巨大な記念碑的存在になっている。

12世紀の終わり近くに、長い内乱が終わって平和が訪れると、宗教思想に新しい動きが起こった。将軍頼朝は、僧侶から世俗権力を取り上げたが、民衆の精神的な指導者として相応の敬意を払った。その結果、知徳ともにすぐれた学僧が次々と登場した。頼朝の後に幕府を継承した北条氏の多くは、仏教を厚く信仰した。彼らは当時の既存の宗派の華美虚飾にうんざりして、禅という瞑想的な仏教の宗派を中国から導入した（1200年）。そして京都、鎌倉、越前に大寺院を建立し、日本に新しい仏教を成立させた。儀式を誇示する旧宗派とは正反対に、秘儀と無限の形而上学を特徴とする新宗派は、上流階級や知識層に歓迎された。民衆も信仰を必要としていたが、それは高度に知的な禅哲学や、近寄りがたく荘厳な旧宗派ではなかった。そのような信仰を民衆にもたらしたのは、源空（法然上人）という僧侶だった。法然は、1207年頃、浄土宗と呼ばれるようになった教えを民衆の間に広めた。浄土宗は、た

leading all the rest. And here as elsewhere assumption of power by spiritual bodies brought in all the attending corruptions. Soon the priesthood became *emperor of emperors*, so much so that one of the latter expressed the annoyance due to his priest-subjects by the well-known saying, "Two things are beyond the power of my control: the water of the Kamo and mountain-priests." Emperor after emperor, and noble after noble vied with one another in building, endowing, and embellishing temples of their particular devotion; and the large city of Kyōto and its suburbs, with their magnificent religious structures,—porches, pagodas, hexagons, bellhouses,—are one huge monument of the faith that once flourished among us.

Near the close of the twelfth century, a pacific settlement of the country after long internecine wars gave rise to a new activity in religious thought. The great Yoritomo crippled the temporal power of the priests, but showed them due respect as the people's spiritual guides; and the result was the rise of many great teachers honorable for their learning and virtue. The Hōjōs who succeeded him were most of them faithful devotees of Buddhism. Tired with the pomp and vain-gloriousness of the then existing sects, they caused the Zen or meditative school of Buddhism to be introduced from China (1200), and several great temples were built, in Kyōto, Kamakura, and Echizen, to perpetuate the new form of worship in the land. The new became a favorite faith with the upper and intellectual classes, its esoterism and endless metaphysics standing in strong contrast to the ceremonial shows of the older sects.—The populace too needed a faith other than the high intellectualities of the Zen philosophy, or the unapproachable sublimities of the older cults. And such a faith was furnished

だ仏陀の名を唱えるだけで浄土へ行くことができると教えたので、念仏宗とも呼ばれるようになった。ただ「南無阿弥陀仏（阿弥陀仏に身命をささげて帰依します）」と、振り鳴らす振鈴の音に合わせて、哀調に満ちた声で唱えられる念仏に、ときに踊りが伴われるという祈りの形態は、従来のいかめしい信仰の形態にまったく新しい特徴を加えた。この分派で、ほぼ同時期に範宴（親鸞上人）という僧侶によって始められた真宗は、広く大衆に信仰されて、他の宗派をすべてしのぐまでになる。この宗派のまったく新しい特徴は、僧侶の一生不犯の禁を解き、戒律をかなりゆるめて、普通の生活の喜びを享受できるようにしたことである。こうして仏教はわかりやすくなり、一般庶民への接近がきわめて容易になった。もう布教のために国家の権威を借りる必要はなく、仏教は民衆の間で力を持つようになり、後世に非常に大きな影響を及ぼすこととなる。日本で民衆の間に広まった仏教には、もう一つ、念仏宗の分派の時宗があり、この3宗派は、当時の知識人に浸透していた深遠な禅宗とともに、ほぼ同時期に民衆に受け入れられていった。このすぐ後に、もう一つ宗派が生まれ、日本の仏教は12宗となった。したがって13世紀は、日本仏教の最後にして最大の形成期であったといえる。この世紀はまさに、日本におけるヒンズーの教えの改革期だった。この時代ほど光に満ちていた時代は他になく、この時代に確信を持って語られた教えを、今世紀に生きる日本人も熱心に聴いているのである。ご多分にもれず日本でも、宗教的熱情は迷信とともに消え、非科学的であることを恐れる我々は臆病になってしまい、目に見える物質世界だけを行動の

them by a priest called Genkū (Saint Hōnen), who, about 1207 A.D., introduced among them what has since been called the Jōdo or "pure land" sect. It taught, above all other things, the possibility of entrance into the Pure Land merely by calling upon the name of Buddha, and hence was otherwise called the Nen-Butsu or Call-on-Buddha sect. The simple "Nam-Amida-Butsu" (I commit myself to thee O thou Amitabha Buddha) was set to music on the hand-bell; and the whole uttered with plaintive voice and often attended with a dance gave entirely new features to, thus far, a very august form of belief. A branch of this was the Shin sect, started at about the same time by a priest named Han'en (Saint Shinran), destined to eclipse all other sects by the influence it was to have over the mass of the people. The very novel feature of this sect was the removal of the vows of chastity from the priest-class, and considerable leniency thus afforded to their free indulgence in the common joys of life. Buddhism thus vulgarized, its approach to the commonalty was greatly facilitated; and now without any imperial authority to forward its propagation, it began to be a power among the people,—a matter of very great consequence to the ages that followed. The addition of one more branch, that of Jishū, to the Nen-Butsu sect completed the development of the exoteric school of Buddhism in Japan, the three coming to be adopted by the people almost simultaneously with one another, and with the esoteric Zen school which invaded the cultured society of the time. The country was to have one more sect,—twelve in all,—immediately following the last we have mentioned. We may say therefore that the thirteenth century was the last and greatest *formative period* of Japanese Buddhism. The century was really the *reformative era* of the Hindoo faith in

基盤としており、人間が今ほど知識がなくとも誠実であり、今ほど生きやすい世の中ではなくとも立派に生きていた時代の影響はかすかになってしまった。ならば、天地がより一層の気高い行為と偉大な犠牲を我々に命じている今、虚飾の信仰を自慢し、見下げはてた安逸にひたる我々を恥じ入るためにも、この時代の英雄を思い出してみよう。

## Ⅱ- 誕生と出家

　**貞**応元年（1222年）のある春の日、波立つ水平線上に朝日が昇り、世界の東の果ての地が朝明けに染まる頃、安房の国の東端、岬に近い小湊村の漁師の家に、一人の子供が生まれた。父は、政治的な理由でこの地に逃れてきた人だったが、今は特に目立つところもない貧乏な漁師だった。母も低い身分の出ではなく、熱心な日輪の信者で、男児を授かるようにと長く願っていたのだが、その願いがついにかなえられたのである。両親は、子供を授けてくれた神にちなんで、生まれた子を善日麿と名付けた。このことは、その子供がこの世での使命を果たそうと決意する時に、大いに関係してくるのだが、それについては後で触れる。誕生に関しては、多くの不思議や奇跡が伝えられている。清らかな泉がその漁師の家の中庭から湧き出し、それを汲んで産湯にし、「出産の不浄を洗い流した」とか、並外れて大きな白蓮華が、まったく季節はずれで

Japan. No such lights as we saw then have appeared since, and we of this century still hang upon the words then uttered with all the conviction of the age. Here, as elsewhere, enthusiasm disappeared together with superstition, and we, afraid of being nonscientific, are cowardly creatures, basing our actions wholly upon the visible, and upon the faint echoes of the time when men were sincere without our knowledge, and heroic without our crowding cares. Let us call up a hero then to shame us in our vaunted faith, and in our love of ignoble ease, when heaven and earth are calling us to nobler deeds and greater sacrifice.

## II– Birth and Consecration

On a spring day of the 1st year of Jōō (1222), as the sun rose above the billowy horizon, and the easternmost outpost of Earth's nations caught its first rosy rays, a child was born to a fisher's family in the village of Kominato (Little Haven) near the most eastern cape of the province of Awa. The father was a fugitive there for some political reasons, now a poor fisherman without any outward distinction; and the mother, also, of no mean birth, a devout worshipper of the Sun-god, of whom the gift of a son had long been asked, and now granted in answer to her prayers. They named him Zen-Nichi-Maro (Good-Sun-Boy) in pious commemoration of the deity who called him into being,—a fact which had considerable to do when the child came to decide his mission to this world, as we shall see afterward. All the wonders and miracles which are reported to have attended his birth,—how a crystalline spring spontaneously gushed forth in the fisher's garden "to wash natal uncleanliness away," how a white lotus of unusual

あるのに家の近くに咲き、「芳香をあたりに放った」などと伝えられている。今世紀に生きる我々は、このような話は、信心深い時代の想像の産物だと思っている。しかし、日蓮誕生の年についてここで特に触れようと思うのは、この信仰に燃えた若者が、後に国を救うという崇高な問題と向き合った時に、よくよく考えたことであるからだ。その年は、仏陀の入滅後2171年であった。すなわち、最初の「正法千年」はすでに終わり、次の「像法千年」も過ぎ去り、最後の「末法千年」に入ったばかりで、一条の光が東方に現れて、末法の世の暗黒を照らすと仏陀が予言した年だった。善日麿が生まれた（陰暦）2月の16日は、仏陀の生涯で誕生と同じほど大きな出来事があった日の翌日だった。仏陀の入滅は2月15日だったのである。このような符合は、日蓮のような心の持ち主にとっては非常に意味深いことであった。

善日麿が12歳になると、信心深い両親は息子を僧侶にすることに決めた。この少年が後年成し遂げたことを考えると、非凡な幼少期にまつわる多くの逸話はおそらく信じてよいのだろう。世を忍んで漁師となった親が、わが子を僧職につかせることで世に出したいと願ったとしても不思議ではない。厳しい身分差別のあった時代においては、低い身分に生まれた天才が世に出る唯一の道は、出家をすることであった。生地からそう遠くない所に清澄という名の寺があり、そこの住職の道善は学徳ともに高いと地元で評判の人物だった。善日麿はその寺に連れて行かれ、慈愛深い師に預けられた。師はこの若者に特別な期待をかけていたようで

magnitude, entirely out of season, opened nearby "to cast fragrance into the air," etc.,—we of this century are accustomed to ascribe to the devout imaginations of the time. But the date of his birth is worth particular mention here, as it was a point much ruminated upon by the young enthusiast as the awful question of his country's salvation afterward came before his mind. The year was the 2171st after Buddha's entrance into the Nirvana; that is, after the first "millennium of the right law" (正法千年) had ended, and the second "millennium of the image-law" (像法千年) had also spent itself, and the third and last "millennium of the latter law" (末法千年) had just been ushered in; when as was prophesied by the Great Teacher, a light was expected to appear to the *east of him* to shine the darkness of the last days. The day was the 16th of the second month (according to the lunar calendar), a day after the same great event in Buddha's life, which was on the 15th of the same month. Correspondences such as these were of immense importance to a mind like our hero's.

When he came to be twelve years old, the pious inclination of his parents decided upon his being made a priest. Considering what he did in after years, we can well believe many stories told about his remarkable childhood; and we do not wonder if the paternal ambition of the fugitive-fisherman saw in his son's consecration to a priestly office an opportunity for the lad's rise in society, as in that age of rigid social distinctions, religion was the only way open for a low-born genius to show itself in the world. Not far from the place where he was born, was a temple, Kiyosumi by name, and its abbot Dōzen had local reputation for his learning and virtue. There the boy Zen-Nichi was taken, and entrusted to the care of the benignant teacher who seems to have taken special

ある。善日麿は4年の修行を終えて16歳で得度して正式に僧侶となり、蓮長と名乗った。その時にはすでに、道善はこの若い弟子の非凡な才能を認め、できれば寺の後継者にしたいと考えていた。若者は、相変わらず両親にとっては希望、師にとっては誇りであったが、その実、心の内では葛藤が大きくなっていて、ついに生まれ故郷を離れ、修学の旅に出ることになるのである。

## Ⅲ- 暗黒の内と外

**蓮**長は仏教の基礎的な知識を一通り学ぶと、いくつかの疑問が湧いてきた。最も明白な疑問は、仏教における多数の宗派の存在だった。彼は自問した。「なぜ、一人の人間の生涯と教えから始まった仏教が、これほど多くの宗派や分派に分かれているのだろうか。仏教とは一つではないのか。まわりを見回すと、どの宗派も他宗派をすべて非難し、仏陀の真実の心にかなっているのは自分の宗派だけだと主張しているが、これはどういうことなのだろうか。どこの海の水もみな同じ味であり、仏陀の教えに二通りあるはずがない。どうして宗派に分裂したのか、そしてどの宗派が、私の歩むべき仏陀が説いた道なのだろうか」

これが、蓮長が抱いた最初にして最大の疑問であったが、これは当然の疑問である。我々も仏教やその他の宗教について同じ疑問を抱いており、蓮長の葛藤に深く同情できる。彼が師とした道善をはじめ、誰もこの疑問を解いてくれなかったため、いきおい念仏に明

delight in the youth. Passing his novitiate of four years, he was formally consecrated a priest at the age of sixteen under the new name of Renchō; and already the good abbot, watching the unusual ability of his young disciple, was beginning to think of nominating him as his possible successor in his office. The youth remained his parents' hope, and his teacher's pride, when behind all outward appearances struggles were going on in his mind, which drove him at last from the region of his birth, to seek enlightenment throughout the country.

## III– In and Out of Darkness

He was fairly introduced into the elementary knowledge of Buddhism when several questions presented themselves to his mind for solution. The most apparent was *the existence of multitudinous sects in Buddhism*. "Why is it" he asked to himself, "that Buddhism which had its origin in the life and teaching of one man is now divided into so many sects and divisions? Is Buddhism more than one? What means that which I see around me, that one sect speaks evil of all others, each maintaining that *it* has Buddha's true mind? The waters of the sea have the same taste, and there can be no two ways in the teachings of Buddha. Oh wherein lies the explanation of this division into sects, and which among these sects is Buddha's way, the way I should walk in?"

Such was his first and greatest doubt, an entirely reasonable doubt, we believe. We also have similar doubt about Buddhism and some other religions, and we can entirely sympathize with our hero in the struggle he had. As neither his abbot nor anybody else relieved him from his doubt, he naturally resorted to his prayers.

け暮れるようになった。ある日、特に信仰している菩薩を祭る堂へ礼拝に行った帰りに、心の重荷に耐えかねて倒れ、大量の血を吐いた。同僚が助け起こしたものの、意識が回復するまでにしばらくかかった。この出来事が起きた場所は、今でも正確にわかっているが、近くの竹藪が、いくらか赤みを帯びているのは、その時散った血の色で染まったからだと伝えられている。ところが、ある夜、この若い僧が仏陀が入滅する直前に語ったという涅槃経を熱心に読んでいると、次の言葉が目に留まり、迷い苦しんでいた心にいい知れぬ解放感をおぼえた。それは、「依法不依人」、真理の教えを信じ、人に頼るな、という言葉だった。すなわち、人がどんなに仰々しく、もっともらしいことを言っても、人の意見を信じてはならず、仏陀の遺した経文を信じるべきであり、あらゆる疑問は経文だけに頼って解決しなくてはならない。蓮長の心は安らかになった。これまでは、すべてが踏むと沈む砂であったのが、拠り所が見つかったのである。この日本の僧侶の話から、400年前にエルフルトの修道院で起きた、似たような出来事が思い出されないだろうか。ドイツの若い修道士は、「意識を失う」ほど多くの疑問を突き詰めて考えた末に、目に留まった古いラテン語の聖書に安らぎを見いだし、以後それを自分の信仰と人生の砦としたのである。

だが、仏僧にとっては、権威ある経典という問題は、キリスト教のルターのように単純ではなかった。このドイツ人の場合はただ一冊の聖書に頼ればよかったが、この日本人の場合には、ときには大きく矛盾する多数の経典があり、その中から最高の権威のある正典を自

One day as he came from his worship at the temple of the Bodhisattva of his special devotion, the burden within him became unbearable, and down he came to the ground with abundant hemorrhage from his mouth. His friends helped him up, and it was sometime before he returned to consciousness again. We are still pointed to the exact spot of this occurrence, a little bamboo bush nearby with certain reddish tints in its leaves being supposed to have taken its colors from the blood that was spattered on that occasion. One evening, however, as his eyes were poring over the Nirvana Sutra, said to have been delivered by Buddha just before his entrance into that blessed state, the following caught the attention of the young priest, to the inexpressible relief of his troubled mind: 依法不依人. *Trust in the Word and not in man.* That is, he was not to trust in human opinions, however plausible and highsounding, but in the sutras as left by the Great Teacher, and he was to decide all questions by them and them only. His mind was now at ease. He found something to stand upon, whereas thus far all had been sinking sand under him. Who, by reading the above account of the Japanese priest, is not reminded of a similar case in the convent of Erfurth four hundred years ago, when after much questionings, "loss of consciousness," etc., the young German monk found his rest in an old Latin Bible that caught his eyes, and clung to it ever afterward as *his* stronghold of faith and life?

But in case of the Buddhist priest, the question of the authoritative scripture was not so simple a one as in that of the Christian Luther. Whereas the German had a single Bible to rely upon, the Japanese had dozens, often of very contradictory natures, from which to make his selection of the canon of the supreme authority.

分で選ばなければならない。しかし、これが比較的容易な作業であったのは、いわゆる高等批評がまったく知られておらず、理由やいわれを問うことなく古人の記録をただ信じるだけの時代だったからである。蓮長にとっては、ある経典の中に、大乗、小乗を問わず、あらゆるすぐれた経典の年代が記載されているのを見つけただけで十分だったのだ。記載されていた経典の年代の順序は、仏陀の民衆に対する初説法が収められている華厳経で始まり、(1) 仏陀が出家してから最初の12年間の教えが収められている阿含経、(2) 次の16年間の教えを収めた方等経、(3) それに続く14年間の教えを収めた般若経、そして (4) 仏陀の生涯の最後の8年間の教えを収めた妙法蓮華経または法華経である。この順序から考えると、最後の経典に仏陀の生涯にわたる教えの神髄が収められているという結論が出るのは当然である。つまり、日蓮の言葉を借りれば、そこには「万物の原理、永遠の真理、仏陀の本心と内証の妙理」がある。それで「妙法蓮華経」という美しい名があるのだ。ここで、仏教経典の正確な年代順や、それぞれの価値を比較して、批評的な考察をするつもりはない。蓮長が重視したこの経典が、仏滅後500年も後世の作であることや、この新しい経典に信憑性と最高権威を与えることを目的として、先に触れた、経典の年代を記載した無量義経が書かれたものであることは、今日ではほとんど定説になっている。しかし、いずれにしろ、蓮長がそこに伝えられている年代順通りに経典を受け入れ、妙法蓮華経に仏教の信仰の規準と、仏教にある多くの矛盾した見方を単純明快に説明する言葉を見つけたことさえわかれば、我々にはそれで十分だ。この

This, however, was a comparatively easy task in the age when the so-called Higher Criticism was wholly unknown, and men put their simple trust upon the records of the ancients without questioning why and wherefore. It was enough for our hero that he found that one of the sutras gave the chronological order of all the great sutras in both Mahayana and Hinayana. The order given was, beginning with the Avatamsaka Sutra, supposed to contain Buddha's first public utterances, (1) the Agamas (Agon Kyō), containing his teachings of the first twelve years of his ministry, (2) the Vaipulya Sutras (Hōdō Kyō), containing those of the second sixteen years, (3) the Prajna Sutra (Hannya Kyō), of the third fourteen years, and (4) the Saddharma-Pundarika Sutra (Myō-Hō-Renge or Hokke Kyō), of the last eight years of his life. Natural conclusions from this order were that the last-mentioned sutra contained the essence of the teaching of Buddha's whole life; or in the words of Nichiren, it had in it "the principle of all things, the truth of eternity, and the secret importance of Buddha's original state and of the virtue of his enlightenment." Hence its beautiful name of "the Sutra of the Lotus of the Mysterious Law." It is not our purpose here to enter into a critical examination of the exact order of the Buddhist canons, or of the comparative value of one above others. I think it is fairly settled now that the sutra that Nichiren thought so much of was a later product, some 500 years after Buddha's death, and that the Amitartha Sutra that gives the order of the different canons here mentioned was written expressly for the purpose of giving authenticity and superlative authority to the new canon. But be these whatever they may, it only suffices us to know that our hero accepted them in the order here given, and found in Saddharma-Pundarika Sutra

結論に達したとき、蓮長の喜びと感謝の気持ちは、涙となって溢れ出た。そして最後に、蓮長はこう自問した。「父と母のもとを去り、このすばらしい教えに身を捧げた自分は、凡僧の古い教えにしがみついて、仏陀自身の金言を求めようとしなくていいのだろうか」。この神聖な志が芽生えたのは、20歳の時であった。もう、田舎の寺に引きこもってはいられなかった。道善と寺の僧侶たちに別れを告げると、深く広く真理を究めるため、蓮長は果敢に世に乗り出した。

　蓮長が最初に向かったのは、当時の幕府があった首府鎌倉だった。首府に入った一介の田舎僧には、ローマに入ったルターのように、目にするものも、耳に入る教えも奇異に映った。鎌倉は、寺院の立派さと僧侶の華美ばかりが目につき、虚偽に充ちていた。禅宗は上流階級を、浄土宗は下層階級を導いていたが、前者は空理空論の泥沼におちいり、後者は阿弥陀への盲信に浸りきり、仏陀の説いた仏教はどこにも見られなかった。それどころか、仏像そのものが玩具として子供に与えられ、作り話の存在でしかない阿弥陀仏が、仏教儀式と称する礼拝で最高位に置かれていたのだ！僧衣をまとった人々が自らの存在を誇示して、恥をさらしていた。彼らは、徳や修行を積むのではなく、阿弥陀仏の名を唱えるだけで救われると教えていた。それで、民衆の間では、南無阿弥陀仏と騒々しく唱えながら、放縦のかぎりが尽くされていた。蓮長は、鎌倉で5年間見てきたことから、彼が奉ずる「聖なる経典の尊師」が予言したように、末法の世はすでに到来して

the standard of the Buddhist faith, and a clear simple explanation of the all-comprehensibility of so many discordant views in Buddhism. As he came to this conclusion, the joy and gratitude within him burst into abundant tears. "I," he finally said to himself, "I who left my father and mother, and gave myself to the service of this excellent faith,—should I cling to the traditional teachings of common priests, and not seek the golden words of the Tathagata (Buddha) himself?" He was twenty years old when the holy ambition rose in his mind. Seclusion in a country-monastery became no more possible. Bidding farewell to his abbot and order, he launched out boldly into the world, to seek the truth far and wide.

His first destination was Kamakura, the Shōgun's capital of the time. A country-priest in the metropolis—a Luther in Rome, —strange phenomena met his eyes, and strange doctrines reached his ears. With the magnificence of its temple-structures and the pomp of its priest-classes, the city was given up wholly to falsities. The Zen sect leading the high, and the Jōdo sect the low, the former into quagmires of futile speculation, and the latter into a delirium of blind trust in Amitabha, Buddha's Buddhism was not to be found anywhere. Yea more, he saw Buddha's very images given to children for toys, and Amitabha of only fabulous existence was given the supreme position in what *they* called Buddhist worship! Men clad in holy garments vaunted themselves in their open shame. Salvation, they taught, consisted only in calling upon the name of Amitabha, and not in acts of virtue and discipline; and so amidst the din of Nam-Amida-Butsu, licentiousness of the grossest kind prevailed among the people. During his five years' stay in Kamakura, he saw enough to convince him of the presence of the Latter Day already in the world, and the need and opportu-

おり、新しい時代に光をもたらすには新しい信仰が必要で、その時期がきていると確信するに至った。ちょうどその頃、誰からも崇敬されていた大阿上人が、全信徒を震えあがらせるような死に方をした。

　上人の体は「子供のように小さく縮まり」、その肌は「墨のように黒く」変色していたのだ。それは、上人が地獄へ落ちたという疑いようのないしるしであり、その教えは悪魔の教えである証拠だった。それに、あの空の怪しさは、どういうことだろう。西の空に、赤と白の3本の筋がくっきりと現れ、2本の白い筋が消えても、赤い筋は「天を突く火柱のように」残っていた。そこへ激しい地震が起こり、多くの寺院が倒壊し、人も家畜も、彼らを救済するために建てられた寺院の残骸（ざんがい）の下敷きになってうめき苦しんだ。「すべては、この国で真の教えが説かれず、誤った教えが説かれ信じられていたからだ。自分こそ、この国に信仰をよみがえらせる使命を与えられた人間なのではないか」。このような思いを抱いて、蓮長は「首府は教えを広めるところであっても、学ぶところではない」と賢明な判断をして、鎌倉を後にした。

　両親のもとに立ち寄ったあと、蓮長はさらに知識を求めるために旅立った。天皇のいる都をあらゆる悪霊から守るために、京都の鬼門の方角にそびえる叡山は、過去1000年の間、日本における仏教修学の中心地であった。海抜2500フィート、高い杉林に囲まれ、穏やかな琵琶湖の壮大な眺めを眼下に見るこの地で、釈迦の説いた道が探求され、熟考され、伝えられてきた。3000人もの屈強な僧兵をかかえ、天皇にも民衆にも恐れられていた最盛期には、全山が喧噪（けんそう）に満ちた居留地

nity of a new faith to bring in a new era of light, as foretold by the Worshipful in his Holy Sutra. Only but recently, Saint Daia, an object of universal adoration, had died a death, which sent horrors to all his followers.

His body "shrivelled up into the smallness of a child," and the color of his skin changed into "pitchy darkness,"—unmistakable signs of his fall into Hell, and evidence of the diabolical nature of the faith he represented. Then, too, what do those monstrosities in the sky signify? Three aerial forms, white and red, hung clear against the western sky, and when the two white disappeared, the red remained "as a pillar of fire piercing through the zenith." The whole was succeeded by a violent earthquake bringing down many temples to the ground, and men and beasts groaned under the debris of the structures intended for their salvation. "All because the true sutra is not preached in the land, and errors are taught and believed in. Am I not he of eternal appointment to revive the Faith in the land?" ...... With thoughts such as these, Renchō left Kamakura behind him, wisely remarking that "the capital of a country is a place for disseminating the truth, and not for learning it."

After a short visit to his parents, he set out for further search after knowledge. Eizan towering in the direction of *Kimon* (Devil's Gate) from Kyōto to ward all evil influences from off the Mikado's capital, has for the last one thousand years been the chief repository of Buddhist learning in Japan. There twenty-five hundred feet above the sea-level, encompassed by tall cryptomeria forests, and with a magnificent view of the placid Lake Biwa below, the ways of Sakya were searched into, contemplated, and transmitted. In its days of prosperity, the whole mountain must have worn the

の様相を呈していたにちがいない。源空もここで学び、叡山で教えられていた教義に反する、一般大衆にわかりやすい宗派を開き、後年、広く一般の信者を集めた。源空の弟子で、真宗の開祖である範宴も、信仰の奥義を会得して全国に高名をはせた多くの僧と同様に、ここの学僧であった。そして蓮長も、日本に真の仏教を広めようという志を胸に、安房の国の漁師のあばら屋から400マイルの道のりを徒歩で旅して、この山へ学びにきたのである。


　蓮長は、叡山で与えられた新たな学問の機会を生かし、手当たり次第に何でも貪欲に吸収した。しかし、とくに力を入れて学んだのは、自分が奉ずる経典としての法華経だった。叡山では法華経の貴重な写本や注釈書を読むことができたのだ。事実、叡山を総本山とする天台宗はこの経典を重んじていた。天台宗の「六十巻物」と呼ばれているものは、60巻からなる法華経だけの注釈書なのだ。法華経のあまりのすばらしさに、中国の天台宗開祖である天台は、30巻もの注釈書を著し、その弟子の妙楽は、師の注釈になお付け加える必要を感じて、さらに30巻を書き加えた。そのうちの10巻は、この経典の名前を構成している漢字6文字について、一字ずつ論じているのだ！　我々には格別にすばらしいとは思えないこの経典が、昔の人には、それほど深い意味のあるものに思えたのだ。蓮長は10年も叡山にとどまって、法華経に関する複雑な資料を徹底的に調べた。ここでは蓮長の達した結論しか述べること

aspect of a bustling colony, harboring, as it did, an army of men-
dicants three thousand strong, a dread of the populace as well as
of the emperors. It was here that Genkū studied, and formulated
his exoteric school of Buddhism so contrary to the tenets taught
in the mountain, and had it afterward so widely adopted by the
people. His disciple Han'en, the founder of the Shin sect, was also
a student here, as were also many others who had had national
reputations for their attainment in the secret laws of the Faith.
And now our Renchō, ambitious of the propagation of genuine
Buddhism in Japan, came four hundred miles on his feet from his
fisher's hut in the province of Awa, to seek enlightenment in the
same mountain.

With the new opportunities for investigation here afforded,
Renchō took in with avidity all that he could lay his hands upon.
But his speciality was the Saddharma-Pundarika Sutra,—*his* Sutra,
—of which valuable manuscripts and commentaries were accessi-
ble in the mountain. Indeed, the Tendai sect, of which Eizan was
the center, made a great deal of this Sutra. What are called "the
sixty volumes" of the sect are so many commentaries upon this
one book. Such a wonderful book is it that Tendai,[*18] the Chinese
founder of the sect, wrote thirty volumes upon it; and one of his
disciples, Myōgaku, finding that the master's commentaries still
needed commentaries, wrote another thirty volumes upon the
first thirty volumes. Ten of these volumes treat separately of each
of the six Chinese hieroglyphics that compose the name of the
Sutra! So deep to the ancient did appear the meaning of the book
which to us appears as nothing very extraordinary.—For ten
long years, Renchō stayed in Eizan, delving into these intrica-
cies. We can only give the conclusions he came to. He was now

はできない。蓮長は、法華経が他のどの経典よりも優れており、叡山の開祖最澄によって原形のまま日本にもたらされたが、その後、叡山の僧侶によって真価がかなり損なわれてしまったことを、はっきりと確信するに至った。蓮長は、京都に数回、奈良と高野山にも一度ずつ遊学して、確信をより強固なものにするために研鑽を積んだ。そして、もう何の疑問もなくなったとき、法華経に生涯を捧げる覚悟ができた。ある時、蓮長の目の前に日本の主だった神々がことごとく姿を現し、蓮長の守護を約束した。神々が空中に消え去る時、「斯人行世間　能滅衆生闇」（この人が世を巡り、人々の内にある闇を滅ぼす）と唱和する神々の声が聞こえた。しかし、蓮長は神が自分に微笑む幻影や訪れを経験しただけの、単なる神秘主義者ではなかった。

32歳になった蓮長には、友もなく名もなかったが、独立不屈の精神があった。真宗の範宴のような、人に言えるほどの家柄の出でもなかった。後年自ら「海辺の旃陀羅が子なり」訳注64 と言っていたように、漁師の息子だった。また、最澄や空海などの「高僧」のように、外国で学んだこともなかった。どのような学問分野についても、秘密を解く鍵の持ち主として日本で認められるためには、海外留学が必須であるのは、当時も今も変わらない。そして蓮長には、どのような種類の後ろ盾もなかった。まして、他宗派の開祖はたいてい大いに享受していた皇室の庇護は皆無だった。当時勢力を誇っていた宗派とはまったく相容れない教義をかかげて、あらゆる権力にたった一人で立ち向かったのである。日本の仏僧で、経典と仏法のために命を賭して立ったのは、蓮長ただ一人であり、その後に続く例を

thoroughly convinced of the view he had entertained of the superiority of the Pundarika Sutra above all the other Sutras; of its
introduction into Japan in its pure from by Saijō, the founder of
Eizan, and of *considerable vitiations introduced thereto by priests who*
*came after him.* Often to Kyōto, and once to Nara and Kōya, he
carried his researches, to establish him further in his conviction;
and when no more doubting was possible, he was ready to lay
down his life for the Sutra. Once he saw with his own eyes all the
principal deities of the land coming to promise protection to him;
and as they vanished in the air, a divine chorus was heard in the
sky, saying, "Shi-nin-gyō-seken, nō-metsu-shujō-an" (this man will
go round the world, and destroy the darkness that is in men). He
was not the only mystic, however, who has had similar visions
and visitations.

He was now thirty-two years of age, friendless, unknown, yet
independent and indomitable. He had no ancestral lineage to lay
his claim upon, as had Hanyen of the Shin sect. He was a fisherman's son, "a sudra of the sea-coast," as he afterward called himself. Neither was his study prosecuted in a foreign land, as were
those of Saijō, Kūkai, and other eminent "theologians,"—a matter
of prime importance, then, as now, of being accepted by Japanese
as a holder of a key to the secret of any branch of knowledge.
Patronage of any kind he had absolutely none; much less, imperial
patronage, as had most other sect-founders in abundance. He
alone began single-handed, against powers of all kinds, with a
view wholly at variance with those of the influential sects of the
day. He is the only case, as far as we know, of Japanese Buddhists,
who, without any example to follow after, stood for a Sutra and a
Law with his life in his hand. His life is interesting not so much

知らない。その一生に関心が寄せられるのは、世間に広めた教えのためではなく、勇敢に自分の教えを主張したためなのである。日本での真の意味での宗教的迫害は、日蓮から始まったのだ。

# IV‒ 宣誓

「預言者が尊敬されないのは、自分の郷里、家族の間だけである<sup>訳注65</sup>」。だが悲しいことに、預言者はたいてい自分の生まれ故郷で、預言者としての第一声をあげる。この世に家のない身でありながら故郷にひかれ、どのような仕打ちに合うかわかっているのに、鹿が谷川の流れを慕いあえぐように<sup>訳注66</sup>故郷に戻っては、拒絶され、石を投げられ、追放されるのだ。蓮長のたどった道も、例外ではなかった。

蓮長が小湊のあばら屋に戻ると、両親は息子の帰りを待ちわびていた。そして、蓮長が出会う数々の試練の中で最初にして最大の試練となったが、息子が若い頃を過ごした寺の住職になるのをこの目で見たいという両親の当然の願いに背いた。そしてこの時、自分を誕生させた神と、これから世に広めようとする経典の名にちなんで、名前を日蓮と改めた。建長5（1253）年4月28日、明るい太陽が東の水平線上の中天にかかった時、日蓮は広大な太平洋をのぞむ断崖に立った。海を前に、山を背にして、そこから感じられる全宇宙に向かい、自ら作った祈りの形式であるお題目を繰り返し唱えた。お題目は、他の宗派をすべて沈黙させ、自分を信奉する者たちをこの世の終わりまで導くための、永遠への合い言葉となるものであった。実際、「南無妙

for the doctrinal views he maintained and promulgated, as for the brave way in which he upheld them. Religious persecution in its true sense began in Japan with Nichiren.

## IV – Proclamation

"A prophet is not without honor save in his own country." Yet it is a pathetic fact to know that a prophet usually begins his public career in his own country. Homeless as he is in this world, he yet feels the attraction of his home, and despite the kind of treatment he is sure to receive there, he resorts there as a hart pants after the waterbrooks, only to be rejected, stoned, and expelled. Renchō's course was not to be otherwise.

In his humble home at Little Haven, he found his parents eagerly waiting for the return of their son; and the first and greatest of all his trials was to protest against their natural desire of seeing him installed as the abbot of the monastery that had nursed him in his youth. He now changed his name to Nichiren, Sun-Lotus, significant of the god who called him into being, and of the Sutra he was to give to the world. On the 28th day of the fourth month of the fifth year of Kenchō (1253), as the rosy sun was half above the eastern horizon, Nichiren was upon a cliff looking toward the broad Pacific, and to the seas before him and the mountains behind him, and through them to the whole universe, he repeated the form of prayer he had framed for himself, the form that was intended to silence all others, to lead his disciples to the end of the earth, and be their watchword to all eternity,—the form,

法蓮華経」というお題目は仏教の核心と、人間そして宇宙の本質を具体化したものであって、正しい法の白蓮の経に身命をささげて帰依するという意味である。


　日蓮は、朝は自然と話し、夕には里人に向かって教えを説いた。すぐに、その名は近郷に広く知れ渡った。鎌倉、叡山、奈良で15年も研鑽を積んだ日蓮ならば、何か新しく、深く、そしてためになる話をするにちがいない。そう思って里人たちは、老いも若きも、男も女も、あるいは真言宗の「ハラハリタヤ」と唱え、あるいは浄土宗の「南無阿弥陀仏」と念仏を唱えながら集まった。寺が人で埋まり「香が四隅に焚かれる」と、「太鼓の音とともに」日蓮が説教壇に立った。男盛りをむかえたばかりで、夜を徹した勤行の跡がそこここにうかがえ、信仰に身を捧げた者の目と予言者の威厳をそなえた日蓮に、集まった人たちの注目が集まり、息詰まる沈黙のうちに第一声が待たれた。日蓮は、自分の経典となった法華経を取り上げて、第6章の一部を読み上げると、「穏やかな顔で、朗々と響く声」で、次のように語った。

　「長い間、あらゆる経典を学び、それぞれの宗派が経典について言っていることを読み聞きしてまいりました。そのうちの一つに、こう記されています。仏陀の入滅後500年の間は、多くの者はまったく精進をしなくても成仏できるだろう。次の500年の間は、精進と禅定につとめれば成仏がかなう。これが正法の千年です。その後に、読経を要する500年と、寺院建立に励まなければならない500年があります。これが像法の千年です。

indeed, that embodied the essence of Buddhism, the constitution of man, and of the universe. It was Nam-Myō-Hō-Renge-Kyō, or [in Sanskrit] Nama Saddharma-Pundarikaya Sutraya, [meaning] "I humbly trust in the Sutra of the Mysterious Law of the White Lotus."

Nature addressed in morning, he was to address his townsmen in afternoon. His fame had already gone around the whole neighborhood. He who spent fifteen years in study in Kamakura, Eizan, and Nara, must have something new, deep, and edifying to say to his countrymen. So they came, young and old, men and women, some repeating *haraharitaya* of the Shingon sect, others the *nam-amida-butsu* of the Jōdo. When the temple was all filled, and "incense perfumed its four corners," Nichiren appeared on the pulpit "at the beating of a drum." A man just reaching fulness of manhood, with many marks of vigils upon him, the eyes of a zealot, the dignity of a prophet,—he was the cynosure of the whole congregation, and his opening words were watched with breathless silence. He took up *his* sutra, the Pundarika, read a part of its sixth chapter, and "with countenance mild, and voice resonant" he thus began:

"Years have I spent in the study of all the sutras, and read and heard all that different sects have to say about them. In one of them we are told that for 500 years after Buddha's entrance into Nirvana, many will attain Buddhahood without any exertion on their part; and for the succeeding 500 years, with diligence and ascetic contemplation. This is the millennium of the right law. Then will come 500 years of sutra-reading, and another 500 years of temple-building. This is the millennium of the image-law. Then will

これが過ぎると『正しい教えがすたれる』500年が始まり、仏陀の教えの功徳はなくなり、人は成仏する道をすべて失います。これが末法の始まりであり、1万年の間続きます。末法の世になってから、すでに200年が経ちました。仏陀の直接の教えから遠く隔たっている我々が、成仏する道は一つしかありません。その道は、妙法蓮華経の5文字の中にあるのです。しかし、浄土宗は人々に、この尊い経典を閉じて、もう耳を傾けないよう求め、真言宗は自分たちが奉じる大日経に比べたら、足を止め履物を脱いで聞く価値もないとののしります。法華経第2巻の譬喩品で、仏教の種を絶滅させる者は必ずや無間地獄に堕ちると、釈尊も説いているではありませんか。聞く耳と見る目がある人なら、このことを理解し、真偽を見分けなければなりません。浄土宗は地獄に堕ちる道、禅宗は天魔の教え、真言宗は国を滅ぼす邪宗、律宗は国賊なのです。これは私の言葉ではなく、経典に書かれているのです。雲の上を飛ぶホトトギスの声をお聞きなさい。あの鳥は時を知り、苗を植える時を教えてくれる。ですから、今植えて、実りの時になって後悔しないようにしましょう。今こそ、法華経を植える時なのです。私は、そのために釈尊から遣わされた使者なのです。」


　日蓮が語り終えると、激怒した聴衆から憤りの声がわき上がった。気がふれているのだから放っておけと言う者もいれば、あのばちあたりな話は厳罰に値すると言う者もいた。集会に出ていた地頭は、日蓮が神聖な境内から一歩外に出たら、すぐに殺そうとはかった。

be inaugurated the five centuries of 'the concealment of the pure law,' wherein the merit of the Tathagata's teaching shall have exhausted itself, and all ways of enlightenment shall be lost to mankind. This is the beginning of the latter-day-law which will continue for ten thousand years.... Now it is two hundred years since the world entered the last millennium. And to us so far removed from the direct teaching of Buddha, there is but one way provided for our attainment of Buddhahood; and that way is contained in the five characters of Myō-Hō-Renge-Kyō. Yet the Jōdo calls upon the people to shut this precious sutra, and to turn no more ear to it; and the Shingon reviles it as unworthy even of loosing the shoes from off the feet of their sutra, the Mahavairo-cana. Are not such spoken of by the Worshipful in the second book of the Pundarika, in the chapter on parables, as the extermi-nators of the seeds of Buddhism, whose sure end will be endless Hell? He that has ears to hear and eyes to see, let him understand, and divide truth from falsehood. Know that the Jōdo is a way to Hell, the Zen, the teaching of infernal hosts; the Shingon, a heresy to destroy the nation, and the Ritzu,[*19] an enemy of the land. These are not my own words, but I found them in the sutra. Hark to the cuckoo above the cloud. He knows the time, and warns you to plant. Plant now therefore, and do not repent when the harvest season comes. Now is the time for planting the Lotus Sutra, and I am the messenger sent by the Worshipful for that end."

He ended, and an uproar of indignation arose from the infuri-ated audience. Some said that his mind was out of order, and hence he might be pardoned; others that his blasphemy was worthy of the severest punishment. The landlord who attended the meeting would see to the blasphemer's being dispatched as soon as he

しかし、老住職は優しかった。自分の弟子は、いつか悔い改め、元の正統の信仰に戻り、夢から覚めるだろうと考えた。暗くなってから、住職は二人の弟子に道案内を命じて、日蓮を地頭に見つからないように、この地から無事に連れ出させた。

## V − ひとり世に抗す

故郷にいれられなかった日蓮は、「法を広めるには最良の地」である首府鎌倉へ向かった。鎌倉に入ると、今日でも松葉ケ谷と呼ばれている、所有者のいない場所に、草庵を建てた。ここに法華経を携えて居を定め、世の過ちを正そうと、ひとり活動を始めた。偉大な日蓮宗の始まりは、この草庵だった。今では身延や池上などの地に巨大な寺院が建ち、全国に5000をこえる寺と、そこに参拝する200万の信徒がいる日蓮宗は、この草庵とこの一人の人物から始まったのである。偉業は、いつもこのようにして生まれる。不屈の精神を持った人物がいて、世間に背を向けられるところにこそ、永遠に偉大なものが生まれる可能性があるのだ。20世紀は、この人物から、その教義はともかく、信念と勇気を学ぶことになるだろう。キリスト教は、日本でそのように始めようとされただろうか。布教の目的で設立した学校や教会、財政援助、人的支援。偉大な日蓮は、そのようなものは何もなく、ただひとり、自分だけで始めたのだ！

　それから1年の間、日蓮は沈黙して、再び修学と瞑想の日々を送った。その間に、初めての弟子を迎えた。後の日昭である。日本の仏教の状態に対する日蓮の考

stepped out of the holy ground. But the old abbot was kind. His pupil might some day repent, resume his former orthodoxy, and so end his dreaming. At dusk, he ordered two of his disciples to take Nichiren out of the district by ways safe from the landlord's attack.

## V – Alone Against the World

Rejected at home, he made his way right into Kamakura, the capital of the country, "the best place for disseminating the truth." There in a spot owned by nobody, in what is still called Matsuba-ga-Yatsu (Pine-Leaf's Dale), he had a little strawhut built for him. Here he posted himself with his Pundarika Sutra,—an independent man,—to begin his conquest of errors around him. The great Nichiren sect had its beginning in this hut. The stupendous temple-structures at Minobu, Ikegami, and other places, with more than five thousand temples in the land, and two million souls that worship in them,—all had their beginning in this hut and this one man. So are great works always born. One indomitable soul, and the world against him,—therein lies the promise of all permanent greatness. The twentieth century may well learn of this man, of his faith and bravery, if not of his doctrines. Had Christianity itself such a beginning in Japan? Mission-schools, mission-churches, allowances in money, helps in men,—great Nichiren, *he* began with himself alone, with none of these!

For a year he is silent once more in study and contemplation. Meanwhile he had his first disciple, named Nisshō afterward, who came all the way from Eizan, attracted by the view they had in

え方に共鳴して、はるばる叡山からやって来たのだ。日蓮は、これで自分の教えがこの国に絶え果てることを恐れずに、いつでも民衆の前に出て、命を投げ出すことができるようになったと、ことのほか喜んだ。こうして日蓮は、1254年の春、この国ではそれまでなかった辻説法を始めた。首府鎌倉の聴衆の嘲罵を浴びながら、故郷で初めて公にした話を、わかりやすく繰り返した。僧の身分にある者が、路傍で説法をするのはふさわしくないという批判に対しては、日蓮はきっぱりと、戦を戦っている者には立って食事をするのがふさわしいではないかと応じた。国の統治者の崇拝する信仰を悪く言うべきではないという非難に対しては、「僧は仏の使いである。世と人々を恐れていては使命を果たせない」と明言した。他の宗派がすべて間違っているはずはないという当然の疑問に対しては、「足場が役に立つのは、寺が建つまでである」と一蹴した。日蓮は6年間絶え間なく、このような説教を続け、やがてその努力と人となりが民衆の注意を引きつけ始めた。弟子の中に、高い身分の者が少なからず数えられるようになり、将軍家の者までもいた。そうなると、手遅れにならないうちに抑えておかなければ、鎌倉中に日蓮の影響が広がると案ずる声があがった。建長寺の道隆上人、光明寺の良忠上人、極楽寺の良観、大仏寺の隆観など、影響力の強い高僧たちが集まって、首府に広まりつつあるこの新興の宗派を弾圧する相談をした。しかし日蓮の大胆な発言の前には、彼らがどんなに力を合わせて反対しても及ばなかった。その頃に次々と国を襲った天変地異を契機として、日蓮は、今なおその種のものとしては他に並ぶもののない名著とみなさ

common upon the state of Buddhism in Japan. Nichiren is exceedingly glad, because he can now appear before the public, and lay down his life there without the fear of his doctrines being lost to his country. So he began in the spring of 1254 what was never heard of before in the land,—*street preaching*. He repeated materially, amidst the gibes and railings of the metropolitan hearers, what he had first proclaimed to his townsmen. To the retort that it was not becoming for a man of his order to preach by the wayside, his decisive answer was that it *was* becoming for a man to eat standing in time of war. To the rebuke that he must not speak evil of the faith adored by the ruler of the land, his plain reply was that "the priest is Buddha's messenger, and fear of the world and men agrees not with his vocation." To the natural doubt that the other forms of worship could not all be mistaken, his simple explanation was that "the scaffold is of use only till the temple is done." For six years he preached in this manner, in season and out of season, till his work and person began to call public attention. Among his disciples were counted not a few of men in high authority, some even of the Shōgun's household, and there was a fear that the whole city might be carried away by his influence, if not checked in due time. There were Abbot Dōryū of Kenchō-ji, Abbot Ryōchū of Kōmyō-ji, Ryōkan of Gokuraku-ji, Ryūkan of Daibutsu-ji, etc., all high dignitaries of vast influence, who took counsel together for the suppression of the rising faith in the capital. But Nichiren's audacity was more than all their united efforts against him. Taking advantage of many calamities that had recently befallen the land, he prepared what is still considered the most remarkable production of the kind,—*Risshō-Ankoku-Ron*, *A Treatise on Bringing Peace and Righteousness to the Country*. Therein

れている『立正安国論』（国に平和と正義をもたらす論）<sup>訳注67</sup>
を著した。その中で日蓮は、国にうちつづく災害を改
めて列挙し、その原因は、誤った教義が民衆に広めら
れたためであるとして、それを経典から広く引用して
立証した。日蓮の考える救済の方法は、最高の経典で
ある法華経を、国をあげて受け入れることであった。
そして、このすばらしい経典を拒んだ当然の結果とし
て、内乱と外敵の侵略に見舞われると指摘した。この
国の高僧に対してこれほど痛烈な言葉が投げかけられ
たことは、かつてなかった。『立正安国論』は、全体が
鬨の声であり、決然とした宣戦布告であった。その戦
いが終ったら、その結果はただ一つ、自分の宗派が根
絶やしにされるか、他の宗派が全滅しているかであっ
た。それは、狂気と紙一重の情熱であり、日本の統治
者の中でも最高の知者の一人であった北条時頼は、こ
の熱狂的な僧を首府から追い出して弾圧することに決
めた。しかし、この政治家には、自分が処罰しようと
しているのが、どのような人物かわかっていなかった。
その人物は、死を覚悟しており、すでに自分と同じよ
うに誠実な人間を生み出したほどの誠実さを備え、後
に数多く実証されるように、あらゆる試練を受ける覚
悟ができていたのである。何物をもってしても、この
ような人間たちを恐れさせることはできず、「謗法に対
する折伏」は変わらぬ勢いで続けられ、ついに、この
小さな教団は力ずくで解散させられ、その指導者は遠
国に流罪となった。

he recounted all the evils from which the land was then suffering, and traced their cause to the false doctrines taught among the people. These he proved by extensive quotations from sutras. The remedy, in his view, lay in the universal acceptance by the nation of the highest of all sutras, the Pundarika; and pointed out, as the sure result of refusal of such a gift, *civil wars* and a *foreign invasion*. Never before were more caustic terms applied to the church-dignitaries of the land. The whole treatise was a battle-cry, declaration of war of the most determined kind, which if fought through, could have but one issue, the extirpation of his sect, or of all the other sects. It was enthusiasm indistinguishable from madness, and Hōjō Tokiyori, one of the wisest rulers the country has had, decided upon its suppression by the removal of the zealot from the capital. But the politic man did not know the kind of soul he was dealing with. It was a soul prepared for death, and with such sincerity in it that it had already begotten other souls like it, no less prepared for encounter with all kinds of trial, as was abundantly proved afterward. Nothing could intimidate these men, and "warfare against Buddha's enemies" was carried on with unabated vigor, till by force the little company was disbanded and its leader carried away as an exile to a far-off province.

# VI – 剣難と流罪

『立正安国論』を上書してからの15年間は、日蓮の生涯にとって、この世のさまざまな権力との戦いの連続だった。まず伊豆に流されたが、その地で過ごした3年の流刑生活の間にも信者を増やした。鎌倉に戻ってきた時、弟子たちから「戦い」をやめ、彼らの教化に専念するように懇願された。これに対する日蓮の答えは断固としたものだった。「すでに末法の世に入った今、邪法の毒はきわめて強く、危篤の病人に薬が欠かせないように折伏が必要なのであり、無慈悲と見えても、これこそ慈悲なのだ」。日蓮は、すぐに以前と同じ、手に負えない僧の姿勢に戻り、身の危険を顧みなかった。ある日の夕暮れ、数人の弟子を従えて布教の旅をしていた日蓮に、剣を手にした一団が突然襲いかかった。襲撃の首謀者は、日蓮が4年前に開宗を宣言した時から、この大胆な改革者の殺害を心に決めていた地頭だった。師の命を守ろうとして3人の弟子が殺された。1人は僧侶で2人は在俗信者だった。ここに、日本で最初の法華経の殉教者が出て、今日、同じ法華経を信奉する無数の信者の貴い記憶となっている。日蓮は額に傷を負いながらも難を逃れたが、その傷は、法に忠実なしるしとなった。

しかし、本当の危難は1271年の秋に訪れた。それまで日蓮の命が助かってきたのは、当時の法律が僧の死刑を禁じていたからだ。日蓮の遠慮のない言動は容認の限度を超えていたが、剃髪した頭と僧衣のおかげで法律の厳しさから守られていたのである。しかし、国

# VI– Sword and Exile

For fifteen years following the publication of his treatise, his life was a continuous battling with the powers and principalities of his world. He was first banished to Idzu,[*20] where he remained three years, making converts in his exile. On his return to Kamakura, he was entreated by his followers to stop "warfare" and devote himself mostly to their edification; to which his decided answer was that "now in the beginning of the Latter Day, when the virulence of errors is so strong, polemic attack is a necessity as medicine to a disease at its crisis, and is a mercy, though it does not appear so." He at once resumed his old attitude,—an incorrigible priest,—heedless of the destruction now hanging over his head. One evening, when on his missionary tour with several of his disciples, he was suddenly attacked by a company of men, swords in hand. The leader of the attacking party was no other than the landlord who had determined upon the removal of the audacious renovator at the time of his proclamation of the new doctrines four years ago. Three of his disciples were killed, one priest and two laymen, in their effort to save the life of their master. Thus the sutra had its first martyrs in Japan, precious to the memory of the myriad who now put their trust in the same. Nichiren escaped with a wound in his forehead, the mark of his fidelity to the Law.

But the real crisis came in the autumn of 1271. His life had been spared thus far, for the law of the time forbade the capital punishment of the priest-class; and though his impudence was now beyond forbearance, his shaven head and sacerdotal robes were his strong protection against the rigor of the law. But when

の既存の宗派に対してだけでなく、聖俗を問わず権力者に対して浴びせる痛烈な攻撃を抑えきれなくなった時、北条氏は、例外的な非常処置として、日蓮を死刑執行人［首切り役人］の手に渡すことを決めた。これが、日本宗教史上名高い、いわゆる「竜の口の御法難」である。その歴史的な信憑性は最近疑問視されているが、信心のあまり後年この事件に付け加えられた奇跡を除けば、「法難」があったことは確かだろう。世間一般に伝えられている話は次のようなものである。「日蓮が法華経の聖なる言葉（脚注・「臨刑欲寿終、念彼観音力、刀尋段段壊」法華経普門品。刑台に命を終えようとした時、観音力を念ずるならば、刀の刃はこなごなに砕かれるという意味）を繰り返し唱えていると、死刑執行人が、首を切り落とそうと刀を振り上げた途端、天から一陣の風が吹き下り、刀の刃が三つに割れて周囲の人々は驚きうろたえ、刀を持つ者の手はしびれ、もはや二の太刀を振り上げることができなくなった。その直後、使者が『全速力で馬を飛ばして』刑場に到着し、鎌倉からの赦免状をもたらした。法華経を広める運動はこのようにして救われたのである」。しかし、奇跡を持ち出さなくとも、この出来事を説明することができる。あの時代ならば、死刑執行人は僧籍にある者の生命を奪うことに、迷信的な恐れを抱いていたはずである。また、威厳にみちた僧が、首を切られるのを従容として待ちながら祈りを唱えている姿を見て、哀れな死刑執行人が、無実の血を流すことに手を貸せば、天罰が下ると恐れおののいたことは想像にかたくない。この異例の死刑を決めた統治者も、同じ恐怖に襲われたに違いなく、死刑に代わって流刑を言い渡す書状をもたせて使者を

nothing could prevent his vituperative attack upon the existing faiths of the lands and with them upon the authorities both civil and clerical, Hōjō decided upon his being delivered to the hand of the executioner as an extraordinary measure in his special case. The so-called "Danger of the Sutra (Go-hō-nan) at Tatsunokuchi" is a most notable event in the religious history of Japan. Its historic veracity has been recently doubted; but the "danger" shorn of the miracles which later piety attached to the event, seems unquestionable. The popular account is on this wise: At the instant when the executioner lifted up his sword for the final despatch, repetition by Nichiren of sacred words* from his Sutra brought down a sudden gust of wind from heaven, and to the utter bewilderment of all around him, the blade was broken into three pieces, and no second stroke was possible by the paralysis of the swordsman's hand. Soon a messenger reached the spot "galloping at full-speed," bringing a writ of release from Kamakura, and the cause of the Sutra was thus saved.—But we can explain the incident without calling in the aid of a miracle. The superstitious fear of the executioner to put an end to the life of a man of the holy order is perfectly natural in that age. And when he saw the calm composure of the dignified priest ready to receive the fatal stroke in the attitude of offering prayer, we can well imagine the poor executioner shaking with fear of heavenly punishment, should he be instrumental in shedding innocent blood. A similar fear must have overtaken the ruler himself who had decided upon this

---

* Rin-kei yoku-ju-shū, Nen-pi Kan-non-riki, Tō-jin dan-dan ne.
   When on the scaffold life is to end,
   And Kwanyin's[21] power is contemplated,
   The blade of the sword to pieces will crumble.

走らせた。間一髪で難を逃れたのは、まったく自然の成り行きだったのだ。

　死に代わる流刑も厳しい刑であった。日蓮は、今度は日本海の孤島、佐渡に流された。佐渡は、当時全国で最も往来しにくい場所であり、最も目障(めざわ)りな罪人の流刑地としてよく使われていた。日蓮がこの島で5年の流刑を生き延びたのは、奇跡であった。ある年の厳しい冬を、法華経を心の糧(かて)とする以外はほとんど何もないまま過ごしたこともあった。この流刑で日蓮が得たものは、肉体に対する心の、力に対する精神の勝利だった。流刑の終わる頃、日蓮の信仰の領土に新たな土地が加わった。以後、佐渡と隣国の人口の多い越後は、日蓮の運動に熱狂的なまでに忠節を守った。

　日蓮の不屈の勇気と忍耐は、今や鎌倉幕府を恐れさせるとともに、賞賛をも呼び起こした。これに重なって、外国が侵略してくるという日蓮の預言が的中して蒙古襲来の危機が迫ったために、日蓮は首府に戻ることを許された（1274年）。日蓮は鎌倉に入ってまもなく、その教義を国中で自由に広めることを許す許可状を手にした。精神がついに勝利をおさめ、その後7つの世紀にわたり、この国で力を持つことになった。

## VII– 最後の日々

　日蓮も52歳になっていたが、その人生の大半は、夜を徹した祈りと世間との戦いに費やされていた。もう、同じ国の人間に自由に話ができる身になったわけだが、布教が許された理由が日蓮には気に入ら

unprecedented execution; and he at once sent out a messenger with the sentence of exile instead of death. The escape we believe was narrow, but was perfectly natural.

The exile which was to take the place of death was a severe one. He was now carried to Sado, a forlorn island in the Japan Sea, at that time the most inaccessible part in the whole country, and the favorite place of banishment for criminals of the most offensive kind. That he survived the exile of five years in this island is a wonder. One severe winter he passed through with little beyond the mental food of his Sutra. His was another conquest of mind over body, spirit over force. At the close of his banishment, he added one more province to his spiritual dominion. Ever since, Sado and the neighboring populous province of Echigo have remained fanatically loyal to his cause.

His indomitable courage and perseverance now called forth the fear and admiration of the authority at Kamakura: and this, together with the fast approaching danger from the Mongol attack in fulfillment of his prophecy of a foreign invasion, secured him permission for his return to the capital (1274). Soon after his arrival there, he obtained a charter for the free promulgation of his doctrines in the land. Spirit conquered at last, and for seven centuries it was to be a power in the nation.

## VII– The Last Days

The man was now fifty-two years of age, and most of his life had been spent in vigils and battlings with the world. He was now free to speak to his country-men; but the way in which the permission was given to that effect did not please him at all. It

なかった。北条氏が布教の自由を認めたのは、恐怖にかられたからだ。だが日蓮としては、統治者も国民も、自ら進んで法華経を信奉することを望んでいた。日蓮は、仏陀にならって山に隠棲し、静かな瞑想と弟子の教育にあたりながら余生を閉じることを考え始めた。ここに日蓮の偉大さがあり、その宗派が永続している理由があると思われる。世間が日蓮を受け入れ始めた時に、彼は退いたのである。日蓮に及ばない人々は、そこでつまずくのだ。

しかし、日蓮の弟子は、教義の禁止令が撤回されると、既存の宗派に拘泥する者を公然と攻撃する活動を開始した。寺は次々と「激しく折伏されて論争に負けていった」という。この熱狂的な信者たちの行動の仕方は、よく知られている。各人が手に太鼓を持ち、一斉に「南無妙法蓮華経」と、お題目を繰り返すのである。お題目を五つに区切って唱和するのに合わせて、太鼓を5回叩く。20人も集まれば耳を聾するほどに響くのだから、何百人も集まって、これまでにない勢いと熱気に満ちて、家から家へ、寺から寺へと、新しい信仰にただちにひれ伏すようにと呼びかけながら、鎌倉中を回った結果は容易に想像できる。開祖の熱意と情熱と不寛容は、今日の信者にもまだはっきりと見られ、本来は攻撃的でなく厭世的な仏教の中で、戦闘的な熱意があるのは唯一この宗派だけである。

日蓮の晩年は平穏だった。富士山の西方にある身延に入山し、南に雄大な大洋をのぞみ、三方を壮麗な山々に囲まれて、日蓮を慕って全国各地からやってくる人々と会った。1281年の蒙古襲来で、自分の預言が実現したこともこの地で知った。これで、日蓮の名声

was fear which induced the Hōjōs to grant freedom, whereas he aimed at the willing acceptation of the Sutra by the ruler and his people. He now began to think of retiring to a mountain after the manner of his Hindoo Master, there to end his days in quiet contemplation and instruction of his disciples. Herein we believe lies his greatness, and the main reason of the permanence of his sect. When the world began to receive him, he left it. Here was an opportunity for stumbling for souls less than his.

But to his disciples, the removal of the interdiction of their tenets was the commencement of open aggressive actions against the adherents of the older sects. We are told of temple after temple "stormed and brought down by vocal attacks." We know what the manner of these zealots is. Each carries a drum in his hand, and all in unison repeat their prayer,—Nam-Myō-Hō-Renge-Kyō, —with five strikes to accompany its five syllables. Twenty of them is stunning to our ears, and we can well imagine the effect of hundreds of them in their new vigor and enthusiasm, going from house to house, from temple to temple, through the city of Kamakura, calling for its immediate surrender to the new faith. The zeal, the fire, the intolerance of the founder, are still distinctly visible in his disciples of today,—the only case of martial zeal in the naturally inoffensive and pessimistic religion of Buddha.

Our hero's last days were peaceful. He established himself in Mt. Minobu to the west of Mt. Fuji, and there with the splendid view of the ocean to the south, and noble mountains beside and behind him, he received the homage of his admirers from all parts of the land. Here he lived to see his prophecy literally fulfilled in

と影響力が一層高まったことはもちろんである。その大事件の翌年、日蓮は乗り物で運ばれて山を下り、池上（大森駅の近く）まで来たところで、在家の弟子の客となったが、そこで1282年10月11日に死去した。最後の願いは、その教えが天皇の都、京都に広まり、ついには「天聴」に達することだった。日蓮は、当時14歳の少年であった日像にその役目を委嘱した。死の床の場面では、日蓮らしい出来事があった。臨終の慰めにと、仏像が運ばれてくると、日蓮はすぐに手を振って持ち去るように合図をした。たいそう不快な様子だった。そこで、見事な筆で法華経の名前が書かれた掛け物を日蓮の前でといた。すると、日蓮はゆっくりと身体をそちらに向けて、手を合わせ、最後の息を引きとった。日蓮は聖典崇拝者であって、偶像崇拝者ではなかった。

## VIII– 人物評

本論で取りあげた人物ほど不可解な性格の持ち主は、日本史上にない。敵にとっては、日蓮は冒瀆者、偽善者、私腹を肥やす者、稀代のいかさま師などであった。そのいかさまぶりを証明するために、多くの書物が書かれ、中には実に巧妙に書かれたものもあった。仏教が敵から嘲られる時、日蓮は格好の攻撃の的となる。日蓮は、日蓮宗以外の同じ仏教徒によって、仏教が受けた侮辱のすべてを担う贖罪のやぎにされたのだ。日本で、日蓮ほど重ねて中傷を受けた人物はいない。そして、日本にやってきたキリスト教も、これに加わり、この方角からも、さらに多くの石が日

the great Mongol invasion of 1281, which of course increased his fame and influence considerably. The year following that great event, he was carried to Ikegami (near Ōmori Station) as a guest of one of his lay-disciples, and there died on the 11th day of the 10th month, 1282. His last wish was to have his doctrines preached in the imperial city of Kyōto, to have "the holy hearings" at last, and he appointed one Nichizō, then a boy fourteen years of age, for this work. One feature of his death-bed scene needs our notice. They brought to him an idol of Buddha as his possible consolation in his last hours; but he beckoned with his hand to remove it at once, with evident signs of much displeasure. Then they unrolled before him a *kakemono* with the name of Saddharma-Pundarika Sutra written in magnificent Chinese characters. Thereto he slowly turned his body, and clasping his hands towards it, he breathed his last. A bibliolater, and not an idolater, was he.

## VIII– An Estimate of His Character

No more enigmatic character has appeared in our history than this subject of our essay. To his enemy he was a blasphemer, a hypocrite, a belly-server, a king of mountebanks, and all that. Books were written, some of them very ingenious, to prove his charlatanism. He is the favorite mark of attack when Buddhism is to be ridiculed by its enemies. He is made the scapegoat of all that is opprobrious in that religion, by his brother-Buddhists out of his own sect. No man in Japan had more calumnies piled upon him. And when Christianity made its appearance in the land, it too took its part in the matter, and many more stones were thrown at him from that quarter as well. I know one of its

蓮に向かって投げられたのである。かつて有名な牧師の一人が、その方面を熱心に研究していた。実際、日本のキリスト教徒にとって、この人物を賞賛することを書くのは、イスカリオテのユダを好意的に取りあげるほど、不敬なことなのだ。

しかし私個人としては、必要とあれば、この人物のために自分の名誉をかける。日蓮の教義のほとんどは、今日の批評の試練に堪えられないことは認める。日蓮の論争術は上品でなく、全体の論調も極端である。日蓮は確かに、バランスを欠いた性格で、一つの方向だけに向いていた。しかし、日蓮から知的な誤りや、生来の気質や、時代と環境の影響の跡をほとんど取り去ってみると、骨の髄まで誠実な人間が、このうえなく正直な人物が、最高に勇敢な日本人が現れるのだ。偽善者は、25年以上も偽善を続けることはできない。彼のためにいつでも命を投げ出そうという何千人もの信奉者をもつことはできない。「不実の者に宗教を立てることができるだろうか」、カーライルは声を大にして言っている。「もちろん、不実の者は煉瓦の家も建てられない」。日蓮が没してから700年たった今、見回せば、4000人の僧侶と8000人の師をかかえた5000もの寺院があり、そこでは150万から200万もの人々が、この人物の定めた通りに祈っている。それでも、これはすべて、恥知らずないかさま師のしたことだと思えと言われる！　私は人間性を深く信じているので、そのようなことは到底信じられない。もし虚偽がこの地上でそれほど長く続くのなら、いったいどうやって、誠実を虚偽と区別するのだろう？

famed ministers once turning his whole attention in that direction. Indeed, for a Christian man in Japan to write anything laudatory this man sounds as impious as to speak good words for Judas Iscariot.

But I for one venture my honor, if need be, for this man. Most of his doctrines, I grant, cannot stand the test of the present-day criticism. His polemics were inelegant, and his whole tone was insanoid. He certainly was an unbalanced character, too pointed in only one direction. But divest him of his intellectual errors, of his hereditary temperament, and of much that his time and surroundings marked upon him, and you have a soul sincere to its very core, the honestest of men, the bravest of Japanese. A hypocrite cannot keep his hypocrisy for twenty-five years and more. Neither can he have thousands of followers ready to lay down their lives for him. "A false man found a religion?" Carlyle exclaims. "Why, a false man cannot build a brick house." I look around me, and I see 5,000 temples manned by 4,000 priests and 8,000 teachers, and 1,500,000–2,000,000 souls worshipping in them after the manner prescribed by this man, now seven hundred years after his death; and I am told to take all these as the work of a shameless mountebank! My belief in human nature is too strong for me to believe in any such thing. If falsity is so permanent upon this earth, by what other means shall we distinguish honesty from it?

この恐れを知らない人物の勇気を支えていたのは、自分はこの世に送られてきた仏陀の特別の使者だという確信だった。日蓮自身は名もない「海辺の旃陀羅が子」であったが、法華経を伝道する能力においては、非常に重要な人物だった。「私は取るに足りない一介の僧侶です」、日蓮はある時、一人の権力者［本間重遠］に語った。「しかしながら、法華経を広める者として、私は釈迦牟尼の特使であり、特使としての私の右には梵天が、左には帝釈天が仕え、日は私を導き、月は私に従い、この国のあらゆる神々は頭をたれて私を敬います」。日蓮にとって、自分の命は重要ではなかったが、そのような正しい法の担い手である自分を、国が迫害しようとしたことは、言い表しようもないほど悲しかった。もし日蓮が発狂しているならば、その狂気は崇高なものであり、自分がその実現を託された使命の価値によって自分の価値を自覚するという最高の形の自尊心と区別するのは難しい。そのように自分を評価した人物は、人類の歴史で日蓮一人だけではない。

　したがって、厳しい迫害を受けている歳月には、聖なる経典、とくに法華経は、慰めを得る不変の拠り所だった。日蓮を流刑地に送る船が海に乗り出そうという時、愛弟子の日朗が師の船に近づこうとして、怒った漕ぎ手［船頭］たちの櫂で打たれ、両腕に不具になるほどのひどい傷を受けた。その日朗に向かって、日蓮はこのような慰めの言葉をかけた。「末世に正法を説く者は、必ず棒で叩かれ流罪になると知れ。2000年前に法華経の勧持品に書かれたことが、今我らにふりかかったのだ。だから喜べ。なぜなら、法華経勝利の日はすぐそこまできているのだ」。流刑の身の日蓮が弟子に

The most fearless of men, his courage was based wholly upon his conviction that he was Buddha's special messenger to this earth. He himself is nothing,—"a sudra of a sea-coast"—but in his capacity as a vehicle of the Pundarika Sutra, his person had all the importance of heaven and earth. "I am a worthless, ordinary priest," he once said to a man in authority; "but as a promulgator of the Pundarika Sutra, I am Sakyamuni's special messenger, and as such Brahma serves me on my right hand and Sakra on my left, the Sun guides me and the Moon follows me, and all the deities of the land bend their heads and honor me." His own life was of no account whatever to him; but that his nation should persecute him, the bearer of such a law, was lamentable to him beyond his power of expression. If demented he was, his dementia was of a noble sort, hard to be distinguished from that highest form of self-respect which knows its own worth by the worth of the mission it was sent to fulfill. Nichiren was not the only man in History who has had such an estimate of himself.

Therefore, the holy sutras, and especially his own Pundarika, were the constant sources of his consolation during years of hard persecution. Turning to Nichirō, his favorite disciple, who to approach his master's boat as it was launched for its voyage to the land of the exile, had his arms painfully disabled by the angry strokes of its oarsmen, Nichiren had this consolation to offer: "Know that staves and exiles are the necessary accompaniments of the preachers of the Sutra in the Latter Day. What was written in the chapter on exhortation in the Pundarika Sutra two thousand years ago, has now come upon thee and me. Rejoice, therefore, for the time of the conquest of the Sutra is at hand." His

宛てた書簡には、いたるところに経典の言葉が引用されている。その中のひとつに、日蓮はこう書いている。「涅槃経に、重きを軽きに変える『転重軽受』の教えがある。現世で重きにあえば、来世では軽きことが保証されている。提婆菩薩は異教徒に殺され、師子尊者は首をはねられ、竜樹菩薩はさまざまな誘惑にあった。いずれも正法の世の、仏陀の国においてである。ならば、末法の世が始まった今、地の果てのこの国においては、どれほど多難なことか。云々」。ルターがキリスト教の聖書を尊重したように、日蓮は法華経を尊重していた。「自分が奉ずる法華経のために死ねるなら、命は惜しくない」とは、危機的状況で日蓮がよく口にした言葉だ。キリスト教のルターと同じほど、日蓮も聖典崇拝者だったのかもしれない。確かに、聖典はあらゆる偶像や力よりも尊い崇拝の対象であり、聖典のために死ぬ覚悟のある人は、英雄と呼ばれている人々以上に尊い英雄である。日蓮を悪く言う現代のキリスト教徒は、自分の聖書が埃にまみれていないだろうか。たとえ聖書の言葉を日々口の中で唱え、聖書がその影響のもとに書かれたという霊感を熱烈に擁護しているとしても、神の使いとして人々の間に聖書を広めるため、15年もの剣難や流罪に耐え、身命を捧げることができるだろうか。聖書は他のいかなる聖典にもまして、人間の行いをより善くするようにできている。その聖書を持つ者が石を投げつける相手として、最もふさわしくないのが日蓮である。

　日蓮の私生活は、当然ながら、このうえなく簡素であった。鎌倉の草庵に居を定めてから30年後の身延でも、同じような暮らしをしていた。その頃には、裕福

exilic epistles to his disciples are full of quotations from sutras. In one of them he writes: "In the Nirvana Sutra, we have the doctrine of 'the turning of heaviness into lightness.' We receive this heaviness in this life, and with it, lightness in the life to come is assured....Deva Bodhisattva was killed by heretics, Aryasimha was beheaded, and Nagarjuna met diverse temptations; and they in the Right-Law Age, in Buddha's own land. How much more then in this end of the earth, in the beginning of the Latter-Law Age? etc." The Christian Bible was not more precious to Luther than the Pundarika Sutra to this man. "If I can die for the sake of my Sutra, I count not my life precious," were his words on many critical occasions. A bibliolater he might have been, as in one sense our own Luther was; but a book certainly is a nobler object of worship than images and forces of all kinds, and a man that could die for a book is a nobler sort of hero than most that go by that name. Let the modern Christian reviler of Nichiren see whether *his* Book is not covered with dust; or if it is daily mumbled in his mouth, and its inspiration hotly defended, whether he could endure sword and exile for fifteen years, and stake his life and soul for it, that it might be adopted by the people to whom he is sent. Nichiren should be the last man to be stoned by the owners of that Book, which more than all other books, did fashion for the better the affairs of mankind.

Nichiren's private life was the simplest that could be imagined. Thirty years after he had established himself in the strawhut in Kamakura, we find him in a similar structure in Minobu, when

な在家信者の弟子もいて、安楽な生活もできたのである。日蓮は「仏敵」と呼んだ者には容赦をしなかったが、貧しい人々や虐（しいた）げられた人々には、誰よりも優しかった。弟子に宛てた日蓮の手紙には、名著『立正安国論』に見られる火のような激しさとはうってかわり、実に優しい気持ちが示されている。弟子たちが日蓮を大切に思ったはずである。

　実際、日蓮の生涯は、性欲のないムハンマド（マホメット）の生涯のようである。激しさと極端に熱狂的なところも同じなら、そのうえ、はっきりした目的のある誠実さや豊かな慈愛の心を持っている点も同じである。日本人の方が、かのアラビア人よりも偉大であったと思うところはただ一点、法華経に対する日蓮の確信は、コーランに対するムハンマドの確信よりも強かったところである。日蓮には、そこまで信奉できる経典があったため、物質的な力は必要なかった。人の力を借りなくても、法華経だけで十分な力であり、法華経の価値を確立するために、どのような力も必要ではなかった。ムハンマドの偽善者の疑いを晴らした歴史は、日蓮をもっと正当に評価する方向に向かうべきだ。

　そこで、日蓮から13世紀という時代の装いをはぎ取り、常軌をはずれた批判の認識の仕方を取り除き、内面に宿る（偉大な人物は皆持っていると思われる）多少狂気じみたところを取り除いてみると、そこには非凡な人物、世界でも最高の宗教家の一人が現れる。日本人の中で、日蓮以上に独立独歩の人は考えられない。実際、日蓮は彼の創造性と独立心によって、仏教を日本の宗教にしたのだ。日蓮の宗派だけが、純粋に日本の仏教であり、他の宗派はすべて、インドや中国、朝

wealthy laymen were his disciples, and ease and comfort were at his command. Very intolerant to what he called "Buddha's enemies," he was the mildest of men when he dealt with the poor and stricken. His letters to his disciples breathe the softest of tempers, in great contrast to the fire in his memorable "Treatise." No wonder that they thought so much of him.

Indeed, Nichiren's life always reminds me of Mahomet *without the concupiscence* of the latter. The same intensity, the same insanoid fanaticism, yet withal the same sincerity of purpose, and much of inward pity and tenderness, in one as in the other. Only I believe the Japanese was greater than the Arabian, in that the former had more confidence in his Sutra than the latter in his Koran. Physical force was *not* a necessity to Nichiren, seeing that he had such a book to trust in. It alone without any human agency is a power enough, and no force is needed to establish its worth. History that has acquitted Mahomet of hypocrisy, ought have done more toward a right estimate of Nichiren.

Divested therefore of his thirteenth century garb, of the aberration of his critical knowledge, and of a little taint of insanity that might have dwelt in him (as it dwells in all great men, I suppose), there stands before us a remarkable figure, one of the greatest of his kind in the world. No more independent man can I think of among my countrymen. Indeed, he by his originality and independence made Buddhism a Japanese religion. His sect alone is purely Japanese, while all others have had their beginnings either in Hindoo, or Chinese, or Corean minds. His ambition, too,

鮮の精神にその起源を持っていた。日蓮の大望もまた、彼の時代の全世界に自分の宗派を広めたいと願っていた。仏教はそれまで、インドから日本へと東に向かって進んできたが、これからは改良された仏教が、日本からインドへと西に向かって進むと日蓮は語っている。このように、受身で受容するばかりの日本人にあって、日蓮は例外的な存在であり、自分自身の意志を持っていたから、ごく御しやすい人間でなかったことは確かである。しかし、そういう人物こそが国家の支えになるのであり、愛想や謙遜、受容、「懇願能力」などという名で行われている行為の大半は国の恥でしかなく、改宗を勧誘する者たちが本国へ送る報告書の「改宗者」数を増やす役に立つぐらいだ。戦闘的でない日蓮こそが、我々の理想とする宗教家である。

embraced the whole world of his time. He speaks of the *eastward* march of Buddhism from India to Japan till his time, and of the *westward* march of its *improved form* from Japan to India from his time on. He was therefore an exception among passive receptive Japanese,—not a very tractable fellow no doubt, because he had a will of his own. But such alone is the nation's backbone, while much else that goes by the name of affability, humility, receptivity or beg-ability, is no better than the country's shame, fitted only for swelling the number of "converts" in proselytizers' reports to their homeland. *Nichiren minus his combativity* is our ideal religious man.

# 訳注

訳注 1 (10頁)　日清戦争は1894〜95年。同書は1894年12月、著者34歳のときに刊行。

訳注 2 (10頁)　自叙伝の*How I became a Christian*（「余は如何にして基督信徒となりし乎」
　　　　　　　1895年刊）などの英文著作がある。

訳注 3 (18頁)　メキシコにあったアステカ帝国の9代皇帝、モンテスマ2世。モンテスマ
　　　　　　　1世が帝国の祖。

訳注 4 (18頁)　東インド会社のベンガル総督として、イギリスのインド支配の基礎固め
　　　　　　　をした政治家、軍人。

訳注 5 (18頁)　1521年に、モンテスマ2世が治めるアステカ帝国を滅ぼし、メキシコ総督
　　　　　　　となったスペイン人。

訳注 6 (22頁)　アメリカの東インド艦隊司令長官。1794〜1858。

訳注 7 (28頁)　琉球。現在の沖縄。

訳注 8 (30頁)　安政の大地震（安政2年11月11日）。

訳注 9 (32頁)　これらの言葉は『西郷西洲遺訓』に収められている。以下の引用文も、
　　　　　　　その多くは同書に収録。

訳注10 (36頁)　一度目は奄美大島、二度目は徳之島（現在は沖永良部島）。

訳注11 (38頁)　当日、江戸城に西郷隆盛たちが入城、勅命が伝達された。4月11日に明け
　　　　　　　渡され、江戸無血開城が実現した。

訳注12 (38頁)　人権宣言のこと。正式な名称は「人間および市民の権利宣言」。

訳注13 (42頁)　征韓論のこと。

訳注14 (42頁)　アメリカの初代大統領。建国の父とされる。

訳注15 (44頁)　1873年8月17日、国交修好全権大使として西郷が朝鮮に派遣されることが
　　　　　　　決定された。

訳注16 (50頁)　西南戦争（1877年）。西郷は私学校の生徒たちに擁されて挙兵。敗れて自
　　　　　　　刃する。

訳注17 (52頁)　トーマス・アクィナス。1225頃〜1274。『神学大全』で知られる、イタリ
　　　　　　　アの神学者、哲学者、聖人。

訳注18 (52頁)　三好重臣中将。

訳注19 (52頁)　山県有朋中将。

訳注20 (60頁)　聖書の教えのこと。

訳注21（64頁）　幕末から維新後の駐日イギリス公使。フランスに対抗し、強力な外交活動を続けた。

訳注22（68頁）　『春秋左氏伝』のこと。中国の歴史書『春秋』の解釈書。

訳注23（72頁）　「旧約聖書」箴言11章24節。訳文は「口語訳聖書」による。

訳注24（72頁）　「新約聖書」マタイ伝6章33節。訳文は「新共同訳聖書」による。

訳注25（74頁）　イギリスの政治家、軍人。1599〜1658。1649年に共和制を樹立。

訳注26（78頁）　イザヤ、エレミヤ、エゼキエルたち。

訳注27（78頁）　ウィリアム・ペン。クウェーカー教徒の移民と共に、デラウェア河畔にフィラデルフィア市を建設。同地方をペンシルヴァニアと命名する。

訳注28（84頁）　現在の山形県。

訳注29（84頁）　日向国高鍋藩主秋月種美の次男。江戸に生まれる。

訳注30（84頁）　儒学者。米沢藩のほか西条、尾張藩にも招かれ、仁政による藩政改革へと導いた。

訳注31（86頁）　鷹山が深く敬慕していた藩祖・上杉謙信が祀られている。第9代米沢藩主である鷹山は上杉家の10代目にあたる。

訳注32（86頁）　1766年に元服し、治憲を名乗る。鷹山の名を用いるのは、藩主を隠退、岳父重定が亡くなった1802年以後のこと。

訳注33（100頁）　楮。クワ科の落葉低木。和紙の原料となる。

訳注34（108頁）　オランダの解剖医書を翻訳し『解体新書』5巻を刊行。回想録『蘭学事始』などがある。

訳注35（116頁）　大大名。元来は、千台の兵車の意味。

訳注36（120頁）　側室のお豊の方は二子を生んだ。

訳注37（120頁）　上杉治広（鷹山の養嗣子）の長女・三姫。

訳注38（122頁）　「なせばなる　なさねばならぬ何事も　ならぬは人のなさぬなりけり」は鷹山の名句として知られている。

訳注39（130頁）　メソポタミアの古代都市。

訳注40（130頁）　現在の神奈川県。

訳注41（136頁）　現在の栃木県。

訳注42（150頁）　現在の成田山新勝寺。

訳注43（170頁）　手賀沼と印旛沼。ともに千葉県。

訳注44（172頁）　フランスの外交官。1869年、スエズ運河を完成させた。パナマ運河建設には失敗。

訳注45（182頁）　モーゼの十戒。「旧約聖書」出エジプト記20章1-17節

訳注46 (186頁)　古代ギリシャの哲学者、教育者。前470/469〜前399。弟子プラトンによる哲学的対話『ソクラテスの弁明』などで知られる。

訳注47 (186頁)　古代ギリシャ最大の観念論哲学者。前427〜前347。著書に『国家論』など。

訳注48 (188頁)　マタイによる福音書10章24節。

訳注49 (188頁)　ヨハネによる福音書10章11節。

訳注50 (190頁)　慶長13年。

訳注51 (190頁)　現在の滋賀県。

訳注52 (192頁)　「大学」「中庸」「論語」「孟子」の四部の書。

訳注53 (194頁)　現在の愛媛県。

訳注54 (194頁)　大州藩主の加藤氏。

訳注55 (200頁)　マタイによる福音書2章7〜12節。

訳注56 (206頁)　江戸前期の儒者。1619〜91。神儒一致を強調。岡山藩家老として治績を上げる。幕府による禁錮中に病死。

訳注57 (208頁)　池田光政侯。

訳注58 (222頁)　慶安1年。

訳注59 (234頁)　三蔵法師の名で知られる。著書に旅行記『大唐西域記』がある。帰国後、訳経に従事。法相宗・倶舎宗の開祖。

訳注60 (238頁)　『平家物語』に、後白河上皇の言葉として出ている。

訳注61 (242頁)　現在の千葉県南部。房州。

訳注62 (248頁)　ドイツの宗教改革者、ルターのこと。1483〜1546。

訳注63 (256頁)　天台大師、智顗。538〜597。著書に「摩訶止観」「法華玄義」などがある。

訳注64 (258頁)　梵語の「チャダーラ」（最下級の賤民の意）が、漢訳仏典でこの文字を当てられた。

訳注65 (260頁)　「新約聖書」マタイ伝13章57節。訳文は「口語訳聖書」による。

訳注66 (260頁)　「旧約聖書」の詩篇42篇1節。「鹿が谷川の流れを慕いあえぐように、神よ。私のたましいはあなたを慕いあえぎます」。訳文は「口語訳聖書」による。

訳注67 (270頁)　1260年、日蓮39歳の著。問答の体裁をとっている。前執権である実力者の北条時頼に呈上された。

訳注68 (280頁)　1269〜1342。京都を三度追放されながらも、妙顕寺を建立、後醍醐天皇の勅願寺に指定される。日蓮宗を京都に広めた。

訳注69 (282頁)　イギリスの批評家、歴史家。1795〜1881。著書に『衣服哲学』『英雄崇拝論』など。雄勁な文体で知られる。この言葉は『英雄崇拝論』にある。

# 英文注*

＊ 1（ 19頁）　　現在、一般的には Moctezuma と表記する。

＊ 2（ 19頁）　　現在、一般的には (Hernán) Cortez とも表記する。

＊ 3（ 25頁）　　一般的には Satsuma と表記する。

＊ 4（ 27頁）　　古めかしい表現で、subjugation, conquest, unification の意味に近い。

＊ 5（ 39頁）　　一般的には Katsu (Kaishū) と表記する。

＊ 6（ 43頁）　　一般的には Korean/Korea と表記する。

＊ 7（ 47頁）　　一般的には Tōkyō と表記する。

＊ 8（ 85頁）　　一般的には daimyō と表記する。

＊ 9（ 89頁）　　一般的には Aizu と表記する。

＊10（ 95頁）　　一般的には Jizō と表記する。

＊11（ 99頁）　　ラテン語。“The voice of the people is the voice of God.”

＊12（107頁）　　一般的には Kōjōkan と表記する。

＊13（111頁）　　この英文は、「新約聖書」のローマ人への手紙12-10に近似している。

＊14（113頁）　　“dance” は social dance のように、自分で踊るという意味が強いが、こ
　　　　　　　　こでは歌舞伎を指すと思われる。

＊15（131頁）　　一般的には Sontoku と表記する。

＊16（187頁）　　フランス語。the prevailing governmental system または the prevailing
　　　　　　　　social system。

＊17（211頁）　　ラテン語。virtue。

＊18（257頁）　　欧米では中国語の発音にならって Tiantai とも表記する。

＊19（265頁）　　一般的には Ritsu sect と表記する。

＊20（273頁）　　一般的には the Izu Peninsula と表記する。

＊21（275頁）　　観音(kannon)の中国式発音。中国ではKanyin と表記する。

（対訳）代表的日本人
Representative Men of Japan

2002年10月 4 日　第 1 刷発行
2008年11月28日　第 5 刷発行

著　者　　内村鑑三

監訳者　　稲盛和夫

翻訳協力　渡会和子

発行者　　富田 充

発行所　　講談社インターナショナル株式会社
　　　　　〒112-8652　東京都文京区音羽 1-17-14
　　　　　電話　03-3944-6493（編集部）
　　　　　　　　03-3944-6492（営業部・業務部）
　　　　　ホームページ　www.kodansha-intl.com

印刷・製本所　大日本印刷株式会社

落丁本、乱丁本は購入書店名を明記のうえ、講談社インターナショナル業務部宛に
お送りください。送料小社負担にてお取替えいたします。なお、この本についての
お問い合わせは、編集部宛にお願いいたします。本書の無断複写（コピー）は著作
権法上での例外を除き、禁じられています。

定価はカバーに表示してあります。

Printed in Japan
ISBN 978-4-7700-2928-7